Bristol Studies in Comparative and International Education

Series Editors: **Michael Crossley**, Emeritus Professor of Comparative and International Education, University of Bristol, UK, **Leon Tikly**, UNESCO Chair in Inclusive, Good Quality Education, University of Bristol, UK, **Angeline M. Barrett**, Reader in Education, University of Bristol, UK, and **Julia Paulson**, Reader in Education, Peace and Conflict, University of Bristol, UK

The series critically engages with education and international development from a comparative and interdisciplinary perspective. It emphasises work that bridges theory, policy and practice, supporting early career researchers and the publication of studies led by researchers in and from the Global

Forthcoming

Decolonizing Education for Sustainable Futures
Edited by **Yvette Hutchinson**, **Artemio Arturo Cortez Ochoa**, **Julia Paulson** and **Leon Tikly**

Assembling Comparison
Understanding Education Policy Through Mobility and Desire
By **Steven Lewis** and **Rebecca Spratt**

Higher Education in Small Islands
Challenging the Geographies of Centrality and Remoteness
Edited by **Rosie Alexander** and **Holly Henderson**

Education and Development in Central America and the Latin Caribbean
Global Forces and Local Responses
Edited by **D. Brent Edwards Jr.**, **Mauro C. Moschetti**,
Pauline Martin and **Ricardo Morales-Ulloa**

Find out more at

bristoluniversitypress.co.uk/
bristol-studies-in-comparative-and-international-education

Editorial advisory board

Find out more at

bristoluniversitypress.co.uk/
bristol-studies-in-comparative-and-international-education

TRANSITIONING VOCATIONAL EDUCATION AND TRAINING IN AFRICA

A Social Skills Ecosystem Perspective

VET Africa 4.0 Collective

BRISTOL
UNIVERSITY
PRESS

First published in Great Britain in 2023 by

Bristol University Press
University of Bristol
1–9 Old Park Hill
Bristol
BS2 8BB
UK
t: +44 (0)117 374 6645
e: bup-info@bristol.ac.uk

Details of international sales and distribution partners are available at bristoluniversitypress.co.uk

British Library Cataloguing in Publication Data
A catalogue record for this book is available from the British Library

ISBN 978-1-5292-2463-4 paperback
ISBN 978-1-5292-2464-1 ePub
ISBN 978-1-5292-2465-8 OA Pdf

Cover design: Nicky Borowiec
Front cover image: Adobe Stock/Diversity Studio
Bristol University Press use environmentally responsible print partners.
Printed and bound in Great Britain by CMP, Poole

Contents

Series Editor's Preface

This is the first volume for the Bristol Studies in Comparative and International Education (building upon the former Bristol Papers series) and one that clearly demonstrates our commitment to 'critically engage with education and international development from a comparative and interdisciplinary perspective'. In content, the book is ground-breaking for the ways in which it challenges traditional, and often northern, conceptualizations of vocational education and training (VET); insists upon analysing both VET and work in broad, relational and inclusive ways; develops and applies original theoretical contributions drawn from political ecology; and moves beyond 'extractive' modalities of research in this important arena. In terms of 'process', the book has further distinction and originality due to the innovative ways in which the 20 core authors/researchers have combined to form the VET Africa 4.0 Collective and wrestled with the decolonial challenges and dynamics of coproduction and joint authorship within the context of an externally funded international Global Challenges Research Fund (GCRF) partnership. For those interested in learning from, and advancing, more equitable international research partnerships, this book has much to offer readers across multiple fields and disciplines.

The book is structured around three sections, the first of which establishes the historical and theoretical context (Chapters 1–4) while introducing the 'social ecosystems for skills' model that underpins the overall framework for the analysis. Section 2 (Chapters 5–8) develops and expands this model through a detailed and critically reflexive examination of the empirical data embedded within four contextually grounded South African and Ugandan VET case studies. Section 3 (Chapter 9) reflects upon the implications of the overall study for future research, policy and practice; and an important and insightful 'Afterword' reflects on the collaborative, multilevel research and writing process in ways that deserve close attention.

This is a complex and sophisticated analysis with theoretical and empirical depth that provides an invaluable resource for all concerned with the future of VET policy, practice and research worldwide. It is a collective book that reimagines more democratic and relational futures for VET, challenges dominant orthodoxies, engages with the implications of both decolonization and climate resilience for the future of skills development, and interrogates the multiple power dynamics involved in advancing innovative international research partnerships within, and beyond, the VET arena. To cite the authors own words: 'As university researchers, we must find ways of balancing the immediacy of the funded project and the need for stronger and longer-lasting bonds in the locations in which we research, while also forming new, oftentimes nontraditional, relations across our institutions and our related partner networks' (afterword).

For these reasons, it is hard to imagine a more appropriate volume for the launch of our renewed book series with Bristol University Press. I am, therefore, more than pleased to recommend this work to readers interested in the contemporary challenges faced by VET in Africa and worldwide; and, most importantly, to *all* engaged with the theoretical and epistemological implications of decolonization for interdisciplinary research, comparative studies and international development.

Michael Crossley
Professor of Comparative and International Education
University of Bristol

List of Figures, Tables and Boxes

Figures

Table

Boxes

List of Abbreviations

AEO	agricultural extension officer
CHAT	cultural historical activity theory
CoE	centre of excellence
DHET	Department of Higher Education and Training (South Africa)
DTP	Dube Trade Port
FCAFTI	Fort Cox Agricultural and Forestry Training Institute
GCRF	Global Challenges Research Fund (UK)
IBLN	Imvothu Bubomi Learning Network
ICT	information and communications technology
ILO	International Labour Organization/Office
INGO	international nongovernmental organization
IOC	international oil company
IPCC	Intergovernmental Panel on Climate Change
KZN	KwaZulu-Natal
LED	local economic development
MEMD	Ministry of Energy and Mineral Development (Uganda)
NGO	nongovernmental organization
NQF	national qualifications framework
PAR	participatory action research
PI	principal investigator
SDGs	sustainable development goals
SEZ	Special Economic Zone
SIP	Strategic Integrated Project
SoE	school of excellence
SOGA	Skills for Oil and Gas in Africa programme
ToT	training-of-trainers
TVET	technical and vocational education and training
VET	vocational education and training
UK	United Kingdom
UKRI	United Kingdom Research and Innovation

UNESCO	United Nations Educational, Scientific and Cultural Organization
UPIK	Uganda Petroleum Institute, Kigumba
US	United States of America
US$	United States Dollars
WRC	Water Research Commission (South Africa)

Acknowledgements and Authorship

Much of the research on which this book is based took place in the context of pandemic and lockdowns. The conventional acknowledgements of all those who gave of their time and knowledge to share with us therefore must be even more heartfelt. We absolutely could not have done this work without the cooperation of hundreds of youth activists, vocational education and training (VET) teachers and administrators, small business owners, farmers, representatives of traditional authorities, and staff of large corporations, development agencies, NGOs and government ministries and agencies. As well as the core writing team, we benefitted hugely also from the support of university administrators, without whom the project could not have made the many adjustments to respond to radically changing circumstances over its lifespan. We benefitted also from the participation of research scholars in our various institutions who attended team meetings and shared insights from their own work, and from the comments of the many external colleagues who attended our presentations along the way, online and in several countries. In particular, we acknowledge Lwande Maqwelane and Phindile Sithole, who provided vignettes for Chapter 7. We also recognize the pioneering work of the late Tich Pesanayi, who established the boundary-crossing foundations of the social skills for ecosystem approach in the Alice case in collaboration with partners from the local economic development office, especially Passmore Dongi, and the Fort Cox Agricultural and Forestry Training Institute, especially but not limited to Chamu Matambo and Louise Madikiza, whose contributions are also acknowledged.

This book would not exist without the financial support of UK Research and Innovation and specifically the funding of the Global Challenges Research Fund (GCRF). As well as the initial funding, GCRF also provided additional support for the UK team in response to COVID-19. All three African chair teams also supported the project financially to cover staffing beyond the GCRF commitment, particularly to extend work on the project and then the book. We should acknowledge the role there of the UNESCO chair at Gulu, and the two South African Research Chairs Initiative chairs, at Rhodes and Wits, funded by the South African National Research Foundation. There were also a number of points where the project benefitted from additional support – for instance, around workshop organization, additional student support and conference attendance – from the partner chairs and centres. In addition, the Water Research Commission of South Africa contributed substantive funding that allowed for the work in the Alice case to develop over a six-year period. The *Journal of Vocational Education and Training* also provided funding that allowed us to cosponsor a conference in Gulu (discussed in Chapter 8) at which members of all the teams presented. Making the book open access was funded by the University of Nottingham, and we acknowledge Professor Robert Mokaya, Pro Vice Chancellor for Global Engagement, for facilitating this.

We have taken the conscious decision to author this book collectively. This was part of a deliberate attempt to move beyond research as extraction. While this was inevitably fallible as still located within the uneven political economy of the global knowledge production system, and our own human frailties, we committed to maximizing the ownership of the project by the wider team. We made early career researcher capacity development an explicit project goal while seeking to grow the whole team. A total of 20 team members were involved centrally in the project and form the collective authorship of this book. All 20 participated in design and case discussion workshops. Most visited both case countries, Uganda and South Africa (although COVID limited some planned travel), and about half of the African team visited England to present at conferences and attend workshops. Several of the less experienced members of the team have gone on to write journal articles based on parts of the project in which they were particularly involved, with support from more experienced colleagues.

Inevitably, contributions varied, as some had far more time to commit to the project, another hard to shift inequality. Eleven of the team were centrally involved as (co)leads of chapter writing and/or as editors. Nonetheless, we have written this as a monograph rather than an edited book as all chapters were extensively worked on by multiple members of the team and edited to cohere. Due to performativity pressures, however, we have named authors for each chapter. These are the team members who were most involved in drafting the chapters, although all have been read and edited collectively. We will return to a reflection on our process in an afterword.

Here, in alphabetical order, we acknowledge our co-authors:

Primo Adoye, Gulu University
Scovia Adrupio, Gulu University
Stephanie Allais, University of the Witwatersrand
Bonaventure Kyaligonja, Gulu University
Heila Lotz-Sisitka, Rhodes University
Simon McGrath, University of Nottingham and Nelson Mandela University
   (University of Glasgow from January 2022)

Luke Metelerkamp, Rhodes University
Palesa Molebatsi, University of the Witwatersrand
David Monk, Gulu University
Sidney Muhangi, Rhodes University
Kenneth Nyeko, Gulu University
David Ocan, Gulu University
George Openjuru, Gulu University
Maxwell Openjuru, Gulu University
Presha Ramsarup, University of the Witwatersrand and University of Nottingham
Glen Robbins, Toyota Wessels Institute of Manufacturing Studies
Jo-Anna Russon, University of Nottingham
Themba Tshabalala, University of the Witwatersrand
Volker Wedekind, University of Nottingham and University of the Witwatersrand
Jacques Zeelen, Gulu University and University of Groningen

1

Introducing VET Africa 4.0

Heila Lotz-Sisitka and Simon McGrath

A new approach to vocational education and training

This book is about vocational education and training (VET). It is concerned with how the current policy and practice orthodoxy is not working despite the efforts of educators and learners. It is driven by a realization that the futures for which VET is intended to prepare people are ever more precarious at the individual, societal and planetary levels. And it is motivated by a sense that while better futures are possible, VET is poorly positioned to respond to the new skilling needs these will require.

Our empirical focus is on Africa, grounded in case studies from two Anglophone countries, Uganda and South Africa. Due to the effects of colonialism and aid dependence, African VET systems have sought to mimic VET in the industrialized world. Yet, these borrowings are often poorly grounded in the realities of the 'donor' northern systems (McGrath, 2010; Allais and Wedekind, 2020) and are even less relevant to African contexts (McGrath et al, 2020a; Allais, 2020b). However, our intention is not simply to make an African account of VET but to engage in a global debate about VET's current weaknesses and the need to transform it to meet the challenges of coming years. Although contexts vary, what we offer in this book has implications for VET in all jurisdictions.

VET systems are not identical. In the Anglophone world in which we are based, VET north and south has been particularly grounded in an individualized human capital development paradigm that drove both colonial and industrialization programmes. Our critique points to the limitations of this modern institutional form of VET. The legacies of colonialism and industrialization continue to this day, producing exclusions from modern institutions and their logics (Patel, 2017). In Anglophone Africa, many locally meaningful forms of VET have been excluded and relegated to 'informality' due to the logics of capital and particular notions of VET's purpose. As we shall argue in greater detail in Chapter 3, this VET is grounded in an extractive view of our relationship to the planet (see also McGrath, 2012).

While they do not escape the link to fossil capitalism (Malm, 2016, see Chapter 3 for a longer discussion), many of the world's best VET systems, by contrast, are less individualistic than in the Anglophone model. Rather, they are based on strong relationalities between VET providers and the associated institutions and work-based communities (both employer and union) that they contribute to and depend on (see, for instance, Deissinger and Gonon, 2021 for a historical review of the German and Swiss systems). These in turn relate to national political economies, especially the workings and contestations of welfare regimes (Busemeyer, 2014). As such, they are located in very different contexts than those that pertain in Africa or the rest of the south. Their potential to provide lessons, therefore, are limited, though they point to some of what is possible in going beyond the Anglophone tradition.

An awareness of historical and comparative experiences leads us to offer a consideration of what a more relational paradigm for VET may look like in contemporary Africa, remembering that such relationalities are argued to have been a feature of precolonial vocational learning, though they are weak in contemporary approaches. This weakness is influenced by contemporary governance systems and histories of exclusion and colonial imposition (see Chapter 2). Although the contexts are different, many other systems globally also need to address path dependence and think about building more relational systems that are fitted for new challenges.

VET, as currently constituted, is out of sync with contemporary experiences of work, and what work means for many young people and communities today in Africa and beyond. Notwithstanding a still strongly held desire for a linear relation between formal training and formal job, this relationship is both complex and rare. The complexity relates back to the historicity of a bifurcated notion of economy that has separated out the meanings and associated institutional structures serving 'first and second economies', with VET traditionally oriented towards the so-called 'first economy' of mining, motors, manufacturing and the like. It has often failed to include the working lives and VET needs of those that are economically active in the problematically termed 'informal' or 'second' economy (see Chapter 5). And it is even worse when it comes to the complex realities of the provisioning economy (see, for example, Power, 2004), or a consideration of the work needed for transformations to sustainability, also conceptualized as inclusive sustainable development.

Much of current VET policy attention is on the 'fourth industrial revolution' and digitalization. However, far less attention has been paid to the climate emergency. Climate change and the global discourse of just transitions and sustainability transformations are driving the need for massive transformation of the global energy system and its historical construction. They also highlight the need to think about new areas of work and learning such as climate resilient agriculture, pollution reduction and improved water resources management (see Rosenberg et al, 2020). This emergency and emerging solutions impact all systems of work, including formal salaried work, less formal and more precarious work, household and livelihood work, and work for the common good. In this book, by way of empirical example, we consider transport, oil, water and food systems (see Chapter 3) as sources of work that transgress the historical binaries of formal and informal work: ecology and economy. Thinking about transport, oil, water and food systems also opens up work for sustainable livelihoods, sustainable development and provisioning work. Beyond these, there are many other such fields of work that need further investigation for their implications for reconstituting VET (including such areas as biodiversity, urban planning, water resources management and healthcare, for example).

At the same time, our critique of VET is part of a wider, parallel critique of how education policies have resulted in systems that are unable to meet the needs of the present and the major challenges that will be faced in making education fit for the future (see Allais, 2020b; Allais and Wedekind, 2020). The latter amounts to nothing less than reframing the purposes of education away from the grip of histories of human capital in its various guises (including as forms of labour for colonial states). In its report to mark UNESCO's 75th anniversary, the International Commission on the Futures of Education points to important quantitative improvements in education over the past 50 years but makes clear that there have also been serious failings. It notes that

> [t]he past fifty years of progress have been vastly uneven and today's gaps in access, participation and outcomes are based on yesterday's exclusions and oppressions. Tomorrow's progress is dependent not only on their correction, but on a questioning of the assumptions and arrangements that resulted in these inequalities and asymmetries. (International Commission on the Futures of Education, 2021: 20)

We argue that a new account of VET needs to take account of these multiple rationalities and must overcome these segmentations of living, working and learning. An important step here is reframing the concept of work, which lies at the very heart of the meaning of VET. The futures of work may be even more different from the dominant imaginary of formal VET than are present realities. However, the VET field shows little concern with how work is being reframed and restructured by economic and technological dynamics, outside of some limited initiatives to introduce digitalization programmes. VET approaches have also been inadequate in responding to the multidimensional nature of complex environmental challenges, partly because these issues have been treated as 'externalities' to mainstream economic activity and work practices, a problem that results from separating economy from ecology and society. Thus, there is much work to be done for VET to engage more substantively with ecological dynamics and influences (see Chapter 3).

Our intention is to go beyond a recounting of 'what works' in VET, or even a critique of what doesn't. Rather, we draw on Bhaskar's notion of an immanent critique (Bhaskar, 1975) (discussed in more detail later in the chapter) to provide a critique of the current state of VET and what underpins its being this way, *and* a vision of what a future, better VET might look like based on emerging visions of a better world (represented by the notion of just transitions) and what we see as the first stirrings of new VET practices that are aligned with this vision. Thus, we intend this book to be part of an opening up of a new phase of VET research (see also Powell and McGrath, 2019a; Rosenberg et al, 2020) rather than harbouring any illusion that it is 'the last word' on these issues.

Introducing the notion of skills ecosystems

As well as reconstituting the notion of work, we must reconstitute the relational system of education and training. This must be done for broader educative purposes (see International Commission on the Futures of Education, 2021) but also to make VET better at providing access to knowledge, learning pathways and pedagogical encounters for a broadening concept of work. In considering this, we have looked at existing VET theories for a thinking tool that could help us start to explore what is needed. Here, we have chosen the notion of the social ecosystem for skills model. This was first proposed for advancing VET in response to rapidly emerging economic sectors. The fundamental premise of this model is that a more complex 'ecosystem' of knowledge, learning and work-based engagement is needed. This can strengthen place-based skills development in collaborative spaces that are enabling work and learning innovation. As we explain in more detail in Chapter 4, the model emerged from contexts such as Silicon Valley and in industrial sectors and cities in Australia and Britain (see also Wedekind et al, 2021). However, it has been identified as a potentially important model for sustainability-oriented education and training programmes where place-based relationally constituted learning around complex problems is needed (Hodgson and Spours, 2016, 2018; Lotz-Sisitka, 2020; McGrath and Russon, 2022). We seek to build on the model and expand it to address other aspects of VET, other contexts and other imagined futures.

Regardless of context, VET institutions are widely understood as important partners in economic development, expected to deliver responsive curricula and engage relationally with employers and work environments. Until Lotz-Sisitka (2020), the social ecosystems approach had not been applied in southern contexts, where work cannot be reduced to formal employment by 'big industries' only, and where sustainability challenges are particularly pressing. Her South African Expanded Public Works Programme case points to the need to think beyond the conventional notion of the VET institution as public and formal, as this applies to only a small part of vocational learning, albeit a crucial one. Relevant to this book, and the work undertaken to further advance our understanding of the potential for this skills development model, Lotz-Sisitka argues that

[t]he Hodgson and Spours (2018) social ecosystemic model also highlights an important role for learning institutions such as technical education and training and further education and training colleges [that is, VET institutions] in cementing ... potential skills development pathways into local economies over time, with a role of not only providing skills, but also operating as developmental 'hubs' in partnership with local development and business entities. In a South African context, this would require a combination of local economic development (LED) structures working closely with relevant learning institutions, such as TVET colleges, agricultural training institutes or community colleges, and where these are absent other training institutions such as non-governmental organisations (NGOs), faith-based organisations, etc. especially in rural areas where formal learning infrastructure is often sparse, or limited to schools. (Lotz-Sisitka, 2020: 118)

In the same volume, Lotz-Sisitka and Pesanayi (2020) reflect on the mediation processes in the early development of a learning network in Alice (one of our case studies) that led to diverse horizontal connections between a range of actors in a regional skills ecosystem for advancing water for food knowledge and practice for local economic development. The mediation processes, while building and supporting horizontal connectivities, were doing this by facilitating links with national policy, curriculum, research and funding systems. A VET learning institution, in partnership with local universities and the local economic development office, provided the 'skills ecosystem leadership', which was extended with the influence of socialized digital technologies (which we reflect on further in Chapter 5). This offered an embryonic reflection on the Alice case as an emerging regional or social ecosystem for skills, which we brought into the current project. We have been reflexively considering this case from the vantage point of what we term here an expanded social ecosystem model for VET Africa (see Chapter 4).

In their reflection on these mediation processes, Lotz–Sisitka and Pesanayi (2020: 159) note that 'establishing regional skills ecosystemic approaches requires mediation, but as yet, not much has been said about this mediation, and how it is to be constituted'. This is an issue that we consider further in this book. Lotz–Sisitka and Pesanayi (2020) also note the need for a more complex systemic view of knowledge flow and dissemination than that traditionally practised in formal VET that can link research, education, extension and social learning activity in more dynamic relations, offering a potential source of curriculum innovation in VET institutions, and social learning innovations in the regional setting. Hodgson and Spours (2018) began to develop such an analysis in London, and we were curious to examine this perspective further in African contexts, hence this book.

In considering what this means for VET in Africa, and building on the earlier work on mediation by Lotz–Sisitka and Pesanayi (2020), we have taken seriously the recommendations by Spours and colleagues (Hodgson and Spours, 2016, 2018; Spours, 2019) that there is a need to mediate between 'facilitating verticalities' (such as policy and funding systems) and 'horizontal connectivities'. We understand the latter in terms of connected, relational organizations and partners in what we describe as a VET 'learning network' (Lotz–Sisitka et al, 2016, 2021; Metelerkamp et al, 2021). We examine the configurations and the functioning of such mediation processes and follow Spours in understanding VET providers as learning institutions with mediating powers that can support VET learning networks along with other partners. In practice, it is not the single VET institution, but rather the connection between learning institutions – for example, universities, VET colleges, workplaces and nonformal vocational providers – that provide mediation in the expanded notion of social ecosystems for skills that we have been investigating and developing, as we also reflect on in this book (see Chapter 8). Therefore, learning networks become important structures that bring multiple actors together in the expanded social ecosystem for skills. Our research also shows that there is need to give attention to how learning institutions reconstitute themselves to provide the types of mediation that can bring horizontal connectivities and facilitate verticalities together in a local, place-based social ecosystem for skills (see Chapters 6 and 8).

As part of our praxis, we have developed insights into the changing nature of vocational learning institutions. In Chapter 8 in particular, we consider the changing nature of the university as a learning institution that, via a transformative orientation and community engagement approaches, is able to provide certain kinds of mediating support within the expanded social ecosystem model. We similarly consider public VET colleges and how they are trying to provide mediating support for VET within the more complex work environment in which they are situated. We note the tensions inherent in this given these institutions' logic is largely formed by the teleologies of industrialization and human capital. It is encouraging, however, that within a 'Futures of Education' framing, African education leaders (in the South African Development Community and UNESCO) are currently contemplating ways in which higher education and VET institutions can better collaborate to strengthen local and national economies and sustainable development. In doing so, they will need to move further towards considering nonformal and informal learning actors and approaches. This is an important strand of this book, explored through expanded social ecosystems and how these support VET in the context of the notions of work outlined earlier (see Chapter 5). Of interest to the expanded social ecosystem model is the role of vocational teachers and their agency for curriculum design enactment and pedagogical praxis development. This is our focus in Chapter 6.

We have taken on this challenge of critically exploring the model in African contexts, via empirical case contexts that reflect the complexity of the notion of work we have just outlined (two each in South Africa and Uganda). Across these contexts, we have considered both a 'large-scale' case (the oil and maritime industries) and a 'small-scale' one (smallholder agriculture and informal work). In each, and despite the scale of the cases, we found that work is far more complex than this simple schema suggests. The complex configuration of work is shaped and influenced by myriad diverse factors, not least the failure of the formal economy to provide 'jobs' for millions of young people (for instance, 64 per cent of South Africans aged 15 to 24 are unemployed [StatsSA, 2021: 30]; 92 per cent of employment in East Africa is in the informal sector [ILO, 2018: 28]). We have found that work is not 'assured', that much learning for such work is informally and relationally constituted, and that learning pathways and transitioning between work and learning are often constructed as complex processes, as Chapters 5 and 8 explore in further detail.

Before proceeding to introduce our cases, it is perhaps time to explain our usage of our key term, VET. We have used it throughout the book as our preferred way of talking about vocational learning experiences, providers and systems. However, this is an area fraught with terminological disagreement (and here we are confining ourselves to the Anglophone debate). Moodie (2002: 258) argues that definitions of VET need to be cognisant of epistemological, teleological, hierarchical and pragmatic dimensions. As Powell and McGrath (2019a) note, there is a huge range of terminology used here for the overall concept, for systems and for institutional types. In South Africa, a further T has been introduced to talk about the system and institutions, 'technical'. When we use TVET later in the book, it is usually in reference to South African public colleges. In Uganda, there has been a recent shift from 'business and technical' as a prefix to 'technical' alone. TVET appears to be the currently preferred (donor-supported) Anglophone term for Africa but 'technical' feels superfluous and is not used globally.

Some prefer to talk about 'skills development' as a broader concept, or to combine the two notions as 'vocational skills development'. Our view is that VET is the most widely understood concept and thus the most preferable. However, it is also clear that ours is an expansive view of VET, one that avoids seeing this as only referring to formal provision, more narrowly to public provision, or even more narrowly still to only that provision that falls under an education ministry. This makes us view conventional boundaries between adult/community/lifelong research and vocational as problematic, though we are concerned to avoid vocational imperialism here. Indeed, we see our concerns as having an important ontological dimension.

Introducing the cases

Our examination of what is wrong with contemporary VET, and why, and how it might be improved is grounded in four cases of regional social ecosystems for skills. Each is geographically bounded, although the boundaries are always porous as each exists within wider systems of political–economy–ecology, education systems and labour markets that are all interconnected. In some, we focus only on one locally important sector, while in others a broader range of economic activities are considered. The cases were selected to illustrate a wide range of contexts of skills formation as part of our wider project of offering an expansive view of vocational learning. We will return to descriptions of each across several subsequent chapters but offer some introductory scene-setting here.

eThekwini

Our eThekwini case is the most conventional in VET research terms. It is centred on a metropolitan area, eThekwini, home to around 3.5 million people. The municipality has grown up around Durban, South Africa's third city and the fourth busiest harbour in the Southern Hemisphere. Other industries have developed around the harbour, including sugar, tourism and automotives, but the transport and logistics sector remain crucial. Our case focuses on this sector and particularly on the maritime skills system and labour market. This concentrates our focus spatially on the north of the city and, as will become clearer in subsequent chapters, additionally on the large bulk port of Richards Bay, around 100 miles to the north.

South Africa's VET system was profoundly shaped by colonialism and apartheid, leading to a racially segmented skills system that was dominated by industrial skills needs, particularly in the mining, metals and motors sectors, but that was negligent of rural subsistence and informal sector skills (see, for instance, McGrath et al, 2004). Since the beginning of democracy in 1994, a complex new skills system has emerged, based on a national qualifications framework, a large public TVET college system and a relatively well-developed industrial training system, organized around sectoral skills bodies, a levy-grant system and learnerships (a form of modern apprenticeship). Originally under two ministries, Labour and Education, the system was reformed in 2009 under the Department of Higher Education and Training, but issues of coordination remain. While intended to be highly facilitatory, the South African skills system is widely seen as containing considerable dysfunctionalities (Allais, 2013, 2020a).

In addition to the wider colonial and apartheid system that racialized access to education and work and built ethnic tensions as part of a regime of control, the Durban skills and work ecosystem around the docks has been shaped further by three important moments. First, a wave of labour unrest in the early 1970s helped develop a strong trade union presence and ideology on the docks. Second, a neoliberal turn by the apartheid state in the 1980s ended a history since the 1920s of using parastatal industries – such as the docks and railways – as a way of oversupplying apprentices to the national economy (see Chapter 2). This had the effect of undermining a historical relationship between public vocational colleges and public employers, but memories of this linger on, largely in views of what current public provision isn't. Third, the coming of multiracial democracy resulted in these historically White colleges merging with historically Black neighbours and a further distancing of the sector from a still largely White managerial cadre.

Theoretically, our interest in this case initially lay in exploring how this evolving skills system was responding to major national government policy initiatives around infrastructural development for economic development. Since the early years of the new millennium, the city has been the site of a series of major infrastructural development projects. These were kickstarted by South Africa's hosting of the FIFA World Cup in 2010, which led to the construction of a new sports stadium and international airport for Durban. These were built upon in the National Development Plan (NPC, 2012), the National Infrastructure Plan (PICC, 2012) and the Operation Phakisa initiative (Operation Phakisa, nd). Within the National Infrastructure Plan, Strategic Integrated Project 2 (SIP2) was the Durban–Free State–Gauteng corridor, linking the port to the country's main industrial region but also promising new industrial development along the route. Within KwaZulu-Natal province (KZN), the project prioritized two Special Economic Zones (SEZs): Dube TradePort, at the new airport, just to the north of the city, and the satellite port of Richards Bay, mentioned already; the expansion of container handling facilities in the Port of Durban; and the development of a new 'dig-out' port just to its south. Operation Phakisa was supposed to balance employment and environment imperatives. However, the economic imperative was clearly paramount, with the environmental element being located within a green growth paradigm.

The South African political system allows for considerable provincial responsibility for economic and related policies. The KZN Provincial Office of the Premier is responsible for overall policy coordination regionally including SIP2 oversight. The provincial Department of Economic Development, Tourism and Environmental Affairs has responsibility for the Dube TradePort Company, a public entity operating the SEZ. The municipality is also an important actor, reflected in its membership of the C40 global cities' alliance. One relevant municipal project is the eThekwini Maritime Cluster, which brings together key sectoral actors.

The municipality has a well-developed education sector with several high performing schools (both public and private), three public universities, three public TVET colleges, a provincial public sector skills academy and many private postschool providers. However, access and educational attainment are highly uneven, reflecting the continuation of longstanding inequalities derived from colonialism and apartheid. Important actors in the maritime skills system include the parastatal Transnet, which has its own training centre for new and existing staff, and Grindrod, a South African-based transnational company with interests in both offshore and onshore aspects of the maritime sector, which also has its own in-house training academy.

One initiative that will feature strongly in subsequent chapters is the new public Maritime Academy, a centre of excellence established at the uMfolozi TVET College in Richards Bay. This has been offering a suite of new maritime studies courses, accredited by the South African Maritime Safety Authority, since 2019.

Hoima

The Bunyoro Kitara Kingdom of Western Uganda, centred on the town of Hoima, historically has been located far from the major economic and political centres of East Africa. At Ugandan independence, the region had relatively little economic or educational development. Economically, it has had a heavy reliance on subsistence farming and fishing, supplemented by largely informal sector activities and remittances from those who have migrated to Kampala or other larger centres. As of 2000, there were no major public education institutions. It is important to stress that although it is called a 'Kingdom', this is a cultural, not political, institution. Moreover, local government is relatively weak.

Into this context since 2000 has come the catalytic economic presence of massive investment in the oil and gas sector, with significant multiplier effects expected for other sectors and across the economy. Lake Albert, which forms the western border of the region, had been identified as having oil and gas reserves nearly a century ago, but it was only in 2006 that it was confirmed that there were significant commercially exploitable reserves. Getting to the point of production, however, has been far from simple. Tullow, the main actor initially, clashed with the government, which eventually took them to court over alleged tax evasion. Combined with the usual oil price volatility, costly technical issues as Ugandan oil requires heating to flow in a pipeline and diplomatic challenges in finalizing a pipeline route for exports given both Kenya and Tanzania wanted it routed through them, the project has been subject to considerable delays.

Nonetheless, progress has been made. As well as early work on an oil refinery, an airport is under construction, and the major roads into the area are being upgraded from their previous unpaved state. Hoima's amenities have improved, and it now has branches of several banks, new restaurants and hotels, and a large new market building. As part of this transformation, Hoima was granted city status in July 2020. However, as we note in Chapter 3, there are crucial political–economy–ecology challenges with the development of a new fossil fuel-based economy.

It was clear to the Ugandan government, the oil companies and aid donors that there was a vast gap between local skills development in the region and the requirements for employment in the new sector. It was only in 2014 that Gulu University began to develop a small branch campus in Hoima, and the district only got a public vocational institution in 2016. Otherwise, there were several small private and church-based vocational providers, each on average enrolling less than 2 per cent of the students of the mean for the eThekwini colleges. These providers offer a broad range of conventional vocational subjects – construction trades, motor mechanics, tailoring – to relatively small classes and with modest resources. Most of this training is geared to local and relatively small-scale economic activity and, indeed, domestic needs such as house building and repairs.

There have been several iterations of development in VET policy, including the 'Ugandan Vocational Qualifications Framework' in 2008, the 'BTVET [business and technical and vocational education and training] "Skilling Uganda" Strategic Plan 2011–2020' and the 2019 'Technical, Vocational Education and Training Policy' (GoU, 2008; MoES, 2011, 2019a). The new policy is intended to focus on the establishment of an employer-led system, develop a vocational qualifications framework harmonized with the regional framework, and promote public awareness and ensure sustainable financing for quality and accessible education (MoES, 2019a). This almost exactly mirrors the 'VET toolkit' discussed in Chapter 2, which has been spread across Africa by international donors, with very limited real impact. The Ugandan policies have been written with major input from donors, and the system is hugely dependent on external funding, in major contrast to the South African picture, although the intellectual impact of donors has been huge there too (McGrath and Badroodien, 2006; Allais, 2007; McGrath, 2010).

Regarding sector-specific skills, the Ministry of Energy and Mineral Development (MEMD) commissioned a British consultancy firm to produce a workforce skills development strategy for oil and gas (MEMD, 2015). This made a case for the development of intermediate and higher skills for the sector within Uganda. This resulted in the decision to build the Uganda Petroleum Institute Kigumba (UPIK), with World Bank support, as one of six new centres of excellence under the Ministry of Education and Sports (MoES, 2019b). The sector is dominated by the use of international qualifications. UPIK has got accreditation to deliver some of these but plans to develop its own qualifications that adapt the international qualifications to the Ugandan context. We shall return to this story in Chapters 6 and 7.

However, the international oil companies were not convinced by the MEMD plan. They expected the peak demand for such skills to come earlier than a new institution could deliver and were sceptical of relying on skills from an unproven provider. This led to the Skills for Oil and Gas Africa (SOGA) programme cofunded by the British, German and Norwegian governments. Influenced by industry views, SOGA concluded in its inception phase that the skills gulf for entry into core industry jobs was too great for more than a handful of locals to bridge (GIZ, 2015). Therefore, it focused primarily on building skills for employment and subcontracting elsewhere in the value chain. This largely consisted in practice of NGO-delivered training programmes in business development and construction trades, the latter to international curricula and resulting in international certification. SOGA had the advantage of being very well resourced and the team clearly had some convening power, being able to get access at senior levels to the oil companies and first-tier contractors and to government, and to work with formal VET providers and local and international NGOs. We will revisit these two interventions in Chapter 6.

Alice

The second South African case centres on the town of Alice and its rural surrounds in the Raymond Mhlaba Municipality, located in the Amathole District in the Eastern Cape. The area was part of the 'homeland' of Ciskei under apartheid. Before that, the colonial Land Act of 1913 had already set up such areas as labour reserves to keep Africans out of urban residence while providing migrant labour for mining and manufacturing. Such areas were never particularly economically viable as small-scale farming regions (also because of poor infrastructural support by the apartheid government) and were always dependent on transfer payments from migrant workers under colonialism and apartheid. This migration and remittance culture endured the transition to democracy in 1994. Today, state expenditure, public sector employment and monthly social grant payments (for children, the elderly and those with disabilities) constitute three further pillars of the financial economy. Public sector maladministration and capacity issues limit the potentially transformative potential of the state's substantial developmental spending in the area. However, at the time of the learning network and skills ecosystem formation process, there was an active and highly functional local economic development office that proactively supported smallholder farmer development into commercialization of their products.

The Eastern Cape Province is a large, primarily rural province, made up mostly of former apartheid homelands, leaving the province with a past and continuing contemporary history of marginalization and poverty. Economic opportunities in the Alice area remain very limited. While there is a substantial citrus industry and game farming, both these industries fail to include large populations, who remain dependent on grants and the land for their livelihoods. The food sector dominates the local informal economy, but there is limited scope for growth in scale due to the intense supermarketization of the South African food system (Frayne and Crush, 2017). In response, informal economic activities are becoming ever more prominent in the region.

Notwithstanding the challenges of going to greater scale, small-scale farming of livestock, mixed crops and home gardening undertaken largely on communally owned land is common. This increasingly has an agroecological orientation through the influence of NGOs and in response to the challenge of limited water. This farming provides a livelihood for many of the region's inhabitants. However, it is striking that much (though importantly not all) of this activity is carried out by the elderly who use it as a means of supplementing the household food basket and, occasionally, its income. There are a small, but still significant, number of formal and informal commercial agricultural enterprises. Despite the relatively abundant water resources in the area, the vast majority of farming activities are carried out without irrigation, leaving farmers to rely on the region's summer rainfall for production.

Yet, these lands were set aside for African habitation precisely because they were not productive enough for commercial farming. This engineered combination of high population densities and marginal agricultural land set up an inevitable environmental challenge. This has been exacerbated by climate change, with water availability a huge constraint, especially in more frequently experienced drought periods. A reliance on rainfed agricultural practices leaves a great many of the region's inhabitants in a critically vulnerable position (see Chapter 3 for the wider political–economy–ecology in which these challenges sit).

In the education sector, Alice is home to the historically prominent institutions of Lovedale School and Fort Hare University. The Amatole District is also home to a tertiary agricultural skills provider, the Fort Cox Agricultural and Forestry Training Institute (FCAFTI), under the Department of Agriculture, Forestry and Fisheries, and a public TVET college under the Department of Higher Education and Training. Educational attainment is still very uneven across the district at school level, with significant consequences for postschool institutions, and youth unemployment is high, at 59 per cent (StatsSA, 2021).

Several state agencies are active in the region. These include the Department of Rural Development and Land Reform, the Department of Agriculture, Forestry and Fisheries, the National Youth Development Agency, and the Agriculture and Water Research Commissions. In contrast to the focus on industrial skills policies in the eThekwini case, the policy environment in the Alice case is dominated by natural resources and community development, including those policies oriented towards issues specific to the agricultural sector in the National Development Plan. However, policies are experienced as top-down and uncoordinated.

As regards skills policies, three challenges are apparent in the region. First, the public TVET college is part of a system that is essentially urban-focused and industry-oriented, with rural colleges, such as this one, largely expected to offer programmes that are misaligned to local labour markets. Second, the gap between what are effectively two agricultural systems is manifested in a disconnect between a high skills ecosystem and both the public VET providers. Third, there is a disconnection between the TVET college and the agricultural college, located as they are under different ministries.

Unlike the large parastatal and private enterprises in eThekwini, the local work and skills landscape is populated by farmers and their organizations, local NGOs, youth groups and community representatives, alongside the local postschool institutions already mentioned and governmental structures. The latter include the Raymond Mhlaba Local Economic Agency, as well as provincial and national government departments with an interest in the development of the local economy and sustainable development. Relationships are often informal and very localized.

The central focus of this case study, the 'Amanzi [Water] for Food' programme, was partially funded by the Water Research Commission (WRC) and the SARChI Chair at Rhodes University (for more extended accounts, see Chapters 5 and 8; Lotz-Sisitka et al, 2016, 2021; and Amanzi for Food, nd). The focus was initially on rainfed water harvesting and smallholder agriculture and the development of a social ecosystem for skills that drew on existing WRC printed resources, and the knowledge of Rhodes academics, members of the community and FCAFTI staff, as well as contributions from University of Fort Hare staff, NGOs, youth cooperatives, farmers' associations and social media partners. A learning network, Imvothu Bubomi (Water is Life), was established. This included an expanding group of horizontally connected partners, intermediary mediators and vertical facilitating groups focusing on a wider range of knowledges and practices relevant to smallholder agriculture and curriculum innovations over an eight-year period of coengaged research and praxis. As we shall show in subsequent chapters (especially Chapter 8), this intervention was able to overcome key institutional weaknesses in the regional skills system and labour market.

Gulu

Gulu, which also received city status in July 2020, is the major urban centre in Acholiland in northern Uganda. Economic activity remains primarily driven by agriculture, but this is hampered by long distances from the major markets of East Africa. The population of the region is very young (around 70 per cent below 30) and unemployment rates are very high.

Until 2006, Acholiland was ravaged by 30 years of civil war, notorious for the use of child soldiers, with much of the population forced to live in internal displacement camps. The war also saw a significant change from the traditional communal and clan-based system to a situation in which much of the land was privatized and many lost access to it. Many of those with little access to land are, unsurprisingly, farming unsustainably. The largely illegal market in charcoal is encouraging deforestation, further exacerbating land degradation. Local markets for agricultural goods are limited, as are opportunities to export nationally and internationally.

Many of the same policies – apart from that on oil – that were described for Hoima apply in Gulu, and there are similar concerns about their lack of coherence and the limits of the state to be facilitatory. City status has not yet led to any significant changes in local government capacity. Given elections and the pandemic, this is hardly unsurprising. Beyond the national and local policy level sits a wider set of political–economy–ecology challenges (see Chapter 3) that also serve to disenable the people of the region.

Nonetheless, 15 years after the war, there is a real sense of transformation as people adapt to postwar settings. Lives are being rebuilt, businesses are growing, roads are being paved and streetlights put up. Gulu is growing as young people from rural areas make their way there, driving *boda boda* (motorcycle taxis), and generally hustling (Thieme, 2013) as they create pathways in their pursuit of decent livelihoods and sustainable futures. The result is a vibrant ecosystem of seemingly chaotic and entangled working, learning and living, as we shall explore in Chapter 5.

The war and its aftermath brought large numbers of humanitarian agencies to the region, often based in Gulu, and one legacy of these is in a large number of programmes aimed at skills development and agriculture development. Consequently, there is a push by the government and NGOs for self-employment. There are a few formal VET institutions in the region, both public and private. Complementing these is a vast array of nonformal training programmes and a large informal sector, with young people learning through apprenticeships at small businesses, in NGO programmes, on YouTube and from each other, as we shall explore in Chapters 5 and 6.

The most important postschool institution in the region is Gulu University, founded in 2002. Its motto is 'for community transformation', and it is increasingly promoting organic farming and sustainability through its Faculty of Agriculture. Many of its graduates are looking to adopt sustainable farming and food practices. As we will explore in more detail in Chapter 8, its UNESCO Chair in Lifelong Learning, Youth and Work plays a key role in animating a network between youth, civil society organizations (including the traditional authority, the Ker Kwaro Acholi), donors, NGOs and nonformal training providers.

Our contribution

Overall, we offer a text that rejects the tendency of too much VET research to accept the world as it is and to see VET simply as a servant of the policy imperatives of capitalism. We *begin* to reimagine VET in Africa in ways that may help to address the problem of a VET paradigm that is stuck in a past *that never was*, one of skills for mass industry or mass empowerment. We provide this primarily as a foundation for an expanded research platform for VET 4.0 in Africa with potential policy implications going forward. As such, we suggest some openings for a reimagining of VET and a futures-oriented research agenda. Here, we highlight the following contributions to that larger project:

- Further development of the critique of existing VET, as offered across this book.
- Further development of the notion of work, as experienced by communities in the everyday, which extends beyond a narrow conception of work for formal employment in the neoliberal tradition.
- Further development of the expanded social ecosystem for skills model as grounded in wider ontological and epistemic debates, and contemporary struggles to connect facilitating verticalities (that is, policy, research and resourcing) to horizontal connectivities (that is, VET system actors in local/regional economies and societies).
- Further development of the internal dynamics of the expanded social ecosystem for skills model such as mediation work and resources (for

example, informal learning approaches that complement formal learning), mediating institutions (for example, learning institutions and learning networks), mediating partners (for example, VET colleges) and mediating actors (for example, lecturers).

- Further development of an account of vocational education that incorporates the variety of sites and modes of learning and teaching that exist.

Our initial intention was to develop a realist evaluation (Pawson and Tilley, 1997) of the emerging VET Africa 4.0 cases. However, we realized that this ambition was inadequate for the task at hand, which is to reconstitute VET in relation to the challenges of contemporary times, where changing work and the conditions and assumptions of work as found in mainstream paradigms of VET no longer seem to 'hold' adequate sway. Therefore, we found that it was more necessary to develop depth of insight into the problematique, via the emerging cases. In so doing, we draw broadly on critical realism:

> The aim of critical realist philosophy is, when the practice is adequate, to provide a better or more adequate theory of the practice; and, when it is not, to transform the practice in the appropriate way. That is to say the aim of critical realist philosophy is enhanced reflexivity or transformed practice (or both). (Bhaskar, 2013: 11)

This leads us to offer an immanent critique, as Bhaskar (1975) uses this older term (see also Cruikshank, 2003). As shown already, we are concerned to demonstrate that current approaches globally to VET contain internal contradictions. Through drawing on a historical sociology of VET in Africa, we argue that these approaches are not fit for their own defined purpose (Chapter 2). Through engagement with the rising tide of political–economy–ecology analysis, we explore the further location of the problem in wider processes that are increasingly being called the logic of the Capitalocene (Moore, 2016) or fossil capitalism (Malm 2016), as explored in Chapter 3. However, Bhaskar (1975) insists that critique needs to move on to at least partially reveal possibilities for emancipatory social change. Realizing these possibilities requires addressing the needs and aspirations of youth, seeing them as key actors in the solution and not as the problem of how current VET policy and practice is failing according to its own criteria. This leads us to consider the implications of an ontologically grounded view of VET in Africa in our analysis and transformed practice experiments.

We explicitly develop a relational orientation in our research via this critique that seeks out resolution of those dualisms that plague VET systems and logics, and their impacts on social life. Such dualisms include that of the bifurcated economy that structures VET systems and therefore also viable learning pathways for young people in particular ways; the dualism of public versus private provision, which ignores the strengths of both; the dualism of economy versus ecology, which fails to admit curriculum innovation for sustainable development in VET; and the dualism of job versus work, which fails to allow a more complex notion of VET's purpose.

We take a relational view of structure and agency, in which 'structure always pre-exists any round of human agency and the heavy weight of the presence of the past precludes voluntarism' (Bhaskar, 2013: 17). Thus, when we consider the VET learners' transitioning pathways or experiences of work (see Chapter 7), we do so understanding the structure–agency relation as one that is relationally, historically and situationally emergent. It is neither voluntarist, entirely open to their agentic actions, nor determinist, something entirely structural.

However, in drawing here from Bhaskar, it is important to be clear that we are not using all the tools of critical realism or providing an explicit critical realist account across all chapters. Alongside critical realism as broadly underlabouring the book, we work with substantive theoretical traditions from the arena of education, training and skills development across the different chapters. As explained already, we use the social ecosystems model as a core theoretical tool. Alongside this, we draw on historical sociology and political economy accounts that show the limited effectiveness of current approaches to VET for economic development and their historical trajectory (for instance, Allais, 2013, 2020b; McGrath et al, 2020a); on participatory action research accounts of VET for community development (for instance, Blaak et al, 2013; Tukundane et al, 2015); on the critical capabilities approach to VET and human development (for instance, De Jaeghere, 2017; Powell and McGrath, 2019a; McGrath et al, 2020b); and on arguments about reorienting VET to address sustainable development concerns (for instance, McGrath and Powell, 2016; Rosenberg et al, 2020).

The book's structure

The book has three sections. In section 1 (Chapters 1–4), we set the historical and theoretical context, including developing the core theoretical tool of social ecosystems for skills. In section 2 (Chapters 5–8), we explore and expand this model through consideration of four aspects of the data from the four case studies. Each of these focuses on an element of how we conceptualize social ecosystems that is absent from or underemphasized in Spours' work (eg, Spours, 2019). In a briefer section 3 (Chapter 9), we reflect on the implications of this approach for future research, policy and practice.

In Chapter 2, we provide a historical sociological account of the development of VET in Africa from precolonial times to the present. We stress the need to have historical depth in thinking about how vocational systems are currently formulated, their present challenges and the possibilities for transformation. Thus, historical depth allows a consideration of both why the current approach is problematic and what are the possibilities and limits of future alternatives. We explain why we use the term 'VET Africa 4.0' by analysis of three previous moments of postcolonial VET discourse and practice.

Our approach in Chapter 3 complements the more conventional approach of the previous chapter by outlining a novel historically and ontologically framed political ecology reading of skills formation. Here, we suggest that conventional approaches lack an increasingly vital engagement with the question of how industrial activity, uncritical human capital theory-dominated skills planning systems, and untrammelled consumption are pushing us beyond planetary boundaries. Rather than the usual focus on skills for metals, motors and manufacturing, we look at how existential challenges, such as climate change, are shaping skills in resource-based sectors (oil, food, water and transport) and what this opens up for us in terms of reframing VET in ways that are more aligned with the challenges of the times. The chapter opens up the possibility for political–economy–ecology framings of VET for sustainable development and just transitions, which we found to be more or less implicit in all our cases.

In Chapter 4, we review and document the evolution of skills ecosystems research as it evolved in the north. We outline its historical evolution and key elements, particularly in the version developed by Spours and colleagues, as the social ecosystems model of skills introduced by them holds resonance for VET in Africa as mentioned earlier. We consider aspects of this model and its application in our cases, deliberating how it can be adapted and extended for rethinking VET in Africa within a multidimensional political–economy–ecology system.

Our focus in Chapter 5 is on the informal economy to develop a notion of inclusivity in VET that builds on the premise of better learning opportunities for more people towards inclusive sustainable development. Using largely participatory methods, we draw on approaches to inclusivity and VET from the Alice and Gulu cases. We centre this chapter on the stories of people within rich learning networks in social ecosystems of connected living, working and learning processes. We demonstrate how the informal sector creates spaces for learning for those who are excluded elsewhere, for example because of poverty, gender, disability or early school dropout. This resonates with Gupta's (2010: 138) view that strategies for inclusive development 'will have to build upon the resources in which poor people are especially rich: their knowledge, values, social networks and institutions'. We argue that a concept of VET in Africa should include informality in its conceptualization of what VET is, or ought to be, in practice.

In Chapter 6, we consider curriculum and teaching activities within the case studies, drawing largely on interviews, focus groups and survey data. This leads us to argue for the centrality of VET teachers (of all types) to a reimagined VET social ecosystem for skills. We suggest that vocational teachers are the mediators of knowledge and learning within incredibly complex skills ecosystems. We contend that they need to navigate the competing demands and expectations of employers, students, the formal and informal curriculum, and the expectations of funders, governments and communities. We draw on illustrative examples of emerging and innovative practices in curriculum and teaching from each of the four cases to understand VET teachers' work fundamentally as curricular and pedagogic actors connected to the world of work, conceptualized broadly as outlined earlier, especially where VET institutions are also needing to engage with more inclusive notions of learning, work and development (as in the Alice and Gulu cases).

Our aim in Chapter 7 is to address how individual learning and work transitions are appearing to be more challenging than the orthodox literature would allow. In particular, the chapter raises the need to look at transitioning in the context of learning that crosses formal and informal contexts, and forms of work beyond institutional workplace contexts. With the ontologically grounded experiential focus of this chapter, we consider the reality that learning and work transitions in Africa have always been challenging given the long histories of exclusion and marginalization, except in the cases of the elite few. Drawing on a set of vignettes, largely based on interview data, we offer a stronger focus on social variables, and argue for an expanded, more complex, view of transitions that encompasses interinstitutional boundary crossing between formal and nonformal learning experiences as well as intra-institutional transitions that are focused on transitioning into different types of work, sectors and occupations, highlighting public good and livelihood intentions embedded in transitioning processes.

In Chapter 8, we draw upon lessons learnt from the Alice and Gulu cases with emphasis on the mediating role played by universities in their relational encounters with VET and regional social ecosystem actors in support of local economies, sustainable development and pro-poor livelihoods construction. In particular, we consider the role of coengaged research and community engagement as two approaches that can contribute to the advancement of an expanded social ecosystem model with positive benefits for VET institutions and communities. The chapter draws on the notion of 'relational agency' (Edwards, 2005), which focuses more directly on the nature of the relationships that comprise a network of expertise, and repositions the university not as a VET institution but as a vital contributor to the emergence of a viable and relevant VET landscape in Africa.

In Chapter 9, we bring together our theoretical insights from section 2 and discuss how they refine the accounts presented in section 1 and point us towards new imaginings and practices as well as critique. We suggest important directions that an immanent critique of VET offers for research. We provide some reflections on implications for policy and practice. We are honest in noting that a 'skills for just transitions' account is still very early in its development and that it more serves as a lens for future imaginings than a reflection on current practices. We note too that there are wider global moves towards reframing educational purposes and reconstituting social contracts for education and training that make education and training more relevant to, and capable of engaging, the future in all its complexity (see the International Commission on the Futures of Education, 2021). We argue that the work offered in this book contributes conceptual tools as well as practical insight into such a process in VET in Africa and beyond.

In an afterword, we offer a short reflection on the process of the project and the collaborative multileveled construction of the book. We deliberately set out to offer a self-critical reading of a project endeavour that was northern funded by the UK's Global Challenges Research Fund (in which real time funded contributions of the global south are not reported, but did exist), and managed out of an English university. Though imperfectly, cooperatively and with a spirit of collaboration and care, we aspired to reduce binaries and historically constituted hierarchies that most often come with development projects and northern-led research and institutional imperatives. We also include a critical reflection on intra-African hierarchies, inequalities and power imbalances, and the correctional measures that we sought to put in place, despite the difficulties that also emerged because of the COVID-19 pandemic. Ultimately, we hope to shed at least some light on how it is possible, but also difficult, to begin to make the move away from uncritical accounts of VET as a servant of extractivism, and VET research as a historically constituted extractive practice.

2

VET and Skills in Africa: A Historical Sociology

Simon McGrath

Introduction

In Chapter 1, we highlighted the pressing need for a new approach to vocational education and training (VET) to support wider processes of just socioeconomic and environmental transformation. In embarking on our journey towards discovering a possible new VET imaginary, we take an initial step in this chapter by offering a brief historical overview of skills development in Africa. We start with a short consideration of the powerful and multifaceted colonial legacy that continues to have major influences on current processes of skills formation in Africa. After the colonial era, we track three dominant trends in VET systems and reform. VET 1.0, immediately after independence, was seen as a limited programme of high-quality provision through a mixture of public colleges and apprenticeships in parastatals and large transnational firms that would mirror the skills formation systems of colonial masters; however, it was relatively marginal to real policy priorities. This was followed by what we characterize as VET 2.0, in which, from the late 1960s onwards, there was a focus on pushing vocational content into secondary schooling, supporting rural community skills programmes and again attempting to build apprenticeship systems. Economic crisis and structural adjustment hit VET along with every other aspect of African economies, leading to what we characterize as VET 3.0: an approach to supporting public VET by emphasizing its failings and offering a 'fix' through a new 'tool kit' focused on targets, quality assurance regimes and outcomes-based funding, reflected in governance reforms, competency-based curricula and national qualifications frameworks (NQFs). The combination of the strong presence of the colonial legacy and these three moments of VET reform has led to the current state of VET on the continent as weak, fragmented and littered with haphazard projects and reforms.

In our imaginings of possible better VET futures, therefore, we need to be aware of both the power of path dependence and the real possibilities for transformational change of both vocational education systems and wider society. Thus, our detailed historical reading of African contexts is intended not to limit our story to those contexts but to make a theoretical and methodological point about the necessity of doing such historical work in thinking about the transformation of any national VET system.

A brief history of VET in Africa

Precolonial skills development

It is impossible to recreate an accurate picture of what precolonial skills development looked like from the fragmentary sources and the existing literature. The latter is largely a literature of education history and philosophy that tends towards an Afro-utopianist nostalgia in which there was a static and golden African communal past, destroyed by colonialism. Nonetheless, what we can see from such a literature is a strong set of claims about the holistic, relational and community-based nature of African traditional education (for instance, Fanfunwa, 1974; Adeyemi and Adeyinka, 2003; Omolewa, 2007). This may be rather oversimplified and too gender-blind – see for example critiques by feminist writers that point out that this has been largely constructed as a masculinist idyll (for instance, Fynn-Bruey, 2021). But it does offer a positive vision of what African education might have looked like at its best, and something that we would want to draw on in thinking about a contemporary relational account that is more consciously gender sensitive.

Strikingly, such accounts include a claim that vocational learnings and attitudes were at the heart of the vision, which saw learning, living and working as inextricably connected. For instance, writing in the early 1970s, Ocitti (1973) argues that Acholi education saw vocational knowledge in a broad way, such that learning to construct a house meant also learning about physical geography (for instance, climate and water availability); geology; human geography (location of and relations with other communities); and building materials, their sourcing and sustainability. This has resonance for our development of a political–economy–ecology approach in Chapter 3.

Traditional apprenticeship is widely seen as a central part of historical African education. There is a large literature on this, or at least on its postcolonial form in West Africa and some less-established variants in other regions (for instance, Callaway, 1964; Hart, 1973; King, 1977; Lave, 1977; McLaughlin, 1979; Fluitman, 1989). However, we need to be cautious about the inclusivity of either colonial or modern forms. In much of Africa, they have been relatively small in scale and scarcely better at reaching the mass of youth than more formal modes of vocational learning. Moreover, although it is often seen as a space for learning opportunities of those with limited formal education, we need to remember that educational levels are actually quite varied (Alla-Mensah, 2021), and that it is also a site of exclusion on grounds of gender, ethnicity, disability and so on. While there are sites of excellent practice, there are also cases where very little learning goes on, and, more seriously, arrangements that are little more than indentured labour.

We will return to these debates in Chapter 5 and highlight new dynamics in informal sector learning. While, inevitably, much precolonial learning would necessarily have been functional, there is a danger of overstressing the extrafamilial elements of this as widespread or overemphasizing its continuities with more modern African forms of apprenticeship, which are unevenly spread across the continent.

From a vocational education perspective, it is important to consider this issue from a labour market angle as well as an education one. The African economic historiography debate provides us with good insights into what African work looked like before colonialism. This literature is well summarized by Austin (2008a and b; 2015). As he notes, the economic debate on the colonization of Africa has tended towards two political poles: one that celebrates colonialism and one that condemns it. Behind both lurk contrasting accounts of what the precolonial economy was like. In the classic colonial account, recreated by modern apologists for empire (for instance, Ferguson, 2003), colonialism saved Africans from ignorance and brought them 'Christianity, commerce and civilization.' In this account, African economies were stagnant in the precolonial era. In the counternarrative, typically from dependency theory accounts (most famously, Rodney, 1972) but more recently from institutional economics (Acemogulu et al, 2001, 2002; Acemogulu and Johnson, 2010), comes an argument that colonialism and the slave trade derailed African economic development (see also Allais, 2020b who explicitly links this to skills formation).

Austin adds nuance to this literature by looking in more depth into African factor endowments over time. He argues that the precolonial African norm was for small polities in which there were relatively low population densities. Land was more abundant than labour, and the usual practice was to farm extensively in the rainy season and to practise handicrafts, and some mining and quarrying where available, in the dry season. Farming was also constrained across much of the continent by endemic diseases that limited the use of draught animals. Moreover, the proportions of unfree labour appear to have been very high in some regions, at least at the start of the colonial era (Austin, 2008a and b).

There were exceptions to this general model in larger urban settlements, where the specialization of the traditional apprenticeship model was more developed, and in areas, such as the East African highlands, where combinations of highly fertile soils and large lakes encouraged more intensive agriculture. In this account, Africa was not mired in poverty but generally did not have major drivers for rapid industrial economic development. Much work was household, communal and subsistence-based, and seasonal, with some specialization.

Colonial experiences

In what follows, we will mainly reflect on the Anglophone literature on British colonies, reflecting both our case studies and our own grounding in that literature more than others. In summarizing this experience, it is important to note that while Britain had an overall attitude towards colonial development and the place of skills formation within that, this was neither static over time nor always consistently implemented across specific colonies. We must also note that all colonies were not the same. They varied according to resources (whether there were minerals or potential for large-scale agricultural exports) and climate (most notably related to the possibility of White settler populations being sustained). Settler colonies were possible in the highlands of Kenya and Zimbabwe, in South Africa and, under South African 'protection' from 1920, in Namibia. The British colonial approach is often characterized as extractive. While this is clearly true, Austin (2015) reminds us that there was a general realization that some investment in the colonies was needed to sustain this, and that colonial lobbies could be successful at times in convincing metropolitan governments to release funds.

Education under colonialism was typified by a focus on a small, elite system, often for the sons of chiefs. Some of this was in state schools, but much of the provision was through Christian missions, which also offered a more widespread elementary education in which literacy and religious instruction loomed large. Functionally, as well as supporting the development of faith communities, this system produced workers for colonial service. Most of the limited vocational education provided was initially linked to the practical needs of missions (McGrath, 2018). This legacy is still very apparent in Uganda, as we shall see later in this book.

The interwar years saw a major debate about the appropriateness of British imperial education in Africa. Drawing on their experience with education of African Americans after the civil war, several American philanthropic organizations started a movement to 'adapt' colonial education to the 'needs' of African populations (King, 1971; McGrath, 2018; Kallaway, 2020). At the heart of this was the Phelps Stokes Fund, which commissioned two hugely influential reports (Phelps Stokes Fund, 1922 and 1925) based on visits to several African countries to explore what might be an appropriate African education. Following in Phelps Stokes' wake, the Jeanes Foundation, which had been training African American teachers in institutions such as the famous Tuskegee, established a series of schools in Africa based on the principle of 'industrial education' (King, 1971). This approach also gained some support in certain colonies. Though now elite academic institutions, Achimota School in Ghana and Makerere University in Uganda both had their origins in vocational institutions opened at this time.

In a 1926 book, *The Essentials of Education*, the secretary of the two Phelps Stokes Commissions, Thomas Jesse Jones, developed the adapted education philosophy most clearly (Jones, 1926). He argued that what Africans needed was an education 'adapted to community conditions' that focused on learning to meet the 'four simples' of what he considered to be ideal African community life:

1. health and sanitation;
2. appreciation and use of the environment, including subsistence agriculture and rural handicrafts;
3. the household and the home, including learning about appropriate house construction and the avoidance of copying Western dress; and
4. recreation, learning healthy and morally upright games and avoiding alcohol and licentiousness.

While there is much in these four areas that progressive educators could find worthwhile in contemporary conditions where issues of health, sanitation and environmental degradation are global challenges, the imposition of such an education by White outsiders (who often also were explicitly racist in their wider pronouncements, see McGrath, 2018), and its clear separation off from elite education, led this approach to be condemned by most African and African American commentators. This meant that adapted education was widely resisted (King, 1971). With the height of the independence movements in the mid-1950s, the overwhelming call was for the expansion of academic education in the interests of new postcolonial state formation objectives, a legacy that still leaves an imprint today (McGrath, 2018).

The formal African labour market under colonialism had a strong emphasis on an extractive economy, whether in mining or agriculture, and on employment by the colonial state. However, though substantial in some colonies, these were not economies for the majority of Africans, and most people were still largely engaged in subsistence agriculture, supplemented by seasonal off-farm activities. It is also worth noting that where African agriculture did start competing with White agriculture, then the state was used successfully to undermine African production (Austin, 2015).

Moreover, where local populations sought to produce crops suited to the environment and local cultural practices, this was often undermined by colonial requirements to grow cash crops for export (Bjornlund et al, 2020), a tension we will return to in Chapter 3. Relatively small numbers specialized in traditional crafts in urban settlements in continuity with the precolonial period. In settler economies, local blacksmithing was undermined by the importation of mass-produced goods.

Thus, at the heart of the colonial education–work nexus was a strong dynamic that education for public employment was the most attractive route, with there being relatively few artisan or technician opportunities in the small formal sectors, and little scope to become a successful commercial farmer. This set up many long-lasting problems with the relationship between learning, living and working, including a powerful positional sense of the importance of academic education over vocational (Zeelen et al, 2010; Allais, 2020a and b). Most African economies still have public sector employment as a considerable component of formal employment. This continued labour market context makes it very hard to change these perspectives through education.

Only in South Africa did a formal vocational system of any size develop, but its evolution was complicated by the complexities of racialized politics under both colonialism and apartheid. The 'poor White problem' of the early 20th century, where many Afrikaner men struggled to find an urban labour market niche between Black and British immigrant labour, was a major driver of the 1922 Apprenticeship Act (McGrath, 1996) and the subsequent growth of apprenticeships, particularly in parastatals, such as those now operating in eThekwini. However, Gamble (2021) shows how this was undermined by attitudes towards working-class schooling that made few suitably prepared for formal VET, mirroring a fundamental weakness of the British system.

Significant elements of these colonial economic and skills formation systems appear to still be exerting influence on educational, and specifically vocational, discourses and imaginaries today, as will become clear in subsequent chapters. This longstanding legacy – both structural and cultural – and related resistances to change are important considerations to return to as we seek to offer a new imaginary.

African VET since independence

Since independence, formal African VET has gone through three main phases, broadly reflecting wider developmental orthodoxies of modernization, basic needs and neoliberalism (see McGrath, 2018). Of course, such a presentation is necessarily highly stylized and tends to underplay local resistance and adaptation and the continuation and development of nonformal and informal alternatives, an important theme of later chapters. It also ignores the overlapping nature of these three phases.

VET Africa 1.0

Our first phase begins around the point of transition to independence in the late 1950s and 1960s. As was noted earlier, there was a strong societal sense across Africa of the positional value of academic education that independence movements, already often dominated by professionals, were quick to embrace. In several countries, this led to the rapid expansion of schooling, although some, such as Malawi and Tanzania, were reluctant to increase secondary-level provision. At the same time, the new economics of education stressed the importance of higher education, as part of a wider vision of rapid African industrialization and nation-building. Thus, the UNESCO Addis Ababa conference of 1961 resulted in a commitment to six years of universal, compulsory and free primary education by 1980, while the next year the Tananarive conference on higher education projected a manpower-related need to expand tertiary education ninefold in Africa in the next 15 to 20 years (McGrath, 2018).

VET received far less attention as it was not seen as important politically in comparison to schools or universities. Nonetheless, there was some understanding from experts and politicians that industrialization would require the localization of middle as well as high skills capacity through investment in public VET. Thus, immediately after independence, formal VET was seen as a limited programme of high-quality provision through a mixture of public colleges and apprenticeships in parastatals and large transnational firms that would mirror the skills formation systems of colonial masters (though Spanish and Portuguese investments were more muted than British and, especially, French).

However, the initial optimism about nation and economy building was short-lived in the face of the challenges to Africa in integrating itself into still largely northern-dominated political and economic systems. VET responses to this challenge were to coalesce into a second phase of interventions.

VET Africa 2.0

The expansion of the supply of school leavers at primary, junior secondary and senior secondary levels, and of university graduates, grew far faster than demand for related levels of skilled workers in the formal, private sector, while expansion of the public sector increasingly came under pressure due to a limited tax base. Insufficient support to small-scale farming led to increased rural–urban migration. Despite the economic development theory of the day's assumptions, these new migrants were not quickly absorbed into the formal economy, which grew more slowly than expected. By the late 1960s, therefore, there were growing concerns about the problem of 'educated unemployment' and youth migration to the cities. This led to a raft of reports and projects designed to keep rural youth in the village through teaching them a trade. Key initiatives here included the 1967 report from the National Christian Council of Kenya, which spawned the village (later, youth) polytechnics, and the work of South African exile in Botswana, Patrick van Rensburg, which generated the Botswana brigades and an adaptation of a socialist approach to 'education with production' (NCCK, 1967; Van Rensburg, 1974). This mirrored a wider development shift towards a basic needs approach focusing on rural poverty and lack of access to basic health and education (Nyerere, 1979). In education, this favoured rural nonformal education, stressing community-based development and adult skills over further school expansion (Sheffield and Diejomaoh, 1972; Coombs and Ahmed, 1974). There was liberatory intent in this movement, and it is worth noting that Julius Nyerere had meetings with Paulo Freire, while the socialist orientation of 'education with production' has already been noted.

In the vocational space, this was complemented by the International Labour Organization's (ILO) 'discovery of the informal sector' in the early 1970s (see ILO, 1976). This overturned the view that informal activities in the growing southern cities were simply transitory and reawakened interest in anthropological literature about traditional African forms of apprenticeship. Authors such as Lave (1977) and King (1977) began to map the complex world that existed in many African towns through which communities of African artisans learnt and flourished, something we revisit in Chapter 5 in particular. The ILO commissioned a range of projects designed to build both rural- and urban-appropriate skills, as did several donors and NGOs such as those from the emerging 'appropriate technology' movement. At the same time, many donors pushed for the insertion of vocational subjects, and sometimes streams, into regular secondary schooling (see Lauglo and Lillis, 1988, for a critical review).

While the public institutions of the earlier phase continued and expanded in scale if not in their relationships to the labour market, this new focus on pushing more vocational content into secondary schooling, supporting rural community skills programmes and supplementing urban traditional apprenticeship formed the core of VET Africa 2.0. It reflected a radically different vision: more massified, more attuned to existing community structures and cultural traditions, and less designed for a relatively high-status future labour aristocracy and more for 'dropouts' (Kallaway, 2001). Clearly, this was a complex shift in VET's perceived status that had positive elements but also served to reinforce the view that academic education is of higher status.

Though VET was never the core of educational planning in the 1960s and 1970s, we have shown that there was a place for it on the policy agenda. Indeed, the moves of VET Africa 2.0 can be seen on one level as an attempt to use VET to solve problems in the school–economy relationship (Allais, 2020b). However, the 1980s and 1990s were to see VET's status as a policy tool eroded. Strikingly, the intellectual origins for this lie in part in work done at the very beginning of the wave of African independence in Ghana. Although his seminal book chapter was published only in 1965, it was from his doctoral research in Ghana in the late 1950s that Phillip Foster developed what became the famous 'vocational school fallacy in development planning' thesis (Foster, 1965). He argued that current African labour markets rewarded general, not vocational education. However, it was not until the 1980s that this argument was combined with rate of return analysis within the World Bank to argue that vocational (and higher) education was a worse investment than primary schooling (Psacharopoulos, 1981, 1985). By 1990, the Bank was prioritizing primary education, a trend reinforced by Education for All and the Millennium Development Goals (McGrath, 2018). African governments were less convinced by this argument, believing that expanding schooling would reopen the educated unemployment issue. However, faced with structural adjustment and the spread of the Bank's position to several donors (notably, not as strongly to the Germanic donors who came from the best-regarded VET tradition), African governments found it hard to maintain investment in VET. Public VET's growing complexity also did not help good system-wide responses. A range of programmes now existed that theoretically targeted different niches of educational attainment and likely labour market destination but that were typically weak in terms of quality and attractiveness.

VET Africa 3.0

In reality, even the World Bank continued lending to VET projects to some extent, largely because this is what their clients wanted as African governments still sought to respond to youth unemployment through VET. Thus, the ideology of the Bank's research needed to bend to the realities of its lending. This resulted in what we are calling VET Africa 3.0. By the late 1990s, the Bank had developed a new intellectual justification for its involvement in VET (Johanson and Adams, 2004) that reflected both a wider development pivoting towards stressing governance and policy reform and the rise of new public management-inspired vocational system reforms in a number of 'Old Commonwealth' countries. VET Africa 3.0 can be characterized as an approach to supporting public VET that highlighted its failings before offering new policy conditionalities for continued support that drew from the wider neoliberal approach of the Washington Consensus.

In VET-specific terms, this was centred on a new 'tool kit' that included new governance structures apparently giving institutions more autonomy but actually controlling them far more tightly through a new set of approaches. These included much clearer targets, quality assurance regimes and outcomes-based funding, which privileged the voices of the business community at local, sectoral and national levels, reflected in governance reforms; and competency-based curricula and NQFs, extended in some cases to the informal sector, though with unsurprisingly limited effects (McGrath and Lugg, 2012; Allais, 2014).

VET Africa 3.0 offered an education solution to an economic problem but has been undermined by the nature of that problem, which is not easily amenable to such an educational response. VET Africa 3.0 began in the aftermath of structural adjustment, which seriously undermined the development of African manufacturing (Allais, 2020b). Although economic growth did improve around the turn of the millennium, this was largely not driven by industrial growth, further undermining the VET Africa 3.0 strategy.

The state of contemporary African VET

Presently, VET in Africa can best be described as fragmented and under 'immense institutional stress' (Kraak, 2016). Public VET systems exist in all countries that hark back to the intentions of VET Africa 1.0. There are pockets of excellence within these, particularly where historical relationships with industry have proved robust. The system, if such a term is accurate, is a palimpsest of various interventions, often initially donor funded. This includes attempts to move up the skills hierarchy into technologist education through institutions such as polytechnics and institutes of technology. In South Africa, for instance, elements of the college system have been carved off and integrated into the higher education system. To give one example, the current Tshwane University of Technology has its origins in Pretoria College (a state technical college), where it was initially housed on one side of the main quadrangle. However, many African polytechnics were upgraded for political reasons and were never either adequately resourced or linked to strong sectors requiring technologists in significant numbers (King and McGrath, 2002).

As well as this upward trajectory for vocational education, there has also been a downward move in some cases into both vocational senior secondary schools and increased vocational offerings in general schools, as reflected in aspects of the VET Africa 2.0 story. However, much of formal, public VET consists of a middle ground of postschool generalist provision that has grown significantly but typically lacks the strong industry linkages of the VET Africa 1.0 model. Rather, it reflects a response of taking those focused institutions and trying to use them to deal with the VET Africa 2.0 problem of mass youth unemployment (Allais, 2020b; Allais et al, 2022). We shall come back to the problems this creates later in the chapter.

On top of this is the further complexity of schools and colleges under other ministerial jurisdictions, such as agricultural, hospitality and nursing colleges, the former being of most relevance to our story in subsequent chapters through the Alice case. Ministries of Labour typically also have trade testing centres for practical assessment, and some training facilities.

At the most formalized end of the spectrum, South Africa has a series of sector education and training authorities underpinned by a levy-grant system. Over time, different countries have followed different routes regarding integration of some or all of these elements into the public VET system.

At the more community-focused end, other initiatives have included the Kenyan youth polytechnics (the successors to the village polytechnics set up after the National Christian Council of Kenya report); Ghana's intermediate technology training units, designed as a way of upskilling the informal sector; and Namibia's community skills development centres, envisaged as nonformal institutions open to those with lesser academic qualifications than required for public VET entry. Other examples such as Botswana's brigades and Tanzania's folk development colleges have survived on the margins of the formal system with which they poorly articulate and that is often hostile to their existence (Rogers, 2019). In later chapters, we will also explore aspects of vocational learning that sit outside even this expanded view of VET.

As we noted earlier in the chapter, churches remain important actors too, both as deliverers of formal – and often highly regarded – programmes and of shorter courses. Additionally, there are a range of NGO, and some donor, initiatives that typically focus on short courses and privilege practical skills over wider vocational knowledge.

As conventionally understood, private-for-profit vocational education and training tends to concentrate in areas of low cost and high demand. This leads it to agglomerate in urban centres and in occupational areas such as business and information technology. In the latter, its willingness to offer international industry-recognized qualifications, rather than national qualifications, gives it an attractive niche among middle-class clientele. The huge importance of such international qualifications for transnational employers too will be an important theme for us in Chapters 6 and 7. However, we also will revisit earlier accounts (for instance, King, 1977) that find pockets of small businesses that have transitioned from supplementing their activities with some training offerings to becoming primarily or solely training providers. While the profit motive is important here, there is also a discourse of community development and concerns about overreliance on international funding, as we will see in Chapters 5 and 6.

Forms of vocational learning of varying degrees of formality take place across the range of enterprises. Some large employers have their own training institutions while others partner with public institutions in classical apprenticeship models of day or block release. At the other end of scale, traditional apprenticeship remains a large-scale route for vocational learning and labour market integration, especially in West Africa, and some other small businesses offer short course training, as noted in the previous paragraph. Finally, if we see work 'broadly to be an activity which seeks to sustain an individual or society' (Moodie et al, 2019: 23) and VET as preparation for this broader notion of work, then it is apparent that there is a far larger world of informal vocational learning than is encompassed by a notion that public VET is the totality. This will form an important part of our story from Chapter 5 onwards.

While there are pockets of excellence in these complex and complicated systems, the overall picture is of weakness (Allais and Wedekind, 2020). Allais (2020b) argues that there are three interrelated factors outside VET that undermine it across Africa. First, the slow pace and limited spread of industrialization means that there are few formal sector jobs and large numbers of people engaged in survivalist activities. Second, this means that formal VET has almost nowhere to send its graduates. Third, the massive growth in secondary education has resulted in massified poor-quality education. This cannot adequately prepare learners for VET and formal employment but encourages many learners to stay on in academic education in the hope that this can lead to the tiny number of professional jobs available (Zeelen et al, 2010; Allais, 2020a and b). Across Africa, the lure of professional jobs has also led to massive expansions of public higher education and a rapid rise of private provision. Several countries experienced tenfold growth in higher education enrolments during the 2010s. This serves to further reinforce the message that academic education is the way to 'real' jobs, even though very many graduates struggle to access them. Here, the colonial legacy discussed earlier appears particularly resilient.

Moreover, African public VET systems have been undermined by two policy imperatives that are in contradiction. First, donors have encouraged African governments to reform their public VET systems using the new public management VET tool kit, referred to earlier as core to VET Africa 3.0. As Allais and Wedekind (2020: 328) note, this reform agenda has not worked well even in the countries selling these ideas: 'Governments in wealthy liberal market economies have been trying to "fix" TVET for decades, without paying attention to the structure of the labour market, the way in which demand for skills is articulated, and the role that workplaces need to play in supporting the development of skills.'

These problems are even more acute in Africa, where such policy fixes have been largely externally driven and poorly grounded in local coalitions for change or local economic realities. Moreover, the smallness of formal, private sector employment and weakness of economies noted earlier also undermine VET reform. As Allais and Wedekind (2020: 328) remark: 'Stagnant economies and deindustrialisation, with some exceptions, make it increasingly difficult to build TVET systems.' Now more than 25 years since these reforms began to be implemented, there is very little evidence of their success (Allais, 2022). Yet governments and donors remain committed to them and, indeed, continue to roll out elements of the programme, sometimes apparently oblivious to having done so previously (Allais, 2014).

One part of the problem these reforms are trying to solve is that vocational provision within the education system is disconnected from industry. What has emerged are new structures at national, sectoral and institutional level that are designed to bring industry and education together (Allais, 2022). However, these reforms misrecognize the problem of limited relationality within VET systems as simply being about the lack of formal structures. In contrast, as we argued in Chapter 1, relationality is complex, and the formal structures that are imposed often ignore underlying economic and social structures. Crucially, we need to move away from formally enacting new relationships between employers and educational institutions to ask questions about how such relationships come into existence, are nurtured and risk collapse, and what VET can do if these are not the primary relations in a local economy structure or system. Moreover, although the sectoral level has received some attention under VET 3.0 reforms, this level of structural change has been less developed than the micro or macro levels. At the heart of our analysis in later chapters is a multilevel perspective, and the importance of both sector and place.

Second, alongside this externally driven VET reform agenda, internal political considerations have led to public VET being ever more dominated by an education logic in which expansion of supply matters far more than demand, and in which 'demand' is also potentially inadequately constructed for the context (Allais, 2020b). This results in the messages of the governance move being swamped by messages from ministries to grow rapidly, which have more to do with political calculations than industry needs. While public providers grow and proliferate, the key institutions of the vocational system do not significantly strengthen (McGrath et al, 2006; Kraak, 2016).

This picture of the formal, public VET system finds parallels in other elements of the VET system. Part of the public policy response was to revisit attempts to vocationalize secondary education (see Mastercard Foundation, 2020) even though these had been judged a failure in the VET 2.0 era (Lauglo and Lillis, 1988; Lauglo and Maclean, 2005; Oketch, 2014). Many of these revived vocational secondary schemes have been abandoned again, while some limp on and new ones are developed by officials still focused on the reasons for introducing them 50 years ago rather than the negative lessons of the intervening half-century.

While there is considerable excellence in enterprise-based training in many African medium to large firms (such as those in the eThekwini case), this is uneven, and its impact constrained by the very limited number of such firms. State interventions here are limited by weaknesses in intermediary bodies and by the very limited financial leverage provided by levy-grant schemes in such settings (Ziderman, 2016; Allais, 2022). Since the era of VET Africa 2.0, attempts to intervene in the informal sector skills formation system have been recurrent. Yet, as Palmer's (2020) review for the ILO notes, there is little to show for this in terms of sustainable change. At the heart of the problem here is an incommensurability between the lifeworlds of the donor-driven interventions and that of informal sector actors. Equally, agricultural colleges have largely failed to address the realities of both small-scale agriculture and the emerging agroecology/organic sector, even though Africa has more than 200 million smallholder farmers who are the mainstay food producers for African societies and communities, an issue that we will come back to later in this book.

Towards a VET Africa 4.0

As can be seen from the preceding discussion, this account indicates that there is as yet an inadequate response to its historicity and to its current contextually emerging demands. We argue that what is required is a radically different theoretical approach and political imaginary that is grounded in both the lived experiences and material conditions of those learning vocationally, and genuine labour market and livelihood possibilities that reflect the desperate need for just transitions and inclusive sustainable development, as discussed in the next chapter (see also McGrath, 2020a; Rosenberg et al, 2020). It also requires a far greater sense of the agency of individuals and the possibilities of collective aspirations and actions while remaining aware of structural injustices and power imbalances. It sees both vocational learning and work in broad terms, avoiding narrowing the relationship to a consideration of public VET for formal sector employment.

We have grounded this historical sociological analysis and subsequent field-based empirical work in four African cases from two African countries. However, our critique is intended to be of wider relevance. Though context is always crucially important, the problems with which this book is concerned are global ones, manifested nationally and locally. It is not just in these two countries that VET faces a crisis of relevance. Many other systems experience many of the problems caused by the wider neoliberal turn and its application to the sector. What we have described as VET Africa 3.0 was largely experienced in much of the rest of the world as part of a set of policies that travelled through aid and other transmission mechanisms from origins in Australia and England (see, for instance, McGrath, 2010). Even continental European systems have not been immune, particularly with respect to qualifications frameworks. Yet, their commitment to relationality and to balancing social and economic concerns remains an important pointer as we think about new African alternatives.

Moreover, mainstream VET, wherever and however constituted, is a child of the Anthropocene. It emerged from the process of industrialization and a realization that initial, though huge, productivity advances could not be sustained without greater attention to formalizing skills development in the industrial sector. In Europe, this led to a reforming of older guild-based apprenticeship models and the rise of forms of dual learning between formal workplace and formal, public training institutions to service factory lines and mines. This linked VET inextricably to highly carbonized sectors such as mining, metals and motors. As formal VET has spread globally, it has remained complicit in unsustainable practices that are embedded in this history. More than a decade ago, Anderson offered a critique of VET as productivist or 'based on a restricted and instrumental view of lifeworlds which reduces people and the environment to the status of human and natural resources for economic exploitation' (Anderson, 2009: 44). However, this critique has largely gone ignored in the VET literature. We want to follow Anderson in insisting that VET *globally* is unfit to address the challenges of a world of work. VET must address sustainability and just transitions if societies are to tackle the complexities of capitalism, which continues to exploit people and planet in ways that are destabilizing the very earth system processes (such as the stability of the climate system) that are the foundation of human existence. What we situate here in African empirical cases is not simply an issue for Africa.

Conclusion

In Chapter 1, we began by mapping out our account of VET, empirically grounded in four African case studies but speaking to global theoretical issues. At the heart of this is a need to develop further a critique of the VET orthodoxy. In this chapter, we have contributed a historical sociological account that summarizes research in the political economy of skills tradition and insists on the historical depth of the issues under examination. However, as we made clear in Chapter 1, we need to move beyond current understandings and historical contexts to imagine a better future for learning, working and living. In Chapter 3, we address this through a political–economy–ecology perspective that helps us focus both on some of the reasons that underlie the critique that we have presented in this chapter and on alternative conceptualizations of VET that might overcome this critique.

3

Water, Transport, Oil and Food: A Political–Economy–Ecology Lens on Changing Conceptions of Work, Learning and Skills Development in Africa

Heila Lotz-Sisitka

Introduction

Not enough has been said about the kinds of skills development that are needed if we are to stem the rising tides and impacts of political economies that have been driving what some call 'fossil capital' (Malm, 2016). In this book, we are producing an emerging argument that it is necessary to also rethink and reframe vocational education and training (VET) logics and approaches if we are to fully consider the implications of a warming future. This chapter provides the context of why this is such an urgent challenge and some thinking tools for understanding where we have come from and where we need to go.

The prognosis is that it is now almost impossible to stop global warming below 2°C. The 2021 Intergovernmental Panel on Climate Change (IPCC) report issued a 'red alert' for humanity, noting climate change to be one of the most severe challenges facing human societies for decades and potentially centuries to come. Scientists are warning that we have entered a new 'geological epoch', named the 'Anthropocene', in which human activity, especially the release of carbon dioxide into the atmosphere through fossil-based pollution, is transforming the stability of the earth system and creating knock on effects such as ice melt and methane release, which exacerbate the impacts of pollutants on the stability of the earth system.

This gains significance if we come to understand that human settlements and especially agriculture (such as food production systems to support those human settlements) became possible due to the largely stable climate patterns in the Holocene period, the geological epoch that we are now moving out of (Steffen et al, 2007, 2011).

The prognosis of the impact of climate change on existing activity and life as we know it has devastating implications for Africa. Southern Africa is particularly vulnerable to climate changes, as the region has already been experiencing changes that are more rapid, with impacts that are more severe, than the global average. This has severe consequences for water security and availability. Existing patterns of global warming and projections for future warming indicate that warming and drying will be greater than the global average, for a vast part of Southern Africa, especially the south-western countries and regions, while the eastern parts will be wetter and subject to more extreme and intense weather events such as floods and cyclones, as has already been seen in the early 2020s. In Uganda, too, climate change threatens food production on a scale that is hitherto unknown. Changes in temperature – projected to be in the region of 4.3°C by the 2080s – are likely to have significant implications for water resources, food security, natural resource management, human health, settlements and infrastructure (DFID, 2008), with a strong likelihood of increased food insecurity and other economic impacts. These challenges arise partly from centuries of political economy thinking that has failed to adequately recognize political ecology and include it in associated VET models and trajectories, ignoring environmental concerns as a result.

Water challenges and associated warming patterns have implications for food production, and especially the provision of adequate water resources for a steady supply of food. In both South Africa and Uganda, agriculture has been identified as one of the sectors that are 'particularly vulnerable' to climate change, with potential drops in crop yields and increased livestock losses projected. This is particularly the case in contexts where there is a high reliance on rainfed agriculture, which characterizes the reality of most smallholder farmers across Africa (such as those in Alice). The scale of the challenge gains meaning when recognizing that roughly 65 per cent of Africa's population relies on small-scale farming (Savage, 2019).

There are numerous calls for concerted action, and multiple studies at national, regional and international levels continue to confirm the seriousness of the impending impacts, many of which are already visible to farming communities. It is not only the challenges associated with water for food that are at issue but those associated with heating of soils and the climatic pattern effects on plant life. Already there are changes to phenology, 'the timing of annually recurrent biological events, which is one of the most sensitive bio-indicators of climate change' (Fitchett, 2021). This provides indicators of how biodiversity and plant life are changing. For example, consistent early blossoming of apple and pear are being observed in South Africa.

The IPCC is already warning that short-term adaptation strategies may not be enough, and that longer-term thinking is needed to fully consider the impending implications of overshooting the 1.5 and 2°C targets.

Oil, transport, water and food: locating VET Africa 4.0

Oil, transport, water and food (which materially partly define our cases in this book) are intimately embroiled in the challenge of rethinking the VET logics and approaches mentioned earlier for their historical, contemporary and future relationships to climate change.

The following summarizes the key messages of the World Bank's country climate risk profiles for Uganda and South Africa (World Bank, 2021), supplemented with other sources. While drawing on this data to give a quick view of the current nature of the climate change crisis in the two countries where our cases reside, in relation to the core focal areas of concern for VET development in these contexts, we recognize the oftentimes 'imperialist character' of global environmental programmes and data, which also have patriarchal overtones as are also found in mainstream sustainable development discourse (Shiva, 1994). Sachs (1993) critiqued mainstream environmental narratives that circulate in international development agencies for being shaped by powerful corporate interests, imperialist agendas, gender biases and racist assumptions. Most recently, these are also being shaped by universalizing behavioural economic narratives (for example, UNEP, 2020; UNDP, 2021). As Tetrault (2017) notes, early political ecology works advocated alternatives such as acting locally, valuing traditional ecological knowledge and strengthening local institutions for collective resource management (see, for example, Agarwal and Narain, 1993; Shiva, 1994; Esteva and Prakash, 1997), arguments we also emphasize in developing the social ecosystems for skills model in this book.

Country climate risk profiles

Both countries will experience the worsening of existing climate challenges. In Uganda, temperatures are increasing, with 1.5°C being projected by 2040, alongside a reduction in annual as well as seasonal rainfall. Since 2000, western, northern and north-eastern regions have experienced more frequent and longer-lasting drought conditions, and extreme events such as floods, droughts and landslides have increased. In South Africa, average temperatures have increased by 1.5°C since the 1960s, with more marked increases across arid, inland areas of the country. Temperature extremes have also increased significantly, both in frequency and intensity. Rainfall has decreased in the west, while an increase in extreme weather events in the east, such as flooding, is already occurring.

Both will face increasing water challenges, although the nature of this challenge is different within and between the two countries. Although Uganda is endowed with both surface and ground water resources, projected climate change and variability are already affecting availability. This is impacting upon sectors such as agriculture and fisheries, forestry and tourism. Water stress is considered highly likely for much of Uganda's population. South Africa is already highly water-stressed and highly vulnerable to a changing climate (a key theme of the Alice case). Projected climate change impacts could exacerbate existing conflicts and further increase inequalities regarding the limited access to potable water. Changes in the quality and availability of water will be the dominant challenge for the country for the rest of the century. As droughts become more frequent and severe, water supplies, biodiversity and agriculture are likely to suffer, with a simultaneous increase in floods posing a serious threat to water quality and a range of economic activities.

Agriculture is significant in both countries, but particularly critical in Uganda, where it employs 70 per cent of the working population and contributes over a quarter of its gross domestic product. Climate change could see a reduction in production of food crops such as cassava, maize, millet and groundnuts by the 2050s, with overall losses reaching up to US$1.5 billion. Gulu is projected to be among the worst affected districts. Increased dry periods will be exacerbated by continued soil degradation, associated with unsustainable agricultural practices (see Chapter 1's introduction of the Gulu case). Major export crops like coffee and tea could also see a reduction in yields leading to combined economic losses of about US$1.4 billion in mid-century. In South Africa, the sector employs nearly 1 million people and contributes to export revenues. More importantly, it is fundamental to local livelihoods, as the Alice case highlights. Climate change is expected to have generally adverse impacts on cereal crop production, high-value export agricultural production and intensive animal husbandry practices. Subsistence, dry-land farmers are more vulnerable to climate change than commercial farmers.

The transport sector has seen massive growth over the past 50 years. In Uganda, new roads continue to be built, currently in the Hoima area, and vehicle use has increased hugely. While this growth has eased human and goods movement, it has also led to high levels of congestion, especially in Kampala, and a significant rise in emissions. Projected climate change trends are expected to have negative impacts on Uganda's road infrastructure and transport sector. In South Africa, emissions from the transport sector account for more than 10 per cent of the country's total greenhouse gas emissions. In the context of our eThekwini case, it should be noted that maritime transport is a very small (recorded) contributor to transport sector emissions in South Africa, but this is due to maritime transport operating mainly beyond South African boundaries.

Energy is a major area of controversy in both countries. The World Bank country climate analysis makes no mention, for instance, of the likely effects of oil extraction in the Hoima region. In late 2021, protests flared along the Eastern Cape coast regarding oil and gas exploration. The Bank suggests that there is high potential for clean energy generation in Uganda. However, the country's legal framework and institutional capacities need to be improved. South African energy is highly dependent on the country's cheap and abundantly available coal, and it is one of the highest carbon emitters per capita in the world. At the 26th Conference of the Parties, the government secured international support for a move towards renewable energy. However, there has been growing trade union opposition to this move (after initial support), and there are clear internal tensions within the government on this policy (Mabasa, 2018; Swilling, 2021).

It is evident from the preceding discussion that findings emerging from the environmental and social-ecological system/earth system sciences have important implications for rethinking dominant development trajectories. Yet, there also remains a need for critical readings of environmental science (such as Forsyth, 2003). More broadly, a stronger link is required between political economy and political ecology discourses in and for rethinking education and training praxis (Rosenberg et al, 2020). In what follows, we mark out some implications of emerging connections between political economy and political ecology, recognizing that more local-level analyses are necessary for substantively connecting these deliberations to skills development praxis, contributing to our argument for investigating the potential of social ecosystem for skills development models as these may also offer better demand analysis for green skills or skills for just transitions (such as Rosenberg et al, 2020). We term this a political–economy–ecology lens, following Malm (2016).

Political–economy–ecology

Considerable work is emerging that provides historical and contemporary vantage points on the deep-seated connections between political economy and political ecology (such as Bond, 2002; Forsyth, 2003; Malm, 2016; Moore, 2016; Scoones, 2016; Satgar, 2018; see also earlier work by Gorz, 1989; Bookchin, 1990). Malm offers a substantive account of the link between carbon-centric development and capitalist accumulation. His work sheds light on early choices made to abandon waterpower in the interests of coal-fired steam power driving the machine age, which Malm attributes to a history of more convenient control of labour than any limitation on availability of waterpower (indeed, waterpower was often cheaper). Coal-fired steam power also allowed the concentration of labour in towns as factory workers, with early carbon emissions leading to protests among workers to 'stop the smoke'. Malm's work shows that carbon emissions were linked to the entrenchment of capitalist social relations, hence the title of his political–economy–ecology work: 'fossil capital'.

Since the early days of the industrial revolution, this story has 'moved offshore' as globally mobile capital continues the search for cheap labour and disciplined labour power by means of the mass consumption of fossil energy and other forms of extractivism (Malm, 2016; Tomaney, 2017). Malm's argument points to some of the struggles that societies are having in reorienting away from fossil capital towards forms of energy that operate via 'flows' (such as water, solar and wind power) rather than 'stocks' (oil, coal and so on), as it is more difficult to develop the cooperation necessary for managing energy flows than it is to control the economy of energy 'stocks'.

Commenting on Malm's account, Tomaney (2017) notes that

> [w]ith this evidence, Malm offers a reformulation of Marxist theory. The production of surplus value is still central to capital accumulation because labour power creates anthropogenic products, but the transformation of fossil fuels into carbon dioxide is intrinsically linked to capital accumulation. Malm extends Marx's notion of a distinction between the formal and real subsumption of labour to the realm of nature to emphasise the way it is subordinated to the production of surplus value. This is a version of Marxism in which an analysis of the production of space is foregrounded, with Henri Lefebvre, Michael Storper and others mobilised in the argument. It is a productionist account which is dismissive of the role of mass consumption as the cause of carbon emissions.

Leff (2015: 33) explains that political ecology emerged as 'a social response to the oblivion of nature by political economy', with subsequent forms of eco-Marxism uncovering a 'second contradiction of capital', namely the 'self destruction of the ecological conditions of sustainable production'. Reframing political economy to include ecology provides new challenges for the foundational narratives that drive VET emerging from this history, especially the now worn narrative of human capital theory, but also the political economy of skills discourse that left out the relation between power, economy, production and nature, turning nature into a resource to be mobilized into the productionist narrative (Moore, 2016). While the political economy of skills account has done much to surface problems with exploitation of labour power, the severity and implications of ongoing ecological exploitation, extractivism and now earth system damage require a broadening of such discourses to include a stronger focus on political ecology (understood broadly as the relationship between politics and the environment). As Leff (2015: 33) states, 'political ecology goes beyond the proposal for conservation of nature ... and policies of environmental management ... to inquire on the conditions for a sustainable life in the ecological stage of economic and technological hegemonic domination'. This needs to be done in ways that also proffer options and ways of moving towards alternative futures that are more inclusive, less exploitative and less damaging of the life-supporting systems that humans and other life forms require to live decent lives and indeed to sustain life in the face of mass extinction of biodiversity and destruction of lifegiving forces such as clean air and water. If they do any work at all, the sustainable development goals (SDGs) (given their largely economically driven environmental management roots, see Martínez-Alier, 2003) at the very least draw some attention to the need for a political–economy–ecology approach to VET.

Burawoy (2013) describes three 'waves' of Marxism, those of capital-labour (1795–1914), production-exchange (1914–73) and production-environment (1973–present), with the latter focusing on societal socialism, real utopias and a sociological-global form of Marxism that also signals shifting relations between theory and practice. For the sociological-global form of Marxism, there is a need to 'search out real utopias that can galvanise the collective imagination but also interrogate them for their potential generalisability' (Burawoy, 2013: 48). Any such generalization needs to be contingent and coconstructed with those most affected. Importantly for our argument in this book, Burawoy insists that this brings the role of civil society into focus, especially its role and contribution towards defending humanity against a growing ecological crisis that emerges from the commodification of nature, which takes the form of 'privatisation of water, land or air'. To this, we add inclusivity of those excluded from mainstream notions of economy, work and VET. Relevant to our approach is Burawoy's (2013: 47, 48) argument that this shift will emerge through the building of what Wright (2010) calls 'real utopias': 'small-scale visions of alternatives such as co-operatives, participatory budgeting and universal income grants that challenge on the one hand, market tyranny and on the other, state regulation'. Such analysis, Burawoy (2013: 48) argues, should focus on 'their conditions of existence, their internal contradictions, and thus their potential dissemination', offering a means of keeping alive the possibilities of alternative capitalism, which he describes as not abolishing markets or states but 'subjugates them to the collective self-organisation of society'.

Raworth (2017) applies similar arguments to a rethinking of the economy, suggesting that we need to include the home, market, state and the commons as four distinct realms. VET, in Africa and elsewhere, tends to only consider the market and, to a declining extent over time, the state. Work that serves the commons and home-based or subsistence work for livelihoods is most often excluded from VET, an issue that we consider via the expanded social ecosystem model. In subsequent chapters, we will show this to be more inclusive of these different notions of work and more inclusive of the types of work in which young African people are actually engaged (see Chapters 5 and 7).

From an environmental perspective, the historical-materialist political–economy–ecology work of Martínez-Alier (1997, 2003; Guha and Martínez-Alier, 2013) on 'environmentalism of the poor' (see also Leff, 2015; Scheidel et al, 2018), which explores power relations that emerge from society–environment relations and materially grounded analyses of unsustainable forms of modern rationality, can be helpful for considering the contradictory and more complex implications of considering a political–economy–ecology perspective as framing for VET 4.0. This extends the perspective of Burawoy. Martínez-Alier, Guha and Leff's work challenges the notion that environmental interest and action stem from affluent societies and their 'post-material' concerns. They draw attention to the significance of historically and structurally constituted ecological distribution conflicts as drivers of environmental concern. As stated by Tetrault, in the global south, such conflicts

> prototypically pit subaltern groups (with their allies in civil society) against private companies and governmental actors. The latter promote capital-investment in the expansion of extractive activities, polluting industries, and environmentally destructive mega-development projects; while the former struggle to protect their territory, productive natural resources, recreational spaces, and cultural landscapes, all of which form the material and symbolic basis for sustaining livelihoods, healthy living environments, and cultural diversity. (Tetrault, 2017: 12)

Rereading the history of African VET

The VET history we outlined in Chapter 2 needs to be read as part of a wider story of colonialism and ongoing neocolonialism. As we noted there, the modern VET system arose in tandem with, and in support of, the industrial revolution and neoliberal capitalist projects of extraction. Even the so-called fourth industrial revolution is not exempt from a significant carbon emissions impact due to the energy used to transfer data and produce the equipment used for such transfers, with claims that this impact is likely to equal that of air travel. By-and-large, VET systems globally have been largely oriented to producing skills for driving the fossil-fuelled industrial economy, with some recent shifts emerging around new value chains related to green information and communication technology and the emergence of an alternative energy economy (mainly in the north). In African contexts, skills systems were developed, and largely remain defined, along extractivist, racist and exploitative lines in support of major industrial and infrastructure development projects of the colonial and postcolonial state and the continuing interests in offshore resource flow (such as oil). Political ecology emerged in the south out of a 'politics of difference rooted in the ecological and cultural conditions of its peoples; from their emancipation strategies for decolonization of knowledge, reinvention of territories and re-appropriation of nature' (Leff, 2015: 34). It has potential to provide a counternarrative to the dominating VET trajectories, but this should not be naively viewed or developed.

After independence, the hope was that African governments would be more accountable to local populations and would end the centuries of foreign domination of African economies and government policies (see VET Africa 1.0 account in Chapter 2). Cheru (2016) explains that this hope, represented and championed by some early liberation movement leaders, had the support of workers, trade unionists and the growing radical student movements, as this was also 'essentially a strategy for more equitable appropriation of the productive forces under a democratic system of government' (Cheru, 2016: 1271). There were important steps in this regard, particularly around health, education and communications infrastructure. However, as Cheru notes, nationalist leaders felt impelled to continue extractivism due to the need to fund development internally. This had the perverse effect of locking Africa into this model.

African development strategies were complicated by the Cold War and a series of military interventions that often linked back to Cold War actors. The 1980s saw the rise of neoliberalism, exported to Africa through structural adjustment at a time when African countries had major debt burdens linked to excessive borrowing fuelled by the 1970s global oil boom. The infrastructural and social development investments of the early independence period were systematically dismantled under a new development regime (Cheru, 2016). As noted in Chapter 2, this led to a new 'VET toolkit' but also to a collapse of the jobs that VET was supposed to support. As Cheru (2016) notes:

[F]ew African countries have achieved credibly in terms of any of the indicators that measure real, sustainable development. Instead, most have moved backwards and experienced growing inequality, ecological degradation, de-industrialisation and poverty. Moreover, with the growing influence of external donors in domestic policy decisions, African governments have become more and more accountable to creditors rather than to their own citizens. Thus, policymaking, an important aspect of sovereignty, was wrenched out of the hands of the African state – amounting to re-colonisation, not development. (Cheru, 2016: 1273)

Ferguson (2006) refers to the impact of this as a form of 'neoliberal transnational governmentality' that even reaches into sustainable development projects. He illuminates how under this trajectory, the needs of foreign capital – for instance in the oil, transport, green agricultural revolution and international conservation sectors – are placed ahead of the needs of African citizens and communities. In such a scenario, the national elite becomes a facilitator of transnational priorities, producing a form of 'recolonisation by invitation' (Cheru and Obi, 2011) as national governments claim ownership of natural resources such as oil and minerals and exploit them ostensibly 'for the people' but, in reality, to benefit political elites. These trends are found in the influence of industrial agriculture's 'green revolution' strategies (Wise, 2020; Belay and Mugambe, 2021) as well as in sectors such as transport where transnational corporations control global movement and flow of resources, and in the minerals and energy sector where natural resources such as oil and coal remain high-value commodities to 'extract and export' (Cheru and Obi, 2011), despite the climate change impacts (Swilling, 2021). As noted earlier, the World Bank fails to mention oil exploration and development in Uganda in its 'climate change risk' reporting, while South African energy policy is contradictory, and the transport sector is failing to take account of maritime impacts as these are said to be 'out of the boundary'.

These neoliberal, transnational political economy interests of elites in African countries also structure the nature of work in its formal sense, and thus also VET systems and their priorities. For example, agricultural education and training programmes are largely oriented towards industrial agricultural paradigms, despite most of Africa's farmers being small-scale producers who could, it is argued, benefit more from advancing their practices through agroecological approaches (Pesanayi, 2019a; Wise, 2020). Additionally, climate-resilient agriculture remains largely absent from these training programmes (Van Staden, 2020). Education on water use in agricultural colleges tends to favour large-scale irrigation, despite impending water scarcity (Pesanayi, 2019a). Technology and engineering VET programmes favour productivism and extractivism and are still largely oriented towards advancing fossil capital imperatives, despite these being in decline the world over, reflecting overreliance on dominant interests still controlling 'free market policies'. Here we note Standing's (2016) critique of 'free market' economic policies as a fundamentally corrupt system that favours rentiers while depressing the incomes from labour, not only in Africa, but globally.

Such paradigms for skills development produce exclusions, most notably around VET for livelihoods, or are increasingly misdirected or impractical given people's current realities (see Chapters 5 and 7). In response, Cheru (2016) argues for three processes that could transform African political economies:

1. promote and sustain democratic governance with an emphasis on broad-based and inclusive governance;
2. improve the effectiveness of the state, including building the human capacity for inclusive economies and poverty reduction; and
3. construct viable social contracts that take seriously the need to reduce socioeconomic inequalities, which will also need to consider the implications of social-ecological risks and impacts.

Strikingly, a political ecology is absent from this. In contrast, Moore (2016) describes the emergence of the 'Capitalocene', resulting from dividing historical change and contemporary reality into 'nature' and 'society'. His argument is that, in fact, history reveals a more connective view of 'environment-making' in which the emergence of capitalism is, and always has been, joined at every step with the biosphere, as Marx also pointed out in his arguments about human control of nature and resource flows in the construction of capital. Altvater (2016: 145) argues that '[c]apitalism changed human existence; it has interpenetrated both earth systems and the mental worlds of each (social) individual', which has implications for our politics and practices as we seek to move out of the capitalist trap in which 'humanity – acting through capitalist imperatives – is organising nearly all its productive and consumptive activities by trapping and depleting the planet's energetic and mineral reserves'.

Thus, in arguing for Cheru's three points, we should see the role of the state not only as one that must build inclusive economies and poverty reduction, but also as being central to 'any realistic effort at climate mitigation and adaptation' (Parenti, 2016: 174). In this, the 'biophysical significance of the state's geography' must be brought into efforts to strengthen the effectiveness of the state. To fail to do this is to further 'free capital from the constraints of territory' and, thus, responsibility for ongoing environmental degradation and the climate and environmental injustices being perpetuated via globalized extractivism and offshore pollution production. This understanding led Hardt and Negri (2001: 297) to argue for the need for 'a theory that connects the role of nonhuman nature's use values to accumulation and the territory of the state', and for reframing the state's role as a responsible environment-making institution that better uses its legal frameworks of property as these are territorially fixed. Parenti (2016) argues that 'states still remain the crucial political

47

units of global capitalism', noting that they are the only institutions that have power left to confront transnational capital institutions. Having said this, there is also a need to recognize the historical role and impact of transnational forms of power and globalization (for instance, IMF policies that focused on 'rolling back the state') and the emergence of new forms of governmentality that tend to 'bypass states altogether' (Ferguson, 2006: 100).

Turning back to our focus on oil and transport, Ferguson describes how transnational topographies of power 'hop' over whole sections of society, developing only those parts of the continent that are valuable for various reasons, a process that creates and sustains structured underdevelopment. He cites examples of transnational mining interests and conservation programmes that alike tend to create enclaves of power and control that fail to benefit larger society, or even the nation states where the natural resource or mineral wealth lies. We have seen this from the history of Africa's oil states, for example. Ferguson (2006: 89) goes on to say that this transnational topography of power makes sustainable development of any kind exceedingly difficult. He argues for a 'heightened level of reflexive scrutiny of our categories of analysis'. Hence, in this chapter, we are arguing for a political–economic–ecological vantage point for analysis of VET systems that can offer a more inclusive and less narrowly constituted foundation for VET in Africa. Here, Bond and Hallowes (2002) argue that mainstream sustainable development is an inadequate response to Africa's development demands and to the environmental conflicts and stresses experienced by the poor. Bond and Hallowes, along with many in environmental justice movements, propose clear and explicit normative commitments to sufficiency, redistribution, equality and 'real' sustainability in development thinking (see also Lotz-Sisitka, 2011).

Cheru points out that even in the context of the inescapable realities of global development priorities and support for these (such as the SDGs), any such relations should 'involve the right of countries to devise, discover and evolve policies that are suited to the local political and economic conditions' (Cheru, 2016: 1279). As stated in earlier chapters, we propose that by giving attention to political economy and political ecology and an expanded notion of social ecosystems for skills, a VET 4.0 system may be developed that is more inclusive and suited to the local political, economic *and* ecological conditions in which the ecological impacts on the economic, and not just the other way round. This is consistent with Burawoy's argument about localized 'real utopias'. Our argument for a political–economy–ecology framing for VET 4.0 in Africa takes us to a consideration of skills development in relation to water, food, transportation and oil (Box 3.1). Very many of Africa's people rely on rainfed agriculture, and all societies, including in Africa, rely on

Box 3.1: The need for a political–economy–ecology lens for VET: views of work, life and learning realities and skills development needs found in our cases

Case 1: Water for food – Alice. As described across the chapters, the driver of the development of a social ecosystem for skills was farmers given back land under the post-apartheid land reform policy, but this was coupled with a failure to provide adequate water. This catalysed a need for collaborative learning among multiple actors to implement locally possible solutions such as use of rainwater harvesting and conservation approaches to bolster smallholder farming production systems, seen to be viable in the water scarce region impacted by drought. Where it engaged with agriculture, the local VET system was privileging high water use irrigation and large-scale commercial agriculture, excluding Black smallholder farmers' aspirations towards economic empowerment and viable commercialization in local economies.

Case 2: Food and diversified livelihoods – Gulu. As described across our chapters, the driver for development of a social skills ecosystem model for skills development in the Gulu region was a history of conflict, exclusion and war. Post-recovery demands included development of more sustainable options for agricultural production based on more equitable distribution and use of land, and a wider range of viable local economic development options, and for further climate resilient development in the longer term for young people, other than those privileged in the existing VET system.

Case 3: Transport – eThekwini. As described across the chapters in the eThekwini case, development of the maritime industry under the centralized Structural Infrastructure Programme of government to develop the ocean economy created a range of VET programmes that were poorly aligned with actual jobs emerging in the sector, due partly to the failure of centralized 'sustainable' development programmes such as Operation Phakisa, which has also been contradictory from a political economy/political ecology perspective, as more recent oil and gas explorations along the coast are showing.

Case 4: Oil – Hoima. As described across the chapters in the Hoima case, the oil extraction in the area is driven by international oil and extractive multinational corporations (IOCs), which operate on principles of extractivism coupled with paternalism. This trajectory of exploitation, followed by strategic reactions to civil society and political pressure and the subsequent engagement in multi-actor partnerships (shaped by sustainable development discourse), is clearly apparent in the trajectory of IOC engagement in skills development initiatives in the Hoima setting. The Skills for Oil and Gas in Africa (SOGA) programme involving donors and IOCs controls skills systems, leaving little room for emergence of local alternatives.

available, clean water for life and economic activity. Equally, all societies, including in Africa, will in future require more sustainable forms of energy and transport for human flourishing, and thus VET systems need to move beyond a stance rooted in political economy in the fossil capital tradition. Rather, we need a political–economy–ecology account as part of a more sustainable and environmentally just society tradition for VET. Indeed, this seems to be a real demand in African societies, as shown, at least in part, by our case contexts here and throughout the book.

Just transitions and emerging skills trajectories

In seeking to reimagine VET, we need to engage with the analysis presented in this chapter rather than continuing to confine ourselves to economistic and productivist thinking. Although mainstream VET research has been slow to respond to this challenge, several approaches are opening up debates here, including work in the education for sustainable development, green skills and just transitions traditions. All these draw attention to the need to include environmental concerns into mainstream development interventions via education, training and transformative social learning (Rosenberg et al, 2020). The green skills discourse, which involves a range of approaches such as greening existing occupations, as well as specialization in green occupations via education and occupational learning pathways in a diversity of sectors, is in itself a complex area of intervention in VET and skills development systems more broadly. However, it is as yet substantively underdeveloped within conventional formal VET programmes (Langthaler et al, 2021). Lotz-Sisitka and Ramsarup (2020) argue that there is a need to bring political economy and political ecology closer together for substantive policy coherence. In this process, new 'demand streams' for green and other adaptive skills become visible, and thus also the possibility for new jobs, reframed jobs or entirely different workstreams that may as yet not even exist. In earlier research, Ramsarup (2017) articulated a transitioning perspective for green skills advancement that indicated that green skills are, in practice, either demanded or neglected at niche levels in a variety of sectors, but for green skills research to 'take hold' and expand, there is a need for regime level shifts in green skills policy and practice instruments. These, in turn, are shaped by landscape level shifts that are ontologically shaped by issues such as climate change and environmental degradation, as well as new sociotechnical innovations such as solar energy advancements. These, as shown by Ramsarup, ultimately make up the 'system of transitioning', which, to be just, must include a sophisticated and consistently reflexive engagement with skills and skills system reorientation processes, along with the political–economy–ecology orientation to education and training praxis argued for earlier.

Since 2010, the discourse of sociotechnical transitions to a decarbonized future in the global south has developed into a just transitions discourse (Swilling and Anneke, 2012). This is being taken up in policy and at national government level, as the implications of transitioning away from a fossil capital foundation in the global economy become more apparent. For example, the Presidential Climate Change Commission in South Africa argues for increased mitigation of carbon emissions as part of a just transition, here meaning a commitment to rapid decarbonization, while at the same time addressing social justice and vulnerability challenges in society:

> A 'just transition' has typically been understood in relation to worker vulnerability to economic shifts from rapid decarbonisation, but it is important to emphasize that social justice is equally important in climate adaptation. Lack of access to productive land, water, energy and safe housing means that poor communities have lower adaptive capacities and are particularly vulnerable. Vulnerability is the propensity to be adversely affected, including sensitivity or susceptibility to harm and lack of capacity to cope and adapt (DEFF, 2019). Vulnerable groups can be identified by factors such as gender, age, disabilities, household income and reliance on public-sector services. Social and economic development including access to basic services are the starting point for strengthening adaptive capacity and resilience. If planned and implemented effectively, increasing adaptive capacities can in turn unlock socio-economic development, create jobs and enterprises, and stimulate local sustainable production and consumption. (PCCC, 2021: 11)

This gains significance for the VET sector when it is understood that decarbonization is likely to lead to a demand for reskilling of existing workers within whole value chains and types of industries (such as the coal and oil industries) (PCCC, 2021). The range of adaptation trajectories are likewise going to demand reskilling of existing workers and communities (for instance, farmers and water users), especially since there is strong evidence – in South Africa at least – that adaptation action is as yet poorly constituted and engaged across society and in all sectors (PCCC, 2021), which is a factor affecting all African countries, as well as countries around the world as societies are really only just beginning to grapple with the full implications of a 2°C+ world order. Beyond sectoral planning (such as energy sector transitions) and important for longer-term planning, mitigation and adaptation scenarios is the understanding that skills for just transitions are not reduced to existing sectors only, but are more widely needed in society, which opens the space for considering alternative models for VET provisioning, a point that we open up for scrutiny in this book.

While perspectives on sector-based transformations are essential for specific VET planning, care should be taken not to reduce 'just transitions' to value chains in transitioning economic sectors such as energy and agriculture. Cock (2019: 862) cautions against 'shallow' green transitions or 'social dialogue' approaches. She argues instead for real transformative change and a 'social power approach' that can embed the 'anti-coal struggle in a social movement for an alternative development path to challenge deepening poverty and inequality' (2019: 872). Just transitions, when interpreted with a depth of understanding of the full extent of policy contradictions and colonial modernity's impact on life, work and living, need to consider the way in which '[t]he real abstractions of Nature/Society penetrated everyday life, reflected in new family forms, new forms of slavery (modern slavery), and the urbanization of rural life through the widespread use of European-style towns' (Moore, 2017: 32). Moore argues that just transitions should reach into the very bowel of life and return to a core point (missed for most of the 20th century) made by Marx that 'value is a specific crystallisation of the original sources of all wealth: human and extra-human work'. In just transitions, both nature fundamentalism and labour fundamentalism need to be deconstructed for their limitations in framing a political–economy–ecology of skills because retaining these fundamentalisms leads to the false conflict between 'jobs' and 'environment'. As also pointed out by Cock (2019) and Africa's young people in Oinas et al (2018), a radical politics of work and life is needed that reaches beyond economism and deep forms of epistemic exclusion (Santos, 2014, see also Chapter 5 and 7). Such a politics of work and life require a fundamental reorientation of education, skills and VET logics as pointed to in Chapters 1 and 2, but more urgently, new imaginaries and applied praxis that can generatively cocreate alternatives that can realize such a radical politics of education, work and life. The chapters in this book show that this is possible via emerging possibilities at the intersections of place, context and history, formal, nonformal, informal and social learning and their respective modes of operation and structuring. As Moore claims (2017: 24): 'Reimagining work in capitalism – beyond labor fundamentalism – provides a way forward in today's unpleasant reality.'

Skills development for just transitions within an expanded skills ecosystem approach

Swilling's work extends just transitions discourse (2020: 29), arguing that ultimately just transitions need to be deepened to include consideration of the 'asynchronous interaction between four long-wave transitions: sociometabolic transitions, sociotechnical transitions, technoindustrial transitions and long-term development cycles'. This gives rise to a discourse beyond the technologies of skills and work, and points to new ways of learning and working to construct new cultural forms, such as ecocultures, new urban visions, sustainability-oriented developmental states and so on (Swilling, 2020: iii). This takes us back to the notion of emergence and Wright's (2010) concept of concrete or real utopias (see also Burawoy, 2013). Our research has shown that these *can* emerge in the cocreation of networked social skills ecosystems (Lotz-Sisitka et al, 2021). As will be shown in later chapters, this surfaces the need to give more attention to relational agency, as well as knowledge and its dissemination in VET. In broadening the notion of work to be inclusive of living and learning considerations, there is a need not only for high-quality knowledge resources and structured learning processes and pedagogies, but also for coengaged approaches to knowledge sharing around practical demonstrations that matter to people. For example, in agriculture, the 'International Assessment of Agricultural Science, Knowledge and Technology for Development' (McIntyre et al, 2009: 7) states that there is need for 'public investments in agricultural knowledge systems to promote interactive knowledge networks (farmers, scientists, industry and actors in other knowledge areas) ... and improving life-long learning opportunities along the food system'. McIntyre et al (2009: 10) state further that 'the resolution of natural resource challenges will demand new and creative approaches by stakeholders with diverse backgrounds, skills and priorities. Capabilities for working together at multiple scales and across different social and physical environments are not well developed.' Approaches that integrate sectors and skills system actors have been largely excluded from the modernist, structuralist social imaginary and institutional support systems.

One form of response to just transitions that addresses the political–economy–ecology perspectives is to develop national or internationally standardized types of VET programmes for new value chains, such as specialized VET programmes for building photovoltaic panels for solar energy generation, or specialized VET colleges for wind or hydrogen economy value chains. Even when such standardized programmes are on offer, there is still a need for locating the VET programmes in local ecologies and economies. For example, the East London Industrial Development Zone in South Africa is oriented towards green economy development and hosts a VET programme on site so that students are engaged in the production of photovoltaic panels within a wider value chain. This is a good example of a formalized local skills ecosystem that draws on universally relevant science and technology knowledge.

However, for a vast range of adaptation responses, and for dealing with more complex issues such as those affecting coal mining communities, smallholder farmers and unemployed youth, as well as the more radically and deeply situated just transitions framed earlier, there is a need to consider VET more contextually and situationally. This means at district or local economy level where ecological conditions, such as availability of water, intersect with historical inequalities and exclusions (such as inadequate access to land and poor-quality education) and have an impact on the type of VET programmes most needed. It is here that the expanded skills ecosystem approach may be most helpful for VET system development. This is not just a contextualization or regionalization argument, but an argument for producing new generative alternatives that are more inclusive of the intersections of work, living and learning in Africa, as we point out across the book. Our analysis of the four cases needs to be seen as pointing towards such emerging new economies and indicative of some of the thinking about VET that will be necessary to support these.

Conclusion

In Chapter 1, we highlighted the need to go beyond the existing VET literature in confronting more explicitly the interconnected need to analyse what is wrong with VET, and why, and the urgency and possibility of imagining alternative VETs. In this chapter, we have introduced a political–economy–ecology frame into VET discussions, an important innovation that we consider necessary to deepen the more conventional critique of Chapter 2. However, Chapter 3 does not only point us backwards into VET's underpinnings and complicity in fossil capitalism. It also begins to point us forward to the challenges and possibilities of a VET reimagining that can be part of a wider move to just transitions. In Chapter 4, we narrow our focus down to substantive VET theory and explore the social ecosystems approach, which shows more of a sustainability sensibility than most rival approaches.

4

Towards an Expanded Notion of Skills Ecosystems

Presha Ramsarup and Jo-Anna Russon

Introduction

In Chapter 1, we introduced the notion of a social ecosystem for skills model and previewed its importance to our approach in this book. In this chapter, we build on that introduction by documenting the evolution of skills ecosystem research and outlining where we are trying to take it forward by expanding the approach. Although our cases are African, our expansion of the model has global salience. We argue that our approach makes a contribution to the wider project of transforming VET for a transformed economy, society and environment.

We begin by tracing the emergence of skills ecosystems within the Anglophone north. In particular, we draw on the version of the approach developed by Hodgson and Spours (2016, 2018; see also Spours, 2019). Their research promotes a more socially oriented application of the skills ecosystems work in diverse contexts more applicable to the African settings for vocational education within which our cases reside. Crucially, they adopt a perspective that connects working, living and learning and enables a more place-based orientation that can also support skills for inclusive sustainable development and regional economies.

We then illustrate how we applied the core elements of the social ecosystem model to the four cases, enabling us to develop a more nuanced and textured understanding of local vocational skill formation. Through this analytical work, we lay the foundation for the theoretical expansion of the notion of skills ecosystems in the final section of the chapter. There we draw on critical realism to help us shape a conceptual and theoretical framework that does not succumb to reductionist conceptualizations of vocational skill formation. In attempting an expanded view, we explore the potential of conceptualizing skills ecosystems as a complex phenomenon that can be resolved into their separate yet related and emergent components so as to identify and relate the various mechanisms as different levels of reality that enable and constrain local skills ecosystems. We developed an expanded model that saw these interactions in a multiscalar, spatiotemporal way.

This expanded notion of skills ecosystems then lays the foundation for the empirical chapters that follow, which explore (i) formal and informal vocational education and training (VET) and the informal economy; (ii) the practice of VET teaching; (iii) transitioning between work and learning, between different disciplines of knowledge and between different levels of learning and levels of practice; and (iv) networking and community engagement in support of inclusive sustainable development and the particular role of universities as mediation partners in promoting this.

Skills 'ecosystems': a construct in transition

Although the skills ecosystem notion is conventionally dated to Finegold's 1999 paper, it also draws on his earlier work beginning in the late 1980s. This early work (most notably Finegold and Soskice, 1988) was focused on the national system level and on the UK in particular. Finegold and Soskice argued that the economy needed to break out of a low-skill equilibrium: a status quo of poorly trained workers and managers amid a self-reinforcing network of societal and institutional interactions that stifled demand for skills improvement. They described the UK as becoming increasingly isolated from more advanced industrialized economies that had far higher levels of general education and training. Their analysis viewed the problem as rooted in deeper systemic issues of supply and demand for skills, rather than just inadequate education and training. They theorized that part of the solution to this challenge lay in 'coordination' between multiple actors in what they viewed as an intrinsically competitive environment, but they did not use the term 'ecosystem'. Their work was quickly picked up as relevant to the South African context (Kraak, 1993; McGrath, 1996; McGrath et al, 2004).

A decade later, Finegold's focus had moved to the regional level (Finegold, 1999). Here, he echoed other traditions going back to Marshall's (1890) work on industrial districts, which argued that economic activities are embedded in social processes that enable certain regions to create and sustain successful clusters (see also the innovation systems tradition, which has also made a spatial leap from the national to the regional: see, for instance, Lund and Karlsen, 2020). Finegold took the case of Silicon Valley and explored how its high-skills ecosystem might inform the UK case. While he stood by his previous overall analysis of Britain's low-skill equilibrium, he noted that this was an oversimplification of reality as high-skill regions and sectors could exist within low-skill economies. He argued that while both 'equilibrium' and 'ecosystem' captured the interdependence of actors within a system, the latter term was preferable as it focused on continual evolution in a self-sustaining high-skill ecosystem. Drawing on natural ecosystems, he suggested that four requirements were necessary to create and sustain a high-skill ecosystem:

- a catalyst (or set of catalysts) to trigger their development;
- nourishment to sustain growth on an ongoing basis;
- a supportive host environment; and
- a high degree of interdependence among actors in the system (Finegold, 1999: 66–71).

The ecosystem metaphor has proved attractive to academics and is increasingly used by policymakers. A related version is that of the entrepreneurial ecosystem. Isenberg (2010) again took the example of Silicon Valley but argued that its success was hugely context-dependent and could not usefully be replicated. Instead, he suggested that entrepreneurship could be nurtured where interventions built on the existing context of the specific place. He identified six elements to this: a conducive culture, enabling policies and leadership, availability of appropriate finance, quality human capital, venture-friendly markets for products, and a range of institutional supports, all of which are always context-specific. These are understood through the 'metaphorical device' of natural ecosystems to retrospectively reflect on the dynamics of tech/financial clustering and rate of 'spin offs' (ecosystem effect) to develop more high-growth firms (Spours, 2021a). While not conceptualized as skills ecosystems, the industrial ecology literature on localized circular economies (Baas, 1998; Yu et al, 2014) also includes issues of system leadership, communication and partnership building, information sharing and transparency, and trust building. In South Africa, the early interest in low-skills equilibria was also followed by a sectoral turn (for instance, Kraak, 2009; McGrath, 2015; Wedekind and Mutereko, 2016; Wedekind, 2019).

The strongest empirical exploration of the notion of skills ecosystems comes from Australia. There, a series of more than 100 pilot projects involved industry associations, enterprise and workplace managers, VET providers, industry skills councils and education authorities. In that context, Buchanan et al (2001: 21) defined a skill ecosystem as 'clusters of high-, intermediate- and low-level competencies in a particular region or industry shaped by interlocking networks of firms, markets and institutions'. They argued that VET policy in Australia also needed to address wider economic development, labour market and employee relations and suggested that 'skill ecosystems' could tackle Australia's skills challenge. The Australian pilots suggest that effective skill ecosystems require leaders with deep knowledge of their domain and analytical and organizational skills. However, they also illustrate that building social coalitions to support skill ecosystem reform is difficult and time consuming, requiring partnerships and trust.

These early iterations of the ecosystem concept pointed to the complex reality of multiple actors interacting within a skills system in a regional context. Despite the expansion of the skills ecosystem work, it faces several core challenges as a model for VET and skills development more broadly. First, critics have argued that a skills ecosystem is constrained by a neoliberal growth model characterized by the absence of strong trade unions, well-regulated labour markets, active industrial policy and robust welfare state arrangements (Payne, 2008). Second, while the focus on context is important and skills in context has intuitive appeal, it is challenging to clarify what in a particular context is problematic. It is thus important to keep the idea that that context is not neutral or self-evident. Analysis and reform in skills analysis needs to acknowledge that most problems arise from the ways that skills in demand are defined, used and developed and have their roots in the nature of work concerned (Buchanan et al, 2017). Third, new knowledge has tended to emerge from applied policy-based research, rather than more fundamental research. Thus, the tradition has been rather weak in its theoretical development (Hall and Lansbury, 2006; Payne, 2008; Anderson and Warhurst, 2012). In the sections that follow, we first expand on Spours and colleagues' conceptualization of a social ecosystem for skills model and then explore our approach to it in an attempt to strengthen its theoretical and empirical basis.

The importance of *social* ecosystems for skills

The preceding chapters illustrate that the issues facing global societies are increasingly seen as complex, multifaceted and integral to social, ecological and economic development. Thus, as societies grapple with the rapid and catastrophic effects of the polycrisis, occupational and educational systems have attempted to meaningfully comprehend the implications. Within Africa, these challenges are especially complex. In a continent facing fundamental transformation on every front, there are significant new challenges for work and learning systems. Lotz-Sisitka (2009: 169) explains that 'change orientated learning and research needs to be located at the interface of local and global as well as past, present and future, creating not only a challenging epistemological frame but also a challenging temporal and spatial frame for such research'. Therefore, understanding local skill formation in these changing times raises interesting challenges.

Drawing on a critique of the entrepreneurial ecosystem and skills ecosystem approaches, Spours and his colleagues developed an alternative ecosystem framework that helped them explore the 'relationship between disruptive economic and technological developments and how they affect local economies, jobs, the shape of urban environments and the living conditions of their populations' (Spours, 2019: 3) with a particular focus on London. Whereas the primary focus of the elite ecosystem was the firm, the primary focus in the social ecosystem is 'local place' as the focal point of economic, civic and educational participation. This shaped a skills ecosystem model that depicts a dynamic, multilevel relationship of temporal and spatial factors as central to skills development.

The social ecosystem for skills model thus offers a useful approach to skill formation research as it seeks to develop skills development approaches that forge stronger connections between working, living and learning, mirroring the best elements of the precolonial skills formation system and the most admired modern systems. It has the potential to learn also from emerging systems seeking to enable inclusive sustainable development, circular economy, industrial ecology orientations that prioritize regional circulation of materialities, and 'the development of a collective knowledge and the development of the collective through knowledge' (Cerceau et al, 2012: 623; see also Habiyaremye et al, 2020).

Spours and colleagues' work on ecosystems uses Finegold's four core elements but attempts to relate these elements both horizontally and vertically through system leadership and common mission. In Figure 4.1, Spours uses Finegold's core elements of ecosystems to illustrate the relationship between horizontal and vertical factors and connects macro and meso elements of ecosystems. Crucially, it emphasizes the social dimension of this, defining a social ecosystem for skills formation as an 'evolving, place-based social formation that connects the worlds of working, living and learning with the purpose of nurturing inclusive, sustainable economic, social and educational development in diverse communities, localities and sub-regions' (Spours, 2021a: no pagination).

Spours' social ecosystem for skills is conceptualized as comprising four related dimensions:

- collaborative horizontalities;
- facilitating verticalities;
- 45° politics and mediation through common mission and skills ecosystem leadership; and
- the concept of ecological time that allows for processes of holistic and deliberative system evolution (Spours, 2021a).

The following discussion expands on these four elements.

Figure 4.1: Combining the Finegold and Spours models

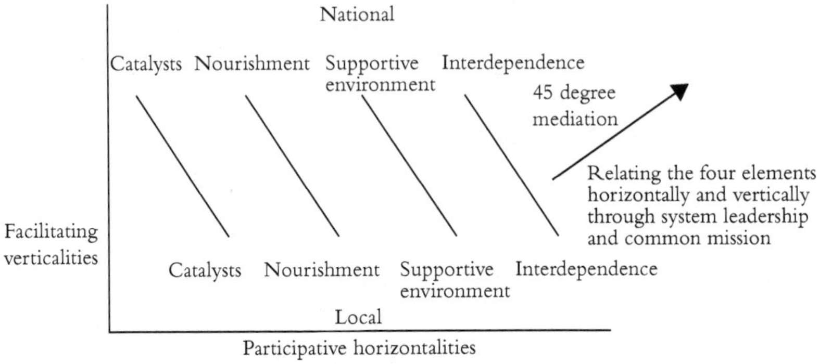

Source: Adapted from Spours (2021a)

Collaborative horizontalities

Extended and participatory horizontal terrains are a fundamental feature of the social ecosystem model, seen as education networks, local anchor institutions and a range of social partners/communities supported by the connective role of digital technologies (though the latter seems highly contextual). The horizontal dimension is understood to be dynamic and multilayered, with spatial characteristics linked to localities, regions and subregions. The idea of 'nested' relationships also opens up a way of explaining how a broad social ecosystem might contain different types of embedded subsystems, such as elite finance and technologically based ecosystems and skills ecosystems involving workplaces. Therefore, Spours argues that the horizontal terrain is layered, interlocking and ultimately collaborative and provides the key elements of 'interdependent relations' and 'nourishment' that sustain ecosystems. The flourishing of the social ecosystem for skills model requires this network-building to progress to institution-building so that it has strong inclusive anchor institutions.

Facilitating verticalities

The emergent social ecosystem for skills model envisages an extended state role – both an enabling national state and an empowered local state – through what is referred to as 'facilitating verticalities'. The verticalities play important roles in sustaining ecosystems as 'catalysts' and in providing the 'supportive environment', including financial boosts, key infrastructure projects and regulatory regimes.

45° politics and mediation

A common mission and ecosystem leadership is needed between the vertical and the horizontal. Spours argues that since these ecosystems are not naturally formed within current economic and political conditions, they require nurturing processes to come into existence and thrive. He explains that this dimension thus embodies 'the role of mediation and connectivity, including the concepts of ecosystem leadership, formative educational activity and socially-designed technological connectivity' (Spours, 2021b: no pagination). In this view, common mission is related, in particular, to the needs of the locality and is concerned with providing the 'glue' between a diverse set of social partners, each with their own specialisms and preoccupations. The common mission is exercised through what might be termed 'ecosystem leadership', the key function of which is to nurture, cohere and educate the different elements or forces of an expanded social ecosystem by relating its horizontal and vertical features. Seen in terms of 'system leadership', Spours draws on Senge et al to highlight three core capacities: 'the ability to see the larger system', 'fostering reflection and more generative conversations' and 'shifting the collective focus from reactive problem-solving to co-creating the future' (Senge et al, 2015: 3–4). In Spours' diagrammatic presentation of this concept, he draws mediation as a 45° line between the horizontal and vertical, drawing on Lawson's (2019) work for an English thinktank that uses the notion of a 45° politics. We do not draw on this aspect of Spours' terminology but simply note his language of the 45°.

Ecological time

The final element is ecosystem construction and evolution over 'ecological time' that allows for processes of holistic and deliberative system evolution. This dimension helps us reflect on how change occurs in systems over long periods of time. Such a reflection emphasizes that social ecosystems are not time-bound. Spours argues that the social ecosystem for skills model should be considered as a long-term project in which continued effort is required to 'understand the configuration of forces needed for the flourishing of such a system and the nurturing of complex relationships over time' (Spours, 2021b: no pagination). Hodgson and Spours (2018) explain that this includes 'the identification and mapping of existing relations and challenges to formulate the common mission, building networked sets of activities to develop new forms of collaborative activity'. These would then create the demand for new types of skills, thus creating a social ecosystem effect.

These elements help us to understand ecosystem change as the interplay of developments at different analytical levels, which interact dynamically in the unfolding skills ecosystem.

Applying a social ecosystems perspective

The VET Africa 4.0 project was premised upon an understanding that VET systems are not functioning effectively and that new approaches are required (see earlier chapters and McGrath et al, 2020). The four cases are situated within a wider systemic perspective and the political economies shaping state-led formal national VET systems that we deem to be largely ineffective. Yet, each of the four cases are also unique locations, chosen to reflect a rural–urban spectrum, with different degrees of economic formality and development trajectories. Within VET Africa 4.0, we required a conceptual and theoretical framework that could capture issues of relationality, in terms of VET networks and connections between individuals and institutions within the geographic bounding of each case and help us to understand how such relationships are hindered or facilitated by regulations, policies and key local actors and institutions. The social ecosystem for skills model encapsulates much of our thinking about the necessity of going beyond productivist notions of skills for work and the economy to thinking more sustainably and holistically about reimagining the purpose and functionings of VET towards just transitions in diverse African contexts.

In the data narratives presented here, we explain how we used and interpreted the social ecosystem dimensions of verticalities, horizontalities and mediation to understand and analyse the skills ecosystem within each of the four cases and guide our cross-case analysis. This process drew upon our prior work synthesizing insights from VET literature for the VET Africa 4.0 project (see also McGrath et al, 2020) and a case-mapping exercise where we developed social ecosystem case maps, drawing on desktop research and contextual work on each case setting. We also drew upon our insights as individual researchers, practitioners and activists in the field and our position as the VET Africa 4.0 Collective. This elucidation involved physically drawing each case ecosystem. Overall, this process expanded our critique of the social ecosystem for skills model in terms of what is necessary for theorizing VET ecosystems in diverse African contexts and led to our expanded notion of skills ecosystems, which we present in the final part of this chapter. For now, we turn to its main elements and how we began to conceptualize these across the four cases and the project more broadly.

'Facilitating verticalities' in African VET ecosystems?

Across the four cases, we began by framing 'facilitating verticalities' as ranging from the international, through to the national and the local. International policies and development frameworks on VET and skills development can be important influencing factors nationally and locally. For example, the policy orthodoxy of VET 3.0 (see Chapter 2) shapes the funding priorities and development narratives of donors and other external actors (for instance, INGOs) operating within the cases. Equally, all the cases are located within globalized economic trends. The way that food, transport, water and oil is experienced in the cases is shaped in important ways beyond the nation (see Chapters 3 and 5–8). Nonetheless, national actors are central to the concept of facilitating verticalities, where it is necessary to understand how state actors, such as regulatory bodies and education and training departments, send signals vertically into the VET ecosystem. These signals are intended to be facilitating verticalities for the local dimension. This local dimension is where the cases sit as place-based locations of VET and the corresponding patterns of living, working and learning.

It was necessary to understand the extent to which vertical policies, systems and investments and hierarchical structures are facilitative of local VET and skills development in each case. We were clear that the possibility for facilitating verticalities existed within and across the international, national and local dimensions of each case. Though we recognized that this consisted of those mechanisms and processes that we could conceive of and empirically seek to understand, from a critical realist perspective, we were aware that the 'real' is far more complex than our knowledge of it. This challenge applies across the entire notion of a VET ecosystem, and we return to this issue in the final section of this chapter.

Unpacking the vertical: South African cases

In South Africa, concepts of a developmental state and infrastructure-led growth are at the heart of government policy initiatives and decision making. The National Development Plan has an explicit focus on large-scale infrastructure projects, and this is central to the eThekwini case, as we noted in Chapter 1.

On the vertical axis, it was intended that the 'visible hand' of the state would ensure that such projects were designed, developed and operated in a manner that secured them as engines of economic transformation, for example by tackling economic disparities in business opportunities and promoting skills access and employment. In the first case, in eThekwini, Strategic Integrated Projects (SIPs) were supposed to be supported by skills investments coordinated from a senior level in the national Department of Higher Education and Training (DHET). Regionally, various state departments were supposed to facilitate the implementation of these policies in the regional ecosystem in partnership with provincial and municipal structures, again as outlined in Chapter 1. However, we were conscious of the stagnation of policy since the actors we had engaged with up to that point attributed none of their activities to the influence of any of these state-led development initiatives. Ideologically, we also saw human capital theory having an immense influence on the activities of the various actors, based on the idea that education is an investment in human capital that will yield dividends in the form of improved livelihoods.

In the second South African case, actors were frustrated by inadequacies in the land reform programme that failed to provide water to farmers who had been given back their land in a context that faces extreme issues of drought and climate change, as outlined in Chapters 1 and 3. We noted in Chapter 1 the range of state agencies that constitute the key actors on the vertical axis. In contrast to the focus on industrial policies in the eThekwini case, the vertical dimension in the Alice case is dominated by policies related to natural resources and community development, including those oriented towards issues specific to the agricultural sector in the National Development Plan. Whereas provincial and metropolitan policymakers are important elements of the vertical in eThekwini, policy is perceived in Alice as largely coming from the distant national level. Moreover, the vertical is shaped by the overwhelming focus on and influence of corporate (and often globalized) control of food and agricultural systems that continues colonial and apartheid processes of deliberate marginalization of small-scale commercial agriculture, as outlined in Chapters 2 and 3. In terms of VET actors on the vertical axis, there are three issues. First, the mainstream public VET system under DHET is essentially urban-focused and industry-oriented, with rural colleges, such as the one in Alice, largely expected to offer programmes that are misaligned to the full scope of local labour markets. Second, the gap between what are effectively two agricultural systems is manifested in a disconnect between a high skills ecosystem and local public VET institutions and agricultural colleges. Third, these different departmental jurisdictions on the vertical axis are reflected in a disconnection on the horizontal axis between the different public vocational providers, located as they are under different policy and quality assurance regimes. Such vertical dynamics could play a critical role in hindering the types of facilitative VET learning and skills development processes that are essential to rural issues such as those faced in the Alice case.

Unpacking the vertical: Ugandan cases

As outlined already, political economy issues – both colonial and postcolonial – in Uganda have contributed both to inadequate skills and livelihood opportunities and persistent negative attitudes to VET and certain skills and livelihoods. Paradoxically, VET is seen both as a current problem and potential solution to broader development challenges. On the vertical axis, this has policy implications for both Ugandan cases. We have already noted the waves of donor-supported skills policy initiatives and have identified these as very much aligned with VET Africa 3.0, despite the longstanding critiques thereof (see Chapter 2).

In both cases, local government is supposed to provide oversight and leadership of VET implementation, but this functionality is limited due to factors such as inadequate funds, policy silos and personnel shortages.

In mapping both cases, it was evident that they were geographically and structurally disconnected from political and economic power on the vertical axis. In addition, there are also distinctive features in each case that influence VET policy and provision at the local level, reflecting the dynamics of postconflict and oil extraction imperatives, as summarized in Chapter 1. In Hoima, this has resulted in the Ministry of Energy and Mineral Development being a major player. Here, the vertical axis is also heavily influenced by the oil sector, its global dynamics, major firms and environmental contestations. However, in terms of VET, the core issue is the impetus that the oil industry has had on shifting policy attention on skills development in the region and the subsequent influx of vocationally related activities and programmes by various international actors on the horizontal dimension. For Gulu, the inflow of major humanitarian aid in response to the conflict still influences the vertical dimension, somewhat muting the human capital discourse.

Top-down verticalities

These first attempts to describe the vertical axis for each case and conceptualize possibilities for facilitating verticalities led us to question who is (and is not) involved in VET and skills planning, when top-down, nationally driven VET strategies appeared to be central to each case. Processes of dissemination and application of VET policy and skills development at the local level were either difficult to visualize or appeared to be primarily top-down in nature. With regard to the possibility of facilitating verticalities that support living, working and learning, it was clear that relevant policy and strategy intent existed in all four cases. However, we recognized that it was also necessary to question how these top-down policies, actors and associated resources could adequately respond to the occupational and skills training mismatch that exists within the cases, not least the levels of employment within the formal sector. This also links to issues of equality, particularly for those individuals outside of formal VET, skills and occupational systems. These insights led to a distinct set of questions about the vertical axis in the social ecosystem model for skills. We opted to include these questions as they offer potential methodological guidance for future work and help to illustrate what might be necessary to facilitate integration among the various policy actors in the dynamic and complex VET contexts represented by our cases:

1. What are the relevant international, national and local policies that have a bearing on the case?
2. What hierarchical governance structures – for instance, government, institutional boards, district level boards and policies (nationally and locally, and internationally) exist – and how might they constitute facilitating verticalities in diverse VET contexts?

3. What are the issues/differences vis-à-vis policy intent and local implementation? What space is there for local VET actors to have agency and be involved in vertical structures? What capacity is there to contribute and have influence (for instance, on policy design)?
4. What is missing on the vertical dimension? For instance, if the local government is missing or appears ineffective, why? How is this compensated for? What/who is included and excluded on the vertical axis? How do issues of segmentation manifest? For instance, are labour markets and learning systems segmented, do certain groups get stuck in lower-status elements of the VET system?

Identifying 'collaborative horizontalities' in complex dynamic multilayered VET contexts

We applied the notion of collaborative horizontalities to the cases to understand the complex, dynamic and multilayered nature of VET-based relationships within each. For this dimension, we sought to understand what key actors and relationships existed on the horizontal terrain. Specifically, we addressed the nature of relationships that may sit within and across various clusters and nested relationships associated with each case. In terms of the core notion of collaborative horizontalities, it was critical to understand what collaborative engagement within each case looked like over time, and which actors appeared to have a mandate to bring actors together on the horizontal dimension collaboratively.

On the horizontal dimension, the eThekwini skills ecosystem consists of a range of public, private and in-house training institutions (the latter both public and private), partially nested in the national skills system, providing a differentiated institutional context, as summarized in Chapter 1. Many of these organizations in turn interact with the public skills policy architecture through DHET and sector education and training authorities. It was evident at the outset that there was a hierarchy of these institutions regarding status within and engagement with the maritime sector, with public VET institutions appearing largely marginal. Indeed, DHET's vertical commitment to linking SIPs and the skills system appeared to dissipate once it moved beyond the walls of the department. However, there were also early signs that one industry body, the eThekwini Maritime Cluster, could play a role in building relationships and facilitating collaboration, though VET was not a priority area therein. As we noted in Chapter 1 (and will return to in more detail in Chapters 6 and 7), a potentially important new intervention at the regional level was the new uMfolozi Maritime Academy in Richards Bay.

In the Alice case, the actors populating the horizontal axis are farmers, local nongovernmental organizations, local economic development officers, extension services, youth groups and community representatives. There are also several students and faculty at local education training institutions. The connections between these actors tend to be contextual and, for the smallholder farmers who are at the centre of the case study, very localized. Despite featuring prominently in the region's history and current demography, small-scale farmers are not at the centre of the VET or agricultural colleges' curricula, nor those of the agricultural faculties of the local universities. As noted earlier, the current formal agricultural education system is mostly geared towards training larger-scale commercial farmers and extension workers. These extension workers, it is intended, will then go on to provide training and support to the much larger pool of small-scale and subsistence farmers in the area. However, historically, due to a bifurcated policy system, universities and agricultural colleges were set up to exist closer to the vertical axis than the horizontal one, reflected in an agricultural expert system that is still not responsive to the needs of farmers on the ground, despite progressive policy. Indeed, in many villages, large disconnects exist between small farmers and the extension services. Political mismanagement and corruption have further complicated issues, leading to breakdowns in trust and a wide divide between actors on the horizontal axis and the verticalities described earlier.

Against this backdrop, it was believed that a multistakeholder learning network, the Imvothu Bubomi Learning Network (IBLN), could provide a model for pro-poor, community-owned approaches to connecting living. This was facilitated by collaborating anchor institutions in the form of the Fort Cox Agriculture and Forestry Agricultural College (FCAFTI) and Rhodes University working with the University of Fort Hare (that is, a cluster of vocational and higher education institutions), with support from the municipality's local economic development office. This provides a model for pro-poor, community-owned approaches to connecting living, working and learning (see Chapters 5 and 8). This learning network has illustrated how such collaborations could improve VET offerings, mediate learning and support inclusive, community-driven skills for a just transition (see Lotz-Sisitka et al, 2021).

In Uganda, the Gulu case also faces a series of development challenges as outlined in Chapter 1. In response, various key actors in the area are seeking to work with young people to transform livelihoods so that they are more just, decent and sustainable. NGOs, both local and national, also play major roles in facilitating vocational skills for development, primarily due to the influence on programmes as determined by strategic funding priorities. They function across various categories with a predominant focus on youth and women. Amid this array of development-oriented actors sit various VET institutions (formal, nonformal and informal), and parents, students, teachers, employers and workers/employees. All of whom are primary local stakeholders on the horizontal terrain. Secondly, Gulu University and Ker Kwaro Acholi (the traditional authority) exist as central community-based resource centres because they connect networks in VET and livelihood opportunities. Finally, there are various youth groups, local communities, traditional institutions, women's groups and cooperatives, who are all central to local initiatives to strengthen VET provision and promote livelihood opportunities (see Chapters 5 and 8).

Finally, in the Hoima case, the discovery of oil in Uganda is linked to a core narrative that oil will contribute to local development through jobs, increased incomes and infrastructure development in the area (see Chapter 3's discussion of African post-independence reliance on extractives). As outlined in Chapter 1, there have been two main skills interventions in the region, the Uganda Petroleum Institute, Kigumba (UPIK) centre of sectoral excellence and the Skills for Oil and Gas in Africa (SOGA) programme. Alongside these are various public and private formal, informal and nonformal VET institutions, all of whom have various training programmes for learners, many of which are not relevant to the oil and gas industry. Similarly, few have the technical capacity, resources or equipment to support anything more than basic skills in subjects such as hairdressing, motor mechanics, carpentry or welding. As with the Gulu case, attached to this ecosystem of VET institutions are important stakeholders including students, VET graduates and parents. Alongside these are growing numbers of local businesses such as transport, hotel, tour companies, land and estate agencies, all of whom represent potential linkages between VET and skills supply and demand either directly or indirectly related to the oil and gas industry. The extent to which this mix of donors, VET managers and teachers, learners and private sector actors (local, informal and those linked to oil and gas) are interacting in ways that resembled collaborative horizontalities for the advancement of local skills remains unclear. Nonetheless, the Hoima case raises the interesting question of whether oil and gas can be a disruption to the current VET model and a catalyst for livelihood changes through a new development paradigm for the region, generated through collaborative horizontalities.

Possibilities for collaborative horizontalities

The horizontal axis pointed towards the possibility for bottom–up, devolved, collaborative elements of governance and leadership within each case. However, this primarily consisted of a theoretical but unrealized potential in most cases, with the notable exception being the learning network example in the Alice case. These preliminary insights on the possibilities and challenges of collaborative horizontalities in diverse and complex VET ecosystems led to the following questions about the application of the collaborative horizontalities concept to VET in Africa:

1. Who are the key actors on the supply side? This may often include VET institutions in multiple guises: formal, nonformal, informal, public, private, religious, alongside NGOs, INGOs and any other actors who are putting skills into the system.
2. What are the key relationships between actors on the horizontal axis, and what are the nature of these relationships?
3. What is the relative status, authority, resourcing and resource flows of the various actors?
4. How is VET-based knowledge and learning transferred within these relationships? Where do people and institutions get their knowledge? How do VET providers learn about what skills they should be providing? Where else are people learning?
5. What, if anything, might be causing a change in people's understanding about VET, and living, working and learning?
6. What/who is missing on the horizontal dimension?
7. What would it take to catalyse more horizontal collaboration? What is blocking or hindering it?

VET learning systems and practices (evidence of mediation)

The third element of the social ecosystem for skills model is the concept of mediation between connecting horizontalities and facilitating verticalities. The process of mediation involves key social actors who 'think and move along horizontal and vertical terrains to arrange exchange and collaborations, to mediate the effects of national and regional government and to use global digital systems to support horizontal collaborative working' (Grainger and Spours, 2018: 6). We used this concept to explicitly think about crosscutting issues of working, living and learning at the intersection of the vertical and horizontal dimensions within the cases, and to explore the possible mediating processes that support a common vision of VET learning systems and practice. Grainger and Spours (2018) talk of mediating forms of leadership that function within vertically organized states and can identify a shared public mission or narrative, as opposed to the narrow objectives related to private wealth production in elite ecosystems. In our case contexts, we questioned what and who has the ability – and corresponding resources and mandate – to bring together processes and key institutions on the vertical terrain with a wide range of actors on the horizontal terrain in collaborations and continuous processes that support working, living and learning. For example, could, or should, community networks and local anchor institutions (for instance, VET institutions and universities) function as mediators? In the Alice case, the focus was less on 'who can mediate' and more on what mediation processes can be collectively developed, which included:

1. contextual analysis and reflection on the need state;
2. training-of-trainers' programmes to introduce new knowledge and options;
3. codevelopment of productive demonstrations as sites of colearning and mutual beneficiation;
4. curriculum innovation; and
5. use of social media communication tools including community radio (see Pesanayi, 2019a; Lotz-Sisitka and Pesanayi, 2020).

This culminated in three overarching questions for case analysis regarding the mediation dimension, and where this might be evident in the four cases:

1. Are there aspects of common vision, mediation and leadership evident within the cases?
2. If so, what type of catalytic actors (institutions, individuals, organizations, others; or configurations of actors) lead and/or facilitate VET ecosystem connections? Are these organizations that sit on both the vertical and horizontal dimension, for instance, INGOs and government agencies? What processes can best facilitate vertical connections between these actors?
3. What differentiates the mediation role from that of collaborative horizontalities? Is it possible and necessary for one actor to do both in VET ecosystems in African contexts?

VET learning systems: reflecting on ecological time

The transformative orientation at the heart of our project could be critiqued as normative or as an aspirational narrative. Aspirational narratives constitute a story of what should be but that evolves over time and through a deep understanding of the tensions and lock-ins between the ground narrative (or present reality) and the aspirational narrative. We remain cognisant that while the aspirational has intuitive appeal, it is important that we prioritize some critical elements that enable us to connect the aspirational narrative to the ground narrative as we frame our local VET agenda. We hence need to understand that the transition is a slow, long-term endeavour that requires multilevel engagement with hidden structures and mechanisms, including history and power relations present, as socioeconomic lock-ins have deep historical roots. We attempted to work across all four cases with a present–future spatiotemporal framing.

A multiscalar, spatiotemporal notion of skills ecosystems

As reflected in the preceding discussion, the social ecosystem for skills model offered us tools to conceptualize a place-based skill ecosystem. However, as we began to analyse the emergent relations and attempted to explore the transformative possibilities, the argument that skills ecosystem approaches hold potential for reimagining VET systems to be more inclusive and with power to address regional sustainable development praxis surfaced some challenges. These led us to explore how we could expand the framing of the social ecosystem approach as a multiscalar and spatiotemporal construct. In doing so, we drew on critical realism.

Critical realists argue that reality is both stratified – real, actual, empirical – and differentiated. This helped us to deal with the multiple levels in nonreductionist ways. By considering these layers of reality as we worked with the idea of multiscalarity, we were able to envisage structures and mechanisms that were operating even where they were 'beneath' the surface. Price (2012) explains that in open systems there is always a multiplicity of such structures and mechanisms operating. It is this multiplicity that generates the complexity of open systems such as skills ecosystems. Working with this idea of a layered reality helped us to conceptualize the interdependent planes constituting our skills ecosystems.

It is important to note that both the generative mechanisms of the real and the events of the actual are not necessarily reflected in the experiences of the empirical. Therefore, one cannot rely solely on the empirical evidence to reveal the causal effects of the phenomenon being researched. In the empirical domain, it is possible to identify experiences of knowing subjects (for instance, individuals working in the catering sector who reflectively shared their autobiographies of transition from learning to work). In the actual domain, one can identify events and their experiences by subjects (for instance, how a particular course or degree programme shaped the transition). In the domain of the real, one can identify both experiences and events, and the underlying mechanisms that generate these events and make them available to experience (for instance, how the existence of courses in a local college allowed an individual to study catering and thus become employed in the sector). However, a full analysis requires looking at all of these and their interactions with structures and their patterns of emergence, which help to understand that what is emergent in each level is related to the causal laws and mechanisms that exist in other levels in an open system.

Thus, from this background, our conceptual work involved conceiving of skills ecosystems as multiscalar phenomena, constituted by interdependent planes. Though presented here as static, they are dynamic, having historical depth and being in the process of transitioning. In considering transitioning, we need to explore what is absent as well as what is present. Our whole approach looks to what is emerging and what might be possibilities and openings for change. This is vital if we are to reimagine and build new approaches to VET.

Critical realism provides a crucial underlabouring to our expansion of the social ecosystem for skills approach. To this, we add a more explicit discussion and application of the notions of relational agency and relational capability, seeing relationality as implicit in previous ecosystems accounts. We also seek to draw on our explicit engagement with political ecology issues and the challenge of just transitions in this and the previous chapter to understand VET's purpose as being about furthering collective human flourishing and integral human development. Spours points in this direction, but our political–economy–ecology analysis takes this much further.

From an analysis of how the cases represented their skills ecosystems, we synthesize the main elements emergent from the four VET Africa 4.0 cases into multiple levels of scale represented in our expanded social ecosystems for skills model, represented in Figure 4.2.

In the figure, we illustrate that within our transitioning skills ecosystem, we studied the transitioning individuals who navigate learning and work

Figure 4.2: Expanded social ecosystem for skills model

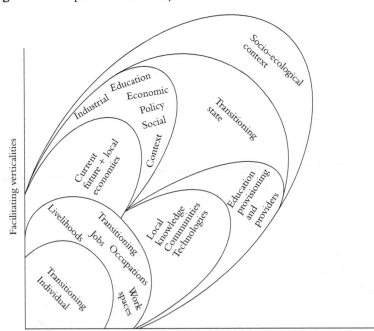

transitions within VET systems into transitioning jobs and occupational roles. Within the ecosystem, it is necessary to understand current and future streams of work especially as we consider work that can strengthen future local economies (as these offer potential VET pathways). In considering this, we needed to examine current and future educational provisioning. For instance, in the Alice and Gulu cases we examined these current and future jobs and provisioning related to formal and informal contexts in Chapter 5. These gave us the related stakeholders, intermediaries and policy contexts that connected the vertical and horizontal within the ecosystem. In trying to illustrate our working model, it is important to consider that the levels are iterative and draw their meaning from each other (what emerges in one level is contingent on the mechanisms at the other levels) and that each level attempts to surface related mediating factors and mechanisms between the vertical and the horizontal. This, we believe, presents challenging epistemological and spatiotemporal frames for future-focused skills ecosystems research.

The multiple processes of transitioning ecosystems depicted across our cases involve multiple actors and systems coevolving in step with each other. This in turn requires a refined lens to examine systemic transitions, agents, their agential capacity and what enables and constrains it. This helps us to deal with an important challenge raised by the first phase of our empirical work, that the current social ecosystem model for skills descriptive language inadequately conceptualizes actors, their agency and their relation to structure. Societies pre-exist the human agents who live in them and are a pre-existing condition for human activity. However, the ensemble of structures, practices and conventions requires human agency for their reproduction or transformation (Joseph, 2002: 9). Agency is linked to social structures, which stand as objects of study in their own right (Norrie, 2010). It is impossible to understand learners' agency in constructing their learning pathways without an understanding of social structures, and how they shape learners' choices, and how agents in turn shape them in the education system. Thus, people do not necessarily work to reproduce the capitalist economy and ignore environmental conditions, yet these results are unintended outcomes of their actions (reproducing structure) and the necessary condition of their acting (grounding and enabling or constraining their agency).

Bhaskar (1979) explains that social structures exist, are exercised and are being continuously reproduced or transformed only by virtue of, in and by human agency. This continuous reproduction or transformation of social structures can be understood through a system of mediating concepts that describe the point of contact between human agency and social structures. This mediation is significant to our argument about emergence within the ecosystem as it is at this nexus that agentive action arises (Archer, 1995, 1998).

This mediation is always evolving, dynamic and unpredictable (Agbedahin and Lotz-Sisitka, 2019). Hence, as we noted earlier, in the Alice case the focus was less on 'who mediates' but how collaborations could occur through mediation.

Conclusion

In the following four chapters, we will revisit the set of issues raised here through empirical examinations of four themes that are central to VET and this expanded notion of a skills ecosystems:

1. inclusivity, relationality and informality;
2. vocational teachers as mediators in complex ecosystems;
3. transitioning processes from learning to work; and
4. the role of the coengaged university as mediation partner in skills ecosystems.

Our intention in addressing this set of themes is to expand the social ecosystems for skills approach. Therefore, we have sought out areas that are not well developed in the literature. Thus, we look beyond the formal frame and at universities as well as conventional vocational providers and highlight the neglected central populations of education: young people and teachers. The chapters that follow are not intended to offer an exhaustive account of aspects of the social ecosystem for skills approach but rather to provide directions forward in exploring the concept of the social ecosystem for skills.

As we have argued in this chapter, the social ecosystem approach offers potentially important insights for thinking about future-focused VET. By extending its focus to Africa, addressing areas neglected in the approach thus far, and providing new insights into its relevance beyond highly formalized settings of work and learning, we will show through these chapters how the approach can work north and south and how our extension of it contributes to global VET debates.

5

Social Ecosystem for Skills Research: Inclusivity, Relationality and Informality

Luke Metelerkamp and David Monk

Introduction

Eighty per cent of Africans work in the informal economy. In this chapter, we consider the highly informal, unregulated and often marginalized contexts that form the majority experience of living, working and learning. Situating the praxis of horizontal learning within these very normal contexts of informality demands renewed analysis into the questions of *how* horizontal learning is facilitated, by whom, with what resources, and why.

Following on from Chapter 4, we develop our approach to social ecosystems further through two empirical case studies offering distinct lenses on to the informal sector. In Gulu, we consider the current dynamics of learning and inclusion among informal traders at a local market and in a set of food and clothing initiatives; in Alice, we reflect on an intentional effort on behalf of established, formal institutions to explore new approaches to teaching and learning through support of expansive informal learning in the context of food growing. While our focus across the book is on the range of labour markets and livelihood opportunities, it is appropriate to start our empirical chapters by focusing on the labour market of the majority.

General context and background

As we noted in Chapter 2, the 'discovery' of the informal sector 50 years ago prompted a flowering of research and programme interventions on how to enhance skills for those already in or likely to enter informal work (King, 2020). The informal economy is the normal economy in much of the world, including across most of Africa (Jütting and de Laiglesia, 2009) where it accounts for around 80 per cent of all livelihoods (Nguimkeu and Okou, 2020). With roughly 800 million youth forecast to enter their working lives over the coming 40 years (Kaneene et al, 2015; Losch, 2016), the informal economy is likely to remain central to how the overwhelming majority of Africans live, work and learn.

However, how we understand the informal sector, its potential development and the role of education and training in supporting it remains a matter of considerable controversy. A good example of the current policy orthodoxy is found in a recent International Labour Organization (ILO) literature review on lifelong learning in the informal economy (Palmer, 2020). This portrays the informal sector largely as a site of poverty and poor productivity, occupied by those with the lowest levels of educational achievement. Yet, apparently these major disadvantages can be easily overcome as the ILO also argues that relatively short interventions can bring significant employment and income benefits to informal sector actors.

From the World Bank, there tends to be a parallel argument about the need to stimulate entrepreneurship, and how easy this is. For education agencies, this then leads to calls for entrepreneurship education (see De Jaeghere, 2017 for a critical review). This is also increasingly being promoted in African vocational education and training (VET) systems based on an assumption that VET can relatively easily flip from a formal employment to an entrepreneurship focus (Allais et al, 2022). Again, there is a sense that there are no structural barriers affecting individual opportunities, and that entrepreneurial success is possible for all, here coupled with a naive faith in current public VET institutions' ability to switch focus.

A third policy trend is towards formalization of the informal sector and its learning systems, on the assumption that this will allow easy access to the formal sector. This includes attempts to bring the informal sector into national qualification frameworks through recognition of prior learning. We are resistant to all these easy policy responses. All have poor track records, similar to many of the VET reforms discussed in Chapter 2. Indeed, they appear to serve more to blame the poor for their alleged culpability than to engage seriously with the obstacles to sustainable livelihoods. Instead, in this chapter, we try to highlight both the structural realities of informal working and learning and the agentic possibilities.

In situating this work on informality, we conceptualize notions of informality and formality as interrelated elements. They are not the binary notions beloved of policy actors. Lives do not operate only in one of the two categories. It is from this perspective that we explore relationships between formality and informality. We also draw on the work of Edwards (2011) and De Jaeghere (2020) and their conceptualizations of relational agency and relational capabilities to underpin our analysis of the dynamics we observed in the Ugandan and South African cases. Collectively, this situates networked ecosystems of actors within the informal economy as the invisible mainstay of the current vocational system across much of the continent and a potentially catalytic driver of inclusive innovation.

Informality, learning and the potential for innovation

The literature on lifelong learning offers richer insights than the VET literature regarding the challenge of vocational learning in African-majority economies. UNESCO codifies lifelong learning as learning to know, learning to learn, learning to be, and learning to live together (International Commission on Education for the Twenty-First Century, 1996). Our attention for the moment is largely on informal learning. Such learning happens in many ways (Hall, 2012). This is characteristically incidental, unplanned and guided by the needs of the learner (Taylor, 2010). It takes place in sites that are collaborative, dynamic and experiential (Monk, 2013). As communities come together to overcome personal and social challenges, they seek out and test diverse and creative solutions together. To that end, informal learning can provide dynamic spaces for (re)negotiation of power and a force for transformative change in communities. McGrath (2020b) suggests that in the context of the human right to education, particularly in countries with low levels of school completion, these spaces of lifelong learning need further attention, something hinted at, but not developed fully, in the 2021 report from the International Commission on the Futures of Education (2021). From a rights perspective, it is important to remember that the colonial model of education has failed to include the majority of youth, resulting in high levels of drop out. This is also due to the political economies of education under structural adjustment, which forced governments to invest in primary education and neglect secondary, tertiary and vocational education (Chapter 2). This has pushed students out of school and made informal learning a necessity, as Openjuru (2010) demonstrates in Uganda (see also Chapter 2).

As we will show later, our research demonstrates disparate spaces of informality that require a great deal of negotiation, coordination and rethinking of assumptions about youth, their life goals and pathways to achieve these. As noted in the previous chapter, skills ecosystems require nurturing processes to come into existence and thrive. Our argument here is that this equally applies to informal learning and work.

From a social ecosystem perspective, informal learning can be seen as a space of potentially remarkable learning and innovation within networks. Learners are not simply individuals but are learning from and with parents, friends, neighbours, YouTube, Facebook and through personal experimentation. Unlike most formal VET institutions, which are criticized for often being overly bureaucratic and slow to change (for instance, Tukundane et al, 2015; Metelerkamp et al, 2020; Jjuuko et al, 2021; and see Chapters 2 and 6), informal vocational learning can shift quickly to meet the immediate needs of individuals, communities and sectors. Informal economy actors can come up with sophisticated methods of getting the knowledge they need and, in the process, necessity drives them to come up with innovative tools to overcome the challenges they face (Metelerkamp, 2018). Many of the youth we speak to call this 'hustling', where they do what they can to survive (Thieme, 2013; Jordt Jørgensen, 2018; Cooper et al, 2021).

Informal learning is not simply a survival strategy for those excluded from formal education and should be appreciated as an important form of vocational learning in its own right. Indeed, data from a 2019 informal economy skills survey in South Africa indicate that most microentrepreneurs actually prefer learning on the job to formal classroom contexts (Metelerkamp and van der Breda, 2019).

However, our intention is not to elevate informal learning to the centre of an account of vocational learning. Rather, it is to insist on its place within wider vocation learning ecosystems that bring together formal, nonformal and informal learning in complex combinations that change over time and according to contexts. The positive view of informal learning for informal work we present here should be read in part as talking back to, or generating a dialectical movement between and with, the formal frame of VET and skills ecosystem research thus far. Through this, we seek to enlarge and enrich the social ecosystem concept.

In our research, we see this dynamism happening in markets, at tailoring businesses, in new enterprises recycling plastic and on (increasingly organic) farms. It takes the form of informal apprenticeship, casual exchanges, observation, practical demonstrations, the sharing of educational content, and short trainings, most typically nonformal in nature. Google and YouTube play important roles in learning, encouraging diversity and innovation through exposure to new ideas and contexts. Likewise, Facebook and WhatsApp connect communities of practice both locally and around the globe. Vocational learning is manifested in both purposive and (seemingly) haphazard ways. For example, a tailor in the market may see another tailor doing something different and observe the methods, an elder may share knowledge of fish farming or blacksmithing with the community, or a mother may teach her child how to 'read' a potential customer. We see young entrepreneurs in Gulu connecting with similar-minded entrepreneurs nationally and internationally. For example, one mushroom farmer worked closely, through Facebook, with mushroom farmers in Ghana and Indonesia to develop his ideas including building a solar dryer. The same entrepreneur then connected with two other youth in Uganda via WhatsApp to buy mycelium (required to start mushrooms) in bulk to reduce the cost. However, learning also takes place where an organization, university or business offers short training programmes, as we will show particularly from the Alice case.

What we observe is that these are all interlinked, and that many people are adept at seeking out the various learnings that they need, whether it is skill related, counselling and guidance, or entrepreneurial. We see that the hustle of everyday life cannot be separated from learning.

The more informal elements of skills ecosystems are not only potential spaces for personal development and life projects but can be important sites of collaboration and transformation that can generate innovation in a way that is often not possible within formal VET institutions. As local people respond and adjust to the world they want, they engage to meet their basic needs for survival and generate new ideas for the future.

However, access into and across even informal learning networks is not always straightforward, and micro networks can be exclusionary. This lack of diversity and cross pollination can lead them to become self-referential, running the risk of entrenching systemic lock-in rather than driving innovation (Spielman et al, 2009). That some are skilled at hustling does not mean that others should be ignored who need more support. Nor is hustling simply agentic, always being shaped also by structural effects.

The two cases explored in this chapter offer insights into learning modalities within the informal economy and the implications of this for how we imagine the institutional boundaries of learning, pedagogy, colearning and participatory methodologies in VET. We direct particular attention towards understanding this system's horizontal components, by which we mean the relational mechanisms and experiences of interpersonal and experiential learning. This implies the need for an interrogation into the many generative aspects of the informal VET systems we observed within our cases, as well as a critical engagement with issues of power, privilege and exclusion that endure across the spectrum of VET in our case study regions.

Case studies: two lenses on informality and inclusion

Our research approach has attempted to shift away from the old productivist model of research in VET (Anderson, 2009; McGrath, 2012; Tikly, 2013). This has led us here to focus on the functionings, voice, relational agency, capabilities and perceived opportunities of the actors in the field as a point of departure. De Jaeghere's (2020) suggestion of considering the ontological and epistemological functional relations of power as individual capabilities to participate in society serves as an important point of departure for capturing the stories of the people we worked with who are pursuing decent livelihoods. This relational capability is central to understanding the power dynamics in this social ecosystem of learning and living. We see youth negotiating informal learning spaces to get the skills they need that are often not available in the formal structures still following productivist models of training. With no clear roadmap towards skills for just transitions within the formal system, these processes of less formalized response are likely to become even more crucial.

The formal VET discourse is also situated within a wider one in which vocational education is of low status and VET learners are typically stigmatized. We see the stories brought out in this research contesting this narrative, despite the formal educational and economic vertical structures that impede their life movements. Rather than linear pathways and simple informal to formal transitions, we see rhizomatic and emergent spaces of learning and learning networks that push and pull and navigate systems and social conditions, crossing formal and informal learning spaces to find the learning they need to progress their lives, even if their modes of work are not radically transformed (see the debate on transitioning in Chapter 7). Thus, we position the relational capabilities and functionings of these spaces within the mediating space of organic learning. This research process has immersed itself in this chaotic and dynamic learning ecosystem that forms the hustle of Gulu City and the rolling rural landscapes surrounding Alice.

Gulu

As we described in Chapter 1, Gulu, the major city in northern Uganda, is in a space of transformation and recovery following 30 years of civil war that ravaged the north until 2006. The north is largely an agricultural area, so the regional focus and many of the urban businesses in Gulu are agriculture related. However, the conflict increased the environmental challenges faced by the region, in part through concentrating land ownership in few hands. This made it harder for the majority to farm sustainably. Furthermore, the shortage of fuel for domestic cooking has stimulated a (largely illegal) market in charcoal, in turn encouraging deforestation and further accelerating land degradation. The response of the Government of Uganda and several donors has been to encourage large-scale agroindustry, with little apparent concern for environmental issues, mirroring patterns we discussed in Chapter 3.

However, the traditional authority, the Ker Kwaro Acholi, has been advancing a cooperative model of development, focusing on the household and broadening to clans and communities. They have a long-term plan to return to the traditional Acholi cooperative model of living, which existed in closer harmony with the surrounding world, and see skills development as crucial to this endeavour (see Chapter 2).

As indicated in Chapter 2, the Ugandan public schooling system is inadequately resourced, and education is increasingly privatized as parents attempt to fill the gaps. It is the same in the formal VET sector. The government launched a new technical and vocational education and training

(TVET) policy and implementation guidelines in 2020. This mandates experiential learning, but it is uncertain if the government will be able to implement the scheme given the allocated resources and a history of limited policy implementation. Gulu University, founded in 2003, is an important centre for community transformation and leads a number of initiatives in the region. In Chapter 8, we come back in more detail to the role of the university in skills ecosystems. There are also a few larger formal VET institutions in the region, both public and private, the latter typically religious. Complementing these is a vast array of nonformal training programmes and a large informal sector with young people learning through apprenticeships at small businesses, in NGO programmes, on YouTube, and from each other.

Compounded exclusion: war, gender and disability

We have stressed human agency and community wellbeing, but it is vital also to note the compounded social exclusion faced by women and people with disabilities. Monk et al (2021a) have documented significant gendered oppression of girls and women in life and education in northern Uganda from a capabilities perspective, claiming that the oppression is systemic and severely undermines girls' and women's ability to participate in society. They explain how women are excluded by the undervaluing of work done in the home, and through fewer quality opportunities in education and paid work. A multitude of studies on conflict in northern Uganda (such as Branch, 2013; Winkler et al, 2015; Meinert and White, 2017; Denov et al, 2018) contextualize the traumatic war experiences of displacement, abductions and (sexual) violence, which have caused enormous trauma that impact on multiple generations. These researchers document that the reintegration process is especially precarious for women, particularly for the estimated 10,000 abducted women and girls who gave birth while in captivity. Furthermore, a report by the Ministry of Gender, Labour and Social Development (2020) details particular difficulties and social exclusion faced by people with disabilities, including access to work, and higher levels of abuse, again with particular reference to the compounded violence faced by women and girls with disability. Monk et al (2021a) depict the liminality and informality of Gulu and the accentuated power dynamics of social structures and norms that exclude many people from participation even in less formalized activities of living, working and learning. As noted earlier, access to land and natural resources is also highly unequal.

Nonetheless, we suggest that informality, especially for the most vulnerable and excluded, can offer significant potential for transgression and development. In the following section, we share some stories of people transgressing informality to develop a shared reality of decent living in a deep entanglement of life and learning worlds.

Youth learning networks

We foregrounded youth and youth voices as a core component of the Gulu research, not only seeing young people as respondents but also as codesigners of the research. Building on existing relationships through the UNESCO Chair in Lifelong Learning, Youth and Work at Gulu University (see also Chapter 8), we asked youth partners to host a series of dialogues about youth livelihoods and VET. Due to COVID-19, they used local radio programmes to host the series. Stories emerged of individual and collective vocational innovation, from mechanics reverse engineering engines to build their own; to artists using recycled materials in their artwork; musicians with music studios; small-scale farmers; and fashion design schools (see also Chapter 7). The stories highlighted potential life pathways available outside of the formal stream of education. Awareness of these pathways is fundamental to strengthening and supporting livelihood opportunities and learning programmes that can keep up to date with the fast-changing needs of youth.

The radio programmes clearly demonstrated the ontological and epistemological functions of social agency at work. They demand that we think how to further develop the rich learning here. People calling in were searching for ways to develop their personal livelihoods, which they saw caught up in the wellbeing of their community. They had ideas and projects, dreams and life aspirations. Even in this short series of radio programmes, we were able to see rich life and learning connections being made, as people started thinking 'I can do that' and signing up to some of the further learning opportunities presented in the shows.

This demonstrates the potential for key actors in the education system to engage in thinking about how to extend such networks, pathways and opportunities. However, this would need to be done carefully, so as not to overcome or control the informality and chaos.

Backyard farming

One good representation of the rich learning networks in Gulu centred on a young urban farmer who started to grow his own food organically during the initial COVID-19 lockdown period to support himself and his family. He used several experimental approaches to gardening in a small space in his backyard. He learned initially from YouTube videos and then sought out broader networks of learning online as he encountered problems with pests. He started a Facebook page to reach out to other youth, who he thought might be doing the same thing, and very quickly it exploded with more than 1,000 followers. He explained that the garden became an important space for learning, "where people could share knowledge, and the various things that they're doing, because most of the things that were being planted are not things that are traditionally grown locally here. So, the need for knowledge is really huge."

He explained how he learned to differentiate between sources of information to find what was authentic and contextually relevant. He moved through stages of learning: first understanding what to grow, then slowly finding which sources were relevant, then growing the confidence and reputation to become a source of information as well. He captured the richness of the learning in the network as participants experiment and learn together. They take accountability for their own learning and responsibility for the learning of the community:

'Initially, it was to know what I want to grow, and then go online, especially on social media. Facebook, more specifically, and just search for any group, any page out there which has people who have similar interests. For example, tomatoes, you'll find a lot of Facebook groups of people who are doing tomatoes, while reading other literature to understand the local context of the application of that knowledge. Because easily when you go online you will find literature, more of different climates, or different zones so you find literature from someone, say, from the Netherlands, but the application of that knowledge into the local context and climate becomes different … It is quite interactive, and people will always share their experiences and knowledge.'

Here we see the entanglement of international networks online with the local context. He was able to find a broad base of learning about the specific plants he was seeking, and he then synthesized this into his own practice and connected it to his local practice network. Another important point that emerges is around trust and reliability. He explained how he was able to connect very quickly with those who are more knowledgeable. This he saw as being measured through their experience, an important distinction in Gulu due to the longstanding faith in formal certificates. Yet, here in the informal learning spaces, people are more interested in practice. We see this coming through in a lot of networks, especially in agriculture where farmers time and again prefer to learn from people they trust and who they see to have proven experience. Indeed, this is often instead of extension officers, who have much higher formal qualifications:

'There are people, platforms, pages that I found over time, more reliable … There's this gentleman from Zimbabwe who is commonly known as Mr Tomato. He has been dealing in tomatoes for about ten years.

Over time you are able to tell that this person has the knowledge ... not necessarily because they are trained in that field, but from the virtue of the experience they have.'

He also explained how these online networks are far ahead of the formal training programmes. He was unable to find any information on their websites, which lag behind informal knowledge sharing. Even reaching out electronically to formal structures did not get him the knowledge he wanted:

'[T]hey have not yet got to the level of serious engagement online. I emailed Operation Wealth Creation [government programme], I emailed one of the research institutes set up by the ministry. Then there is also a specific institute which is doing research in bananas, then I think I reached out to two agriculture extension agents also. I wrote them all emails. I think it's been over a year now. None have ever responded. So, where feedback is not in time, it becomes difficult to rely on them.'

This story of backyard farming is representative of many examples we have of youth learning in similar fashion. Another example is of a young woman who has taken up coffee farming, along with some local crops. She is part of a vibrant international women's network across Africa that is more formalized than the Facebook groups to which she also belongs. They participate in regular online meetings with guest speakers providing workshops about various skills. They seek out markets together, as well as opportunities for trade among each other. She is simultaneously providing outreach services to her local community in a cooperative style while providing quality products to reach the international networks. Then there is the mushroom farmer mentioned earlier who has established dynamic learning networks through Facebook where he has taught himself everything from how to build structures for growing, storing and drying mushrooms to designing a website.

Bringing an environmental perspective to bear, we can see that several local youth entrepreneurs are starting to make money from recycling and reusing goods. For example, one collects plastic and converts it into building tiles and, during the pandemic, plastic visors (in a global context where there is twice as much plastic as living biomass – Elhachan et al, 2020: 442). Others are making crafts, artwork and household items (such as sponges and mats) out of recycled goods. These innovators are part of an emerging sustainable skills learning network that sits within the youth network anchored by the university (McGrath and Russon, 2022) and points in the direction of skills for just transitions as outlined in Chapters 3 and 4. All these youth are committed learners and knowledge sharers. They have developed significant networks of practice around them in the informal sector both locally and internationally.

We have presented some examples of very different informal learning that show people coming together to learn from each other, often developing friendships as they do. Inevitably, some are more successful than others. Many are far more constrained by their life circumstances. However, all are struggling to find their way and are seeking out learning from their networks to advance themselves. Their life experiences are deeply entangled in their own and in each other's learning. The examples of success and leadership draw people in.

A major differentiating characteristic of this successful learning is finding something that individuals enjoy doing or think they are good at, where they have a 'vocation'. We see people starting with an idea that resonates with themselves, who find and receive mentorship in business, and who have strong networks to ask for support and mentorship. In all the learning spaces, we see people trying to find the skills they need to be successful in markets, which are not simply constrained by poverty but that also see increasing demand for quality, innovation and differentiation. We also see expanded and expanding notions of work as young people explore what work means for them and how to advance relational and societal goals, as well as individual and economic. As noted earlier, we also see emerging practices pointing towards a more ecological understanding of work and skills.

Alice

In Chapters 1 and 3, we noted how the history of colonialism and apartheid, the development of supermarketization in the democratic era and a worsening climate emergency have all negatively shaped livelihood opportunities in the area surrounding Alice.

A protracted water crisis triggered and sustained the momentum for collective action. In 2015, the South African Water Research Commission (WRC) partnered with Rhodes University. This was to better understand why the curriculum materials that the WRC had developed to support smallholder farmers with rainwater harvesting and conservation were not being applied in practice. Substantial investments had been made into the development of these materials, but they were not getting to farmers and/ or not being made use of in practice.

Addressing this knowledge-flow issue began with a process of developing and nurturing an ecosystem around the smallholder farmers' water challenges, using the farmers' challenges and existing WRC learning materials as a starting point. Following establishment of a learning network, which in the first meeting was named 'Imvothu Bubomi' (the Imvothu Bubomi learning network [IBLN]), meaning 'Water is Life' (reflecting the core concern of the network), a series of training-of-trainers' (ToT) courses based on the WRC materials were developed and run by the team at Rhodes University in partnership with the Fort Cox Agriculture and Forestry Training Institute, the Local Economic Development office, and NGOs, a story we also revisit in Chapter 8 (see also Pesanayi, 2019a; Lotz-Sisitka et al, 2021). The project team presupposed that systemic learning across the activity system could assist in embedding these rainwater harvesting practices into the fabric of the predominantly informal, agrarian system. Two mechanisms were initially used to achieve this.

The first was to include the creation of productive demonstration sites into the assessment criteria of the ToT curriculum. This was a practical groupwork task through which course participants had to select a rainwater harvesting practice and apply it in a useful way to their own contexts. This involved interdisciplinary teamwork and resulted in three functional demonstration sites selected for implementation in three sites in the network in the first iteration. These became a key feature of the IBLN's practice going forward, as the sites had both practical value to farmers, and colearning value for teaching others in future. The inclusion of practical, interdisciplinary groupwork into the curriculum also instilled an important culture of horizontal learning and institutional boundary crossing into the foundations of the learning community. In the absence of formal workplaces in which to embed learners, these groups provided an alternative form of collegial support and mentorship as well as a space in which to translate theory into practice.

The second mechanism was to invite a diverse range of actors within the local agricultural system to join these ToT courses. Instead of targeting college faculty to familiarize them with the WRC's teaching material, or extension workers to encourage them to disseminate the information, or farmers to use the material, a broad spectrum of these actors were jointly enrolled in a five-module course that was officially certified by Rhodes University. Concerns surrounding the drought combined with the perceived status of this large academic institution lent gravitas to the process, creating a high level of buy-in and cohesion within the mixed group, allowing an emphasis to be placed on the notions of learning with, from and for each other, irrespective of assumptions and perceived hierarchies.

Formal certificates were awarded at a ceremonial ToT graduation. However, these were noncreditbearing certificates that were not targeted at a fixed outcome level in the national qualifications framework. The use of noncreditbearing certification assisted in making the course inclusive of members with low literacy, without putting it 'below' the level of the more formally qualified college faculty and extension officers. As with the interdisciplinary group work projects, this method of certification fostered a collaborative, horizontal learning culture in which it was understood that the utility of the qualification was in its direct application to the crisis at hand, rather than as a means of access to or progression through formal learning or employment pathways.

This culture of learning for the sake of practical problem solving remained at the heart of the IBLN as it evolved, and the personal relationships formed in the training process supported ongoing multi-institutional collaboration as the network evolved.

Mapping learning networks

In 2020, five years into the IBLN's evolution, a network mapping exercise was undertaken with a mixed sample of actors from across the learning network. This mapped out the networks of knowledge exchange that different actors within the learning network had, and the relative importance they attributed to individual actors within their knowledge networks. These nine network maps made no distinction between formal or informal learning and sought simply to understand where actors were drawing information and knowledge from in relation to their work in agriculture. Figure 5.1 provides an example of the difference between a farmer who had only recently joined the network via a connection they had to a local youth group and the knowledge network of another who was deeply embedded at the centre of the network. This mapping offers a stark comparison of the knowledge resources different farmers have to draw from as they conduct their livelihoods and clearly illustrates the process of relational agency development.

Phases of network evolution

During the first phase of the network, the initial flow of information into and within the network followed several distinct information pathways around central anchor institutions. Information about rainwater harvesting and conservation that flowed from the WRC, via Rhodes University, to the participants in the ToT course was reflected in six of the nine maps drawn and is the clearest example of this first phase of these knowledge pathways being developed.

Building on this, it was observed that the relationships established around these knowledge pathways opened up a fertile environment for broader exchanges between previously unconnected individuals and organizations to begin taking place. Beyond the initial pathways established around rainwater harvesting and conservation, three more loosely defined phases of this broader exchange warrant mention.

Figure 5.1: Two farmers' knowledge acquisition pathways

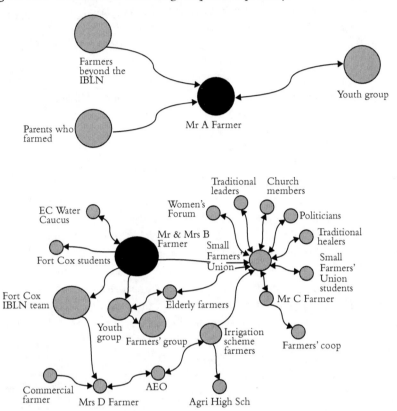

Phase 2 saw an emerging exchange of information between the original network members on a range of topics not related to the initial training they engaged in. Topics ranged from seed and tool exchanges to soil fertility management practices.

Phase 3 (emerging in an overlap with the second phase) then saw a more diffuse engagement around the fringes of the network beginning to emerge as founding members began to share their knowledge with widening circles of secondary actors. For example, based on the WRC's rainwater harvesting and conservation material, FCAFTI staff took advantage of a scheduled curriculum review process to update the institute's curriculum on rainwater harvesting and conservation. Similarly, in a nearby village, an active local youth group that took part in the ToT programme began independently running rainwater harvesting and conservation training for their extended communities.

Figure 5.2: Four phases of learning network evolution

1. Initial knowledge pathways on RWH&C established through ToT course

2. Broadening exchanges along initial knowledge pathways

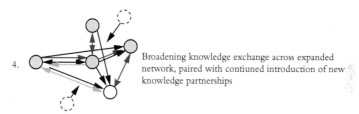

3. ToT graduates extend RWH&C knowledge pathways to new actors

4. Broadening knowledge exchange across expanded network, paired with contiuned introduction of new knowledge partnerships

At the time of writing in 2022, a well-organized system of exchange activities is in place. This includes quarterly network meetings, community radio slots, *ilimas* (collective workdays) and an active WhatsApp group. These are helping to develop a fourth phase of network evolution in which existing pathways of exchange are widened to include a growing list of topics. At the same time, this is providing a new space for IBLN members to invite valuable pre-existing relationships and information into the learning network.

These four phases, summarized in Figure 5.2, provide a conceptual framework for understanding the evolution of this course-activated learning network over time.

The forms of relational social infrastructure that Figures 5.1 and 5.2 represent support many of the learning needs of the loose ecosystem of actors who surround smallholder farmers in the Eastern Cape.

However, despite the growing network of relationships, Rhodes and Fort Cox accounted for 48 per cent of the total weighted contribution to the network. This weighted institutional 'anchoring' by established, better-resourced players is a common feature of skills ecosystems elsewhere (Kilelu et al, 2011; Hodgson and Spours, 2018). We also explore this issue in Chapters 6 and 8 and the extent to which this should be seen as a successful feature of responsive public providers, rather than them crowding out other knowledge actors.

Discussion

Relational capability, relational agency and distributed expertise

In reflecting on these two lenses on informality and inclusion, the notion of relational agency (Edwards, 2005, 2010) is key. Relational agency involves a capacity for working with others to strengthen purposeful responses to complex problems. It arises in a two-stage process within a constant dynamic consisting of:

1. working with others to expand the scope of the task being worked on by recognizing the motives and the resources that others bring to bear as they, too, interpret it; and
2. aligning one's own responses to the newly enhanced interpretations with the responses being made by the other professionals while acting on the expanded scope (Edwards, 2011: 34).

Mkwananzi and Cin (2020: 5) pick up on this notion of relationality from within the capabilities approach when discussing collective agency in primary- and secondary-level education of refugees in South Africa, noting that social structures such as 'self-help initiatives, or organised collectivities ... grassroot groups, village councils or churches, work as fundamental spaces that encourage people to formulate shared values and pursue them to achieve what they have reason to value'. This mirrors our experiences in Uganda and South Africa. Mkwananzi and Cin further demonstrate that there are powerful forms of collective action that coalesce within these spaces and become capable of delivering very high-quality education 'despite limited resources such as books, computers, a functional library, and science laboratories, all of which may be seen as necessary for successful teaching and learning' (Mkwananzi and Cin, 2020: 9).

They argue in turn that 'collective agency leads to access to resources (in this case, education), leading to the advancement of other capabilities and resulting in public good aspirations' (Mkwananzi and Cin, 2020: 9) and assert that while every human being is responsible, sharing this responsibility with others results in a collective agency that naturally forges socially good aspirations.

In Alice, the learning network's social structure acted as an enabling precondition for the emergence of trust, shared values and collective responsibility for an aspirational vision of a vibrant agricultural sector. We also witnessed the emergence of an implicit ethical and environmental compact within the learning community that mirrors Mkwananzi and Cin's observations of public good aspirations. In Gulu, the learning networks we see forming are also grounded in a shared experience of hardship and a goal of improving community wellbeing. Rather than competing with each other, there is a sense of moving forward and working together for everyone's benefit. Another example is a woman who has developed a learning network in her community to improve markets, but also because "when I see those women, I see my mother and I know the hardship she went through".

In both cases, we observed that where forms of basic but structured social institutions were established, be these in the form of a learning network or youth café , these acted as an enabler for the pooling and sharing of local assets (physical and intellectual) in support of quality VET in a resource-constrained context.

Gardening for change: facilitator skills for supporting richer horizontalities in the informal economy

This kind of rhizomatic working across boundaries between actors and organizations requires emergent and highly contextualized forms of cooperation, pathfinding and trust building, among myriad other things. Because efforts to implement horizontal boundary crossing in top-down ways so often fail (Metelerkamp, 2018), Christensen and Laegreid (2007) liken the role and competencies of a successful network facilitator to more of a gardener than an engineer or an architect. This seems congruent with Edwards' approach:

> Working across practice boundaries in this way makes demands on practitioners. Responsive collaboration calls for an additional form of expertise which makes it possible to work with others to expand understandings of the work problem as, in activity theory terms, an 'object of activity'. It also involves the ability to attune one's responses to the enhanced interpretation with those being made by other professionals [read also as actors/stakeholders]. Relational expertise is therefore based on confident engagement with the knowledge that underpins one's own specialist practice, as well as a capacity to recognise and respond to what others might offer in local systems of distributed expertise. (Edwards, 2011: 33)

However, the examples that Edwards and others draw on emanate almost exclusively from formalized, institutional and highly regulated contexts such as child welfare in the UK (Edwards, 2011), public administration in Australia (Christensen and Laegreid, 2007) and industrial organization in the United States (Santos and Eisenhardt, 2005).

We have already noted that 80 per cent of Africans work in the informal economy. So, what of these highly informal, unregulated and often marginalized contexts that form the majority experience of living, working and learning? Situating the praxis of horizontal learning within these very normal contexts of informality demands renewed analysis of questions of *how* horizontal learning is facilitated, by whom, with what resources, and why.

While it was beyond the scope of our case methodologies, it could be that approaching such horizontalities from the perspective of an anthropology of friendship (the culture of *ilima* or collective helping out, which exists in most African cultures, see Pesanayi, 2019a) would yield rich insights that enable a meaningful southern grounding to the northern skills ecosystems literature. Pesanayi's (2019a) research pointed to the significance of collective empowerment and empathy in horizontal relationships. That said, both the Alice and Gulu cases suggest that designing learning processes in ways that proactively open up spaces for the formation of meaningful interpersonal connection, while increasing the likelihood of friendships developing, are important methodological considerations for anchor organizations seeking to foster collaborative learning networks in informal rural contexts. This is demonstrated in the successful ventures that are community development oriented and that emerge in a form of learning cooperatively. Such intentional friendships emerge in the ontological context of *Ubuntu* and an urgent pulling towards developing peaceful relationships in chronically distorted and piercingly severed historical contexts of colonization, war, class, corruption, racial discrimination and social upheaval. Within this space, youth are seeking to heal themselves, and they see this process as emerging together rather than in competition with each other. This focus on healing themselves is beginning to expand out to an awareness of the importance of healing the planet too.

Unpacking horizontalities

The Alice netmaps and Gulu interviews clearly indicated how relational isolation can limit farmers' ability to respond, develop and adapt. Despite their real possibilities, described in this chapter, local communities of practice can also be insular and often self-referential. In such instances, actors have little access to new ideas and information, and limited economic, technological and social capabilities to engage in knowledge acquisition either horizontally via peer groups or more vertically through formal training.

The typical VET response to this challenge has been to invest in more top-down knowledge provision in the forms of agricultural extension services and training institutions. What our cases illustrate is both that a far wider spectrum of realities exists, and that through investing into, and building on to these realities, more inclusive and adaptive models of lifelong (and vocational) learning can be developed. Importantly, the models provided by the Alice and Gulu examples are not posed as an alternative, or in opposition, to more traditional, institutionalized VET responses. Instead, they offer a more expansive approach that places the formal VET institution into a richer set of relationships with a range of approaches to learning and working.

As was noted from the Gulu case, where windows of opportunity for horizontal learning and collaboration emerge, tremendous energy exists to drive these forward, with, or without, the support of enabling verticalities such as labour law or formal institutional curricula. There is a rich opportunity for governments to connect to these learning networks, without overtaking them.

Thus, while there is no denying the structural limitations faced by so many across the continent when it comes to vocational learning, both the Alice and Gulu cases provide examples of the kinds of rich relational networks centred on actors within the informal economy and the power of such networks to act as an integrative force, softening and stretching traditionally rigid boundaries between everything that has typically constituted the formal systems of education, and the vast landscape of learning that exists beyond it.

Facilitating mechanisms in horizontal learning in the informal economy

The examples of the use of social media by farmers in Uganda provides a potent account of young people in the informal economy building relational agency networks. The ability to freely search and join subject-specific Facebook groups provides an unprecedented opportunity for tech-savvy youth to plug into communities of practice that span local and international knowledge resources, as well as private sector and familial ties, in sophisticated ways. This experience of the enabling role of technology is mirrored in the Alice case, where WhatsApp has played a vital role in the life and evolution of the learning network. Vital features of these enabling digital technologies are that they use existing communication channels through which people can request and offer support at no cost within a caring community of practice. This is not to deny the presence of a digital divide, but to stress that connectivity can exist in otherwise marginalized spaces.

Facilitating mechanisms were not only digital, and digital mechanisms on their own appear (in our experience) to lack the life and energy required to catalyse and sustain network engagement. This horizontality in our cases drove fairer access to learning opportunities. However, this sense of justice came at a price. It demanded that participants assume a far greater shared responsibility for the education of their peers.

Hence, we argue that the role of specific technological and methodological tools employed in the two cases was threefold. First and foremost, it was to foster spaces of greater epistemic equality in which it becomes possible to balance an individual's right to education with an equal responsibility for supporting the learning of others. Second, these mechanisms served to expand the knowledge horizons of individuals and networks, bringing new knowledge to bear on localized challenges (and in turn offering their knowledge to others) and developing a deeper understanding of the interplay of local and global in these challenges. Third, it was to support new knowledge creation through place-based processes of experimentation and reflection. We will return to these issues from a teaching perspective in the next chapter.

Boundary crossing: why is it important and how does it happen?

Edwards defines boundaries within learning communities as spaces where 'practices intersect and common knowledge can be built' (Edwards, 2011: 34). While contextually quite different, the two cases both offer new insights into the ways in which boundaries are understood, engaged with and transgressed.

Seen from a generative perspective, boundaries are the spaces in which

> resources from different practices are brought together to expand interpretations of multifaceted tasks, and not as barriers between the knowledge and motives that characterise specialist practices. Importantly, the learning that occurs in these spaces is not a matter of learning how to do the work of others, but involves gaining sufficient insight into purposes and practices of others to enable collaboration. (Edwards, 2011: 34)

However, within contexts of radical socioeconomic inequality in which informal livelihoods and exclusion from formal vocational education is the norm, there is a need to critically engage with Edwards' notion of boundaries. For those within the informal economy and rural contexts, where people's learning networks have traditionally been quite insular, boundary crossing involves not only learning how to work with others, but also learning to seek out, access and contextually validate the knowledge and expertise of others.

Reflecting on the two cases, we witnessed boundary crossing taking place when knowledge was understood not as a commodity, but as a public good. However, as was demonstrated in the Alice case, the world does not lack open-source resources, and the existence of publicly available knowledge alone is insufficient. For meaningful boundary crossing to take place, new pathways for knowledge flow need to be established and nurtured with empathy as shown in Pesanayi's (2019a) study on boundary crossing in the Alice case. Examples of such pathways from our cases included:

1. Opportunities for collective participation in generative practical work, in which people come together to create work of tangible value, through

this also reclaiming an African culture of agricultural practice that was being eroded (*ilima*).

2. Personal friendships and connections with others associated with the activity system that span existing social, geographical and institutional boundaries.

3. Individuals or networks were able to gain access to digital technologies that enabled the discovery of, and communication with, others associated with their field of practice while also radically reducing the cost of communication with these people. Facebook and WhatsApp are examples of this.

Much has been written on the importance of knowledge brokers who can serve as guides and pollinators, helping to bridge gaps, provoke alternative perspectives and signpost unknown unknowns (Klerkx et al, 2009; Kilelu et al, 2011). Our experience corroborated the importance of these pollinators in boundary crossing, and they emerged from all sectors of the networks we studied. For those emerging from within existing institutions, it was important that sufficient institutional wriggle room existed to allow them to bend their roles and institutional mandates enough to allow engagement with actors historically considered beyond their institutional mandate.

Ultimately, however, people across the network need to have dignity and feel their efforts and insights have a meaningful contribution to make to society (De Jaeghere, 2020). That said, boundary crossing is not a passive act. It requires all stakeholders to lean into the process and exercise courage in seeking out and laying claim to the knowledge of others, while equally reciprocating in kind when others seek out their knowledge in pursuit of the common good.

Conclusion

Tracing the evolution of the knowledge pathways in Alice alongside more recent, formative mobilization work within Gulu supported existing observations by Spours (and others) of the important role that individual knowledge brokers, anchor institutions and social media platforms can play in setting the initial pathways of exchange within learning networks. However, equally, our observations within these predominantly informal ecosystems go on to tell another set of stories.

In expansive informal economy contexts, the actor landscapes were highly fragmented, consisting of many thousands of continually shifting individuals, microenterprises and familial ties. In such contexts, the anchor institutions and other formal partners are spread very thinly on the ground, and their spheres of influence are exceptionally limited. While existing skills ecosystems work makes an important step forward in uniting a diversity of actors into an integrated theory of living, working and learning, the profound differences in the structural nature of the labour economy are inadequately explained using the current skills ecosystems models. In such situations, the notion of an anchor institution may be necessary but not sufficient. Network catalysts, providing frameworks for fractal processes of deepening relationality, in which the formal institutions play a marginal day-to-day role, might be a more accurate conceptualization of the ways in which formal institutions can and should engage.

These more informal elements of skills ecosystems are not only spaces for personal development and life projects, but are important sites of collaboration and transformation, generating innovation in a way that is not possible within formal VET institutions. On a continent where 80 per cent of people find work in the informal sector and 90 per cent of the population is excluded from postschool qualification, informal components of skills ecosystems offer spaces of inclusion and participation often better suited to accompanying young people into the world of work.

As this overwhelming majority of people respond and adjust to the world they want, they engage to meet their basic needs for survival and generate new ideas for the future, which increasingly include concerns about the environment in which they live, learn and work. The solutions this generation requires are not known by the generation that preceded them. Never before have tailors in Gulu had to keep pace with rapidly changing fashions while competing with exports from massive Asian factories. Nor have young farmers in Alice had to contend with the complex set of ecological and economic challenges they face today. Philosophically speaking, we can say with certainty that solutions are not yet known, cannot yet be taught, and therefore need to be developed based on what we have at hand in open systems of potential emergence. This does not place the burden of solving the world's problems on to the shoulders of this generation, or on those of some academic or technocratic elite, but instead pedagogically frames the learning process as a democratic and interrelational dance between visioning and problem solving.

Therefore, it was unsurprising that in both case studies we observed that the nature and structure of relationship superseded the specific nature of content. Yes, access to useful information was an important driver, but relationships were ultimately the starting point for the value created for participants across the different types of networks in both countries. Given young people's need to remain highly adaptable, opportunistic and resilient in the face of unexpected shocks, it was relationships that allowed people to assemble, repurpose and reconfigure knowledge into dynamic responses.

6

Vocational Teachers as Mediators in Complex Ecosystems

Jo-Anna Russon and Volker Wedekind

Vocational teachers in complex skills ecosystems

At the heart of much of vocational education and training (VET) is an educational process that includes teaching, learning, a curriculum, the learner–teacher relationship and daily decisions taken by vocational teachers in response to contextual factors that affect learning in local settings. This educational process in VET is incredibly complex and often poorly understood. More significantly, VET systems are both criticized and reformed at institutional and curriculum policy levels, but the implications for vocational teachers remain under-researched. Vocational teachers differ from schoolteachers in both status and location within the skills ecosystem. They often exist as both teachers *and* members of a particular occupation and sector. They work in various public and private locations in general or specialist vocational training institutes, training organizations, work-based training programmes or as mentors or coaches in master–apprenticeship relationships (both formal and informal).

The cases within the VET Africa 4.0 project typify contexts where vocational teaching has often been ineffective or behind the curve in terms of knowledge and teaching practice. While our interactions with vocational teachers in South Africa and Uganda reinforced some of these findings, many were frustrated or disillusioned, and confronted daily challenges of limited, outdated or nonexistent resources and equipment, inappropriate curricula, lack of professional development and inadequately prepared or unmotivated students. These concerns were mirrored to a degree by employers and students, reflecting the nonfacilitating verticalities outlined in earlier chapters.

Such challenges can also be exacerbated by crises such as climate change, migration, conflict, poverty, inequality (particularly for women and girls) and more recently COVID-19. All of these affect the world of work and the corresponding role of vocational teachers. They need to face students as individuals – not just robotic productive agents – while also meeting the needs of diverse employers and workplaces and dealing with the expectations of government and the local community. Moreover, they must hold all these factors in balance when working through a learning task with students. While this is an enormous challenge, it is also a potentially exciting and creative space at the heart of a skills ecosystem.

In this chapter, we understand skills development as a complex social ecosystem, as outlined in previous chapters. Vocational teachers are at the centre of this, albeit often without adequate resources and recognition. The skills ecosystem literature to date does not engage with the concept of vocational teachers and their role, positionality and agency within the skills ecosystem. We believe that vocational teachers should be playing a broader mediating role within the skills ecosystem and are central to any reimagining of VET. In what follows, we review typical narratives about low-quality vocational teaching and the challenges vocational teachers often face in contexts such as South Africa and Uganda. We show how subsequent trends undermined the notion of the vocational teacher, drawing on more recent work to argue for a broader version of this notion. The case examples then provide the basis for the discussion of the possibilities (or otherwise) for vocational teachers as mediators. We argue that an expanded notion of vocational teachers needs to be reimagined and embedded horizontally and vertically within the skills ecosystem to facilitate learning that aligns with the broader aims of VET Africa 4.0.

Foregrounding vocational teachers in the skills ecosystem

Vocational teaching is a surprisingly under-researched field in Uganda and South Africa. The limited research available focuses almost exclusively on teachers in formal public VET institutions and generally suggests that they are poorly qualified, undervalued and needing training. In the critiques of African VET in the 1980s and 1990s (outlined in Chapter 2), claims by Psacharopoulos (1981, 1985) about poor rates of return were explained in part by an argument about VET quality. Similar arguments were advanced by northern governments (especially Anglophone) as youth unemployment rose. While the core problem was labour markets, the rise of the new governance agenda in VET (see Chapter 2) included a critique of VET teaching quality and led to serial drives to improve initial and continuing vocational teacher education. Paradoxically, these included narrowing the content of such education and lowering required qualifications levels (for instance, see Smith and Yasukawa, 2017 and Schmidt, 2021 for reviews of the Australian experience). The situation in Africa has generally been seen as more acute, with vocational teacher programmes and qualifications often lagging behind wider changes in the system and not reaching enough new or existing teachers (for instance, Tukundane et al, 2015; Papier, 2017; Muwaniki and Wedekind, 2019). National and Africa-wide policy documents stress the centrality of teacher quality: 'The delivery of quality TVET is dependent on the competence of the teacher; competence measured in terms of theoretical knowledge, technical and pedagogical skills as well as being abreast with new technologies in the workplace' (African Union, 2007: 9). Consequently, both Uganda and South Africa have seen major new initial vocational teacher qualifications in the past decade, though inservice provision has been slower to emerge.

In South Africa, Blom (2016), Wedekind et al (2016) and Buthelezi (2018) accept the general argument about a problem but, helpfully, root this both in limited lecturer qualifications and occupational experience and the wider, impossible challenges faced by vocational teachers. They note that few vocational teachers possess the perceived ideal triple package of significant industry experience, good academic qualifications and sound pedagogical knowledge alluded to in policy documents. However, they highlight the scale of the challenges faced, including major curriculum reforms and institutional mergers; a massive growth in enrolments, mainly consisting of younger learners with lower average prior attainment levels than previously; low salaries, morale and staff retention; and inadequate equipment and resources, despite recapitalization efforts. These concerns resonate widely with work on vocational teachers in other parts of Africa (for example, Okumo and Bbaale, 2018; Muwaniki and Wedekind, 2019).

A key criticism VET teachers face is their lack of relevance to contemporary labour markets. Industry and employers are often cited in public fora complaining about the poor quality of VET graduates and the fact that they have not been taught the skills needed to be work-ready. This thinking was evident in Australia in the mid-1970s, where VET teachers were seen as providing the skills *they* thought were important rather than what industry needed. As a result, VET teaching was recast with the shift to a demand-driven system, which effectively 'teacher proofed' the curriculum by focusing on industry-determined units of competency (Buchanan et al, 2017). This focus on units of competence and their assessment has been widely embraced by policymakers and embedded in the proliferation of qualifications frameworks (Allais, 2007), itself part of the 'VET toolkit'. However, by focusing on responsiveness and competence, the role of the teacher was reduced to that of a trainer or facilitator, negating their educational expertise. This runs counter to a broader notion of a skilled vocational teacher being what Barnett (2006) called 'Janus faced', facing both the world of work and the world of education.

What then is a good vocational teacher? While the literature on vocational teachers internationally broadly agrees with the need for vocational teachers to have a complex mix of foundational knowledge underpinning the occupation, practical knowledge about the work (including experience of work), and pedagogical knowledge and skill, not all systems require teachers to master all aspects of this. For instance, in a dual system where theory is taught in a vocational school and practice is taught in the workplace, there is a division of labour between teachers in these two sites of learning. Similar divisions exist in systems where workplace simulation occurs in school-based settings (with, for example, technicians running the practical workshops). Thus, it is not always necessary for all teachers to have all dimensions equally.

Some writers have argued for a greater emphasis on developing the underpinning theoretical knowledge as this is seen to equip learners to progress and adapt as the world of work changes. These researchers point to the need to strengthen teachers' theoretical understanding and develop curricula that are broader and cover occupational fields (Wheelahan, 2007, 2015). In contrast, ensuring that teachers understand the often-tacit forms of knowledge and skill needed in work processes, in order for them to make these explicit to students, requires a much stronger connection to specific workplace settings and requires a stronger integration of theory and practice (Gamble, 2016).

In addition to these broad areas of competence required by teachers, there is increasing research focused on vocational pedagogy (Lucas et al, 2012; Wedekind et al, 2016). This literature attempts to draw a distinction between general pedagogical and andragogical principles and a specific set of vocational pedagogies, that is, distinct ways of teaching unique to vocational education. The approaches to this vary, including lists of methods deployed by vocational teachers, the identification of signature pedagogies or the sequencing of specific knowledge and skills. One of the central debates has been the role of real world work settings for vocational learning. An extensive literature exists on workplace learning, internships, simulation, education with production, training with production, mentorship, coaching, apprenticeship and so on that explores how best to learn while working and what the role of the teacher is in these settings (see, for example, Mikkonen, 2017; Olsen and Tikkanen, 2018). More recently, vocational teaching has begun to grapple with the implications of information technology and how this interfaces with teachers or potentially replaces them (Cox and Prestridge, 2020; Vaganova et al, 2020). As we saw in Chapter 5, the growth of video-based platforms such as YouTube have made it possible for many learners to access material and teachers at any time or place.

The engagement with skills ecosystem thinking in the Anglophone north sought to move thinking beyond the supply side bias by focusing more on the wider contexts within which skills are developed (Spours, 2019). However, as we noted earlier, despite various theoretical and conceptual iterations of the skills ecosystem, the specific role of vocational teachers within the ecosystem is never explicitly considered. One of the implications of the ecosystemic perspective is the regional focus (Wedekind et al, 2021). By implication, teachers should be understood much more in the local context rather than through the default national lens. For example, a teacher's skills and needs may vary depending on the nature of the skills ecosystem in which they are embedded. Similarly, access to workplaces, and what those workplaces are, is also contextually dependent. For instance, we saw in Chapter 5 that few of these were in the formal sector in Alice or Gulu. This suggests that within a skills ecosystem, vocational teachers might also play a mediating role, a perspective that was confirmed in the case of Alice by Pesanayi's (2019a) research.

The conceptualization of mediation – social actors thinking and moving along horizontal and vertical terrains to arrange exchange and collaborations – opens up the theoretical space to consider the world of working, living and learning and the connective role of education in diverse communities and localities (Grainger and Spours, 2018; Spours, 2019). The preceding chapters have discussed the complex challenges confronting VET, and we are not suggesting that the mediating role of a vocational teacher within the skills ecosystem can solve these challenges. However, an ecosystem perspective suggests that a reimagined VET requires vocational teachers who can recognize the role's mediation aspects and are facilitated to undertake that role. To unpack this, we turned to our four cases to answer the following questions:

1. Where are the teachers within the four cases according to a broader conception of vocational teachers?
2. What are they doing? What distinct types of vocational teachers, curriculum and pedagogical practices are enabled or constrained in the various settings where we find vocational teachers?
3. What are the implications for VET teachers functioning in the mediation space within the skills ecosystem?

In what follows, we present our observations of the 'where' and 'what' of vocational teachers within the four cases, before discussing the implications for vocational teachers functioning in the mediation space with the skills ecosystem.

The 'where' and 'what' of vocational teaching: case observations

Conventional institutional settings

Throughout the cases, we found vocational teachers located in traditional vocational institutional settings including VET colleges, agricultural colleges and universities of technology (or polytechnics). In eThekwini, there is a well-established set of institutions including three public TVET colleges, three universities and specialized vocationally focused schools. In Alice and surrounding areas, there are two universities, an agricultural training institute and a TVET college. Gulu and Hoima have an array of public and private institutions, most notably Gulu University, as well as several vocational training institutions. Thus, there are multiple sites where vocational teachers are located.

In many of these settings, teachers were constrained by national policies, such as curriculum and qualification prescriptions. In South African public colleges, for example, programmes were developed in a national process with little flexibility to adjust the curriculum to local specificities. Thus, the three eThekwini multicampus public colleges have a very limited specific maritime focus across their offerings. Similarly in the Alice region, there is an urgent need for programmes directly related to small-scale farming in drought-prone contexts. In Hoima and Gulu, most vocational institutions remain rooted in traditional subjects (such as motor mechanics and tailoring) and traditional modes of teaching focused on delivering curriculum content, with limited evidence that these are closely aligned to local labour markets. One of the difficulties experienced by vocational teachers in these colleges is that the standard qualifications on offer appear to have little value in local labour markets. This makes it difficult for vocational teachers to build connections within the ecosystem, and so teachers remain isolated from workplaces.

This is not to deny that some innovation is happening at the programme level. One eThekwini college had started offering a qualification for building yachts and pleasurecraft to align with the strategic imperatives of the Oceans Economy initiative of Operation Phakisa, but this programme was equipping people for jobs that did not exist. This made it virtually impossible for the teachers to develop linkages to local firms. An important example already introduced in Chapter 1 is the local instantiation of the national programme of centres of excellence through the uMfolozi TVET College Maritime Academy. This was established in 2020 to respond to the Ocean Economy initiative. However, national decision making meant that it was located 100 miles from the sectoral hub in eThekwini port. This meant that students and teachers were physically removed from the major existing economic activity associated with the Oceans Economy, making it difficult for vocational teachers to develop strong industry linkages for learners. In addition, much like the boat building programme, actual job opportunities in this sector were lagging behind policy intentions expressed in the Oceans Economy strategy, as we noted in Chapter 4.

A similar challenge exists in Hoima, where skills are needed in anticipation of the jobs that will arise when oil and gas developments take place. However, there is no real opportunity for teachers to facilitate linkages between their students and employers at present. Thus, colleges and their teachers were trying to position themselves ahead of demand. Furthermore, in Hoima, formal VET institutions are very small by international standards. As noted earlier, they typically offer a broad range of conventional vocational subjects to small classes and with modest resources. Most of this is geared to local and relatively small-scale economic activity and domestic needs such as house building and repairs. Such characteristics make these institutions and vocational teachers ill-equipped to respond to a rapidly emerging sector such as oil and gas where there is an extreme mismatch between skills required and the skills available in remote rural areas. For example, pipeline welding for the oil industry involves vastly different skills and techniques than welding burglar bars, fences or metal window frames, and there are also significant consequences for weld failures. The oil industry is used to commencing operations in remote rural areas and has developed a strong tradition of relying largely on a globally mobile population of highly skilled and experienced artisans. Entry into these occupations is carefully regulated through a set of international certificates that are recognized across the sector globally. Finding skilled vocational teachers that can train to these standards is a challenge, not least because teaching pay scales cannot compete with those in the labour market for similar skills. One principal of a well-regarded institution confided to us that it was difficult to see how this skills gulf was to be bridged.

In response to this skills gap, in much the same mode as the South African centre of excellence (CoE) model, the Government of Uganda built a sectoral CoE, the Uganda Petroleum Institute, Kigumba (UPIK), to maximize insertion into technical and technological jobs in the industry (introduced in Chapter 1). Staff shared with us how features such as a high-quality curriculum developed in consultation with industry and other relevant stakeholders, along with accredited instructors and quality infrastructure, helped set UPIK apart as a CoE. As vocational teachers, there was a source of pride at the standard of the buildings and the equipment on offer, and we heard that the CoE vision and culture cascaded through the institution to teachers and students. This was a source of inspiration to other vocational institutions.

Elsewhere, within the cases, the universities in eThekwini, Gulu and Alice (the latter in partnership with Fort Cox) pointed to some of the benefits of educational providers and vocational teachers having a greater degree of autonomy over their curriculum. As we discussed in Chapter 5, the Imvothu Bubomi Learning Network (IBLN) used noncreditbearing short course certificates to bring together groups of stakeholders within an activity system around a shared learning objective. This approach is very different from a diploma or four-year course that must meet national learning outcomes alongside teaching things such as citizenship. Its aim of stimulating social learning around a shared matter of concern in a learning network was also different.

In varying ways, these institutions have responded to top-down policy signals, coordination efforts and the funding opportunities that have arisen. There is evidence of curriculum innovation in the form of new programmes, though in eThekwini some of the responses are essentially a reorganization or repackaging of existing programmes. The two largest and most prestigious public universities, the University of KwaZulu-Natal and the Durban University of Technology, have both created maritime-focused institutes and tailored programmes to offer maritime law, engineering for shipping and maritime studies, among others. They have also created coordinating committees to draw together the disparate strands of work (research, teaching programmes, consultancies) related to the maritime sector and have been able to draw on local industry expertise to enhance their offer. In Alice, Fort Cox went through a curriculum revision process that included a range of internal and external stakeholders to better align the curriculum to developments in the field. This level of autonomy is not present in most of the other institutions in our cases, and consequently teachers can only add to or enhance the official curriculum in often marginal ways.

Flexibility can be critical in vocational teaching. Vocational teachers involved in agriculture spoke of the tension between the organizational cycle of an educational institution and work cycles in the ecosystem. Formal semester structures and conditions of service among staff that mirrored schools rather than businesses meant that both teachers and their students would be absent from campuses for significant periods of time. Thus, an agricultural college attempting to run a fully functional farm has periods where the supply of labour (students and staff) disappears, and so the normal annual cycle of crops or livestock cannot be replicated. This highlights the perennial challenge faced by educational institutions and their teachers when they attempt to simulate working conditions and work processes in educational settings.

Despite these challenges, we also encountered several examples of vocational teachers in conventional formal settings developing innovative practices and overcoming constraints to support their students in accessing work opportunities. One teacher used their networks to source older equipment from companies to expose students to functioning tools used in workplaces. Several stressed the need to demonstrate workplace expectations in the college, such as health and safety regulations and punctuality rules, to instil behaviours that are expected in the workplace. These practices point to the fact that teachers do have degrees of control over their teaching even when constrained by policy and institutional settings.

External interventions in the conventional system

Within the cases, we also observed several external interventions within the local skills ecosystem. In Hoima, the Skills for Oil and Gas in Africa (SOGA) programme was an intervention cofunded by the British, German and Norwegian governments (see Chapter 1). Influenced by industry views, SOGA concluded in its inception phase that the skills gulf for entry into core jobs in oil and gas was too great for most local citizens. Therefore, it focused primarily on building skills for employment and subcontracting elsewhere in the value chain. This largely consisted of NGO-delivered training programmes in business development and construction trades, the latter to international curricula leading to international certification.

SOGA had the advantage of being very well resourced with a degree of access to oil companies, first-tier contractors and government, and a remit to work with formal VET providers and local and international NGOs. For selected institutions, this created opportunities through several programmes, one of which involved staff and selected students being trained to international standards in welding, electrical engineering and scaffolding. One local Catholic vocational provider was a preferred institution of choice for both funders and private sector actors linked to SOGA. In our survey of vocational teachers in Hoima, teachers from this preferred institution most frequently cited "engagement with the private sector" as one of the professional development opportunities open to them as vocational teachers. However, for all other training institutes, the most frequently cited professional development opportunity was "networking with trainers in similar subjects". From this survey and our observations across the case, it appeared that this particular intervention enhanced the capacity of vocational teachers to be more responsive to industry demands through their connectivity with funders and external stakeholders.

However, beyond this, SOGA's wider influence on vocational teaching appears muted. It prioritizes neither national qualifications nor public institutions. While some staff did gain international certification as artisans, there was no intention to change national curricula or qualifications, and the interventions were only in some trades. Ironically, one inadvertent impact of SOGA arose from its focus on health and safety, an imperative for working in the oil and gas sector. This SOGA-funded training had clearly been well disseminated to vocational teachers in the region as this topic was regularly mentioned, even by teachers in vocational institutions not directly linked to oil and gas. However, in our survey, many responded to a question about environmental sustainability by describing aspects of occupational safety and health and safety certification. This perhaps illustrates how vertically derived and disseminated curriculum interventions do not always get adopted by VET teachers or take root in vocational institutions as planned.

A second intervention was an initiative by an INGO, which aimed to counteract top-down, rigid, curriculum-driven teacher training processes in Uganda. Many vocational teachers were clear that they wanted more support, and some spoke of having to teach topics for which they had no practical experience. One lecturer, for instance, recounted watching YouTube videos in preparation for such teaching. The NGO intervened in this space through targeted programmes and funding. However, they decided to avoid the bureaucratic hurdle of trying to influence the nationally derived curriculum and instead focused on exploiting areas of the mandated curriculum to enhance teacher training. The NGO primarily delivered a curriculum intervention linked to teacher training placements. This involved teaching trainees about student centred and experiential learning, hands-on production and enhancing skills such as creativity, teamwork, initiative and problem solving. The impact on vocational teachers was evident. In our engagement with graduate teachers, it was obvious when they had gone through the NGO's training as they would talk confidently about what they had learnt. However, as with very many teachers globally, they often struggled to put this into practice due to challenges such as lack of resources, time constraints and unmanageable class sizes.

Vocational teaching embedded in work contexts

There is significant teaching of vocational and occupational skills outside formal VET institutional settings. Vocational teachers are found in private sector training organizations, incompany training centres and a wide array of work settings where they mentor, train and supervise students and colleagues. This diversity is only likely to increase as economic organization takes on new forms. Such activity can be linked to formal qualifications or be part of an official internship. However, there is also significant vocational teaching (paid and voluntary) that is not tied to a formal programme. In the main, these teaching settings are embedded in work contexts or adjacent to them, allowing teachers to remain very close to practice.

Within the eThekwini case, there are various private training providers (large and small) offering training in aspects of freight handling, port management and logistics. A prominent example is Transnet, a state-owned rail, port and pipeline company that operates the Transnet Maritime School of Excellence (Transnet SoE). This offers inhouse training for existing and future employees in areas such as marine operations, terminal operations, port management and port engineering. The embedded nature of Transnet SoE ensures that programmes and vocational teachers are strongly aligned with the skills needs of the biggest employer and role player in the port, with access to state of the art equipment and immersed in the latest procedures and regulations. Consequently, Transnet SoE overcomes perennial challenges faced by vocational institutions (particularly traditional public ones), namely of being out of date or recruiting teachers that are insufficiently experienced in the field of practice.

Incompany training academies like Transnet SoE have a distinct advantage in that they can staff programmes with vocational teachers who are employees in the sector. Within Transnet SoE, these teachers remain company employees and retain their titles and status such as being called captain and wearing the relevant maritime uniform. In this example, we see how vocational teachers are embedded in a work setting in a way that enables them to remain in touch with the workplace, retain their company conditions of service, make use of the workplace for practical components and facilitate student–employee interaction. This trend is also true for smaller, specialist private providers who are also able to recruit teachers from industry on a part-time basis. To create similar conditions in a public college is extremely difficult as the organizational logic is determined by the priorities of a public college with multiple programmes and conditions of service associated with the public sector.

In a contrasting example from the Gulu case, we encountered a catalytic individual (hereafter referred to as Farmer X) who offered vocational training to the local farming community. Farmer X had a family background in agriculture and an agriculture degree from overseas. He began adopting the role of a nonformal vocational teacher after making the life-changing decision to leave a stressful city job and return to Gulu to start farming. He began by offering an open invitation to the local community to work and learn with him if they wished. What initially started as a small community farm developed into an important provider of agriculture training in Gulu.

Through ongoing processes of learning and colearning with others, Farmer X developed various modes of vocational teaching including online training via video calls and an online learning platform; satellite demonstration farms; taking on students sponsored by NGOs; bringing farmers together to develop quality products for the region and take them to market; and starting a primary school on the farm with a focus on teaching agriculture to children in rural areas. As various strands of vocational teaching developed, some elements began to be more formally connected to different parts of the local skills ecosystem. He designed nonformal practical short courses in agriculture, which were in the process of being formally certified by the Directorate of Industrial Training. He took a significant number of interns and postdoc students from Gulu University and other Ugandan universities. He sent his instructors to a local public provider to get officially certified. This process of gaining accreditation based on practical experience reverses the standard process of classroom-based theoretical learning and examination-based certification. It is being trialled with Farmer X with a view to becoming formalized within the institution.

Farmer X has become a prominent and outspoken member of the agricultural training community, influencing policy and practice. For example, he received funding to travel overseas as part of a government programme promoting farming, which in turn influenced his practice, and his modular curriculum design is beginning to influence Directorate of Industrial Training policy. However, there is a fundamental problem to this approach in that the original farm now functions as a training farm, as it is not financially viable. Critically, this is a model that other actors in Gulu are also embracing (see Box 7.7). We heard of various VET students, university graduates and innovative individuals aspiring to set up a business to gain NGO funding to train others. Similarly, other individuals who had set up businesses in farming and tailoring found they had to develop their own hands-on quality training to bridge the skills gap in the local labour force but were then becoming reliant on external funding for training provision. Here we see both a market for quality vocational training and a market for NGO funding that complicates simple notions of supply and demand in a training market.

The potential dependence on NGOs raises a question about the sustainability of this model financially. So does the situation where this type of innovative community-based vocational teaching is tied to one individual and thus may collapse without their central role. However, there was evidence that the vocational teaching initiatives established by Farmer X were on their way to becoming institutionalized in some form through structures such as a board and increased participation of other members of the team and partner organizations involved in the qualifications process.

This example illustrates how one individual can generate benefits in the vocational teaching space for a community and the scope that exists for different actors, including the state, to be flexible across formal, informal and nonformal modalities in ways that support innovations in vocational teaching and curriculum design.

Vocational teachers and collaborative horizontalities

Finally, our cases provided insight on vocational teachers from the perspective of collaborative horizontalities within the skills ecosystem. In some instances, we found examples where policy-driven mechanisms actively sought to connect more marginalized vocational teachers with institutions that theoretically had closer ties with industry. For example, a senior manager at UPIK reported that it has a mandate to work with other provider institutions so that quality "trickle[s] down" to other institutions. However, UPIK does not currently work in this way, and it was acknowledged to us that, other than programmes linked to international accreditation, UPIK had not seriously considered how it might connect to other institutions and vocational teachers in the region. This is arguably a missed opportunity. Moreover, building a good relationship with major oil industry actors also remains a challenge for UPIK, with inevitable implications for enhancing the capacity of vocational teachers in UPIK and the wider region to respond to industry demands and place their students in viable jobs.

The vocational teachers we engaged with in Hoima spoke of their desire for a more networked peer-to-peer process in which practitioners could share experiences. While these vocational teachers exist in marginalized, resource-poor contexts and might easily be dismissed as ineffective, disillusioned and behind the curve in typical VET narratives, many of them did not fit this stereotype. They were often educated to degree level, with a range of previous experience working in the civil service, the private sector and the community. Many reported improvising in the face of their resource constraints, but it appeared that this was a largely individualized practice, with considerable lost opportunity for knowledge sharing. However, they were also aware of the political sensitivity of establishing and maintaining such structures and the inherent tensions between a professional development and a labour relations focus in educator organizations (Stevenson, 2020). UPIK was linked to the formation of the Oil and Gas Trainers Association, but beyond this no other formal networks appeared to exist.

Indeed, in planning to become involved in Hoima, SOGA identified a lack of collaboration as a key weakness across East African VET systems (GIZ, 2015). However, as we noted earlier, the programme was not aimed at bringing the horizontal and vertical together. It does not aim to implement national policies and build national (public) systems primarily, mindful of the poor track record of donor interventions in these areas. Nor is it a conduit upwards of messages from the horizontal axis. Rather, it is primarily a bridging mechanism between private actors and locals as individual clients. Once again, this is perhaps a missed opportunity to engage more explicitly with vocational teachers who live and teach amid a rapidly changing skills ecosystem.

In eThekwini, from an ecosystem perspective, public and private vocational trainers ideally interact in the form of collaborative horizontalities within the local skills ecosystem. Given the complexity and breadth of initiatives around the port and the maritime economy, there are a range of national and regional mediating bodies to connect the potentially disparate role players on both the vertical and horizontal axis (see Chapters 1 and 4). Several employers and mediating and coordinating organizations have developed internship programmes that enable young graduates to learn about the sector. For example, the eThekwini Maritime Cluster (effectively an NGO), and the Special Economic Zone (SEZ) management company, Dube Trade Port (DTP), take on graduate interns and report that these interns have found work in the sector upon completing their internship. Supporting students to find opportunities for work experience is a crucial mediating aspect of the vocational teacher role. Doing so in a sector that is still being developed is a challenge, and these internships give students the opportunity to both experience work and develop important networks in the sector. The DTP has also facilitated training for employers within the SEZ and developed opportunities for trainers and staff to specialize, for example in cargo handling or hi-tech facilities in the DTP Agrizone.

However, despite the existence of several mediating organizations and structures, the case highlights more absences and potential than actual examples of enabling the curriculum and pedagogical practices of vocational teachers and their capacity to mediate within the skills ecosystem. There is limited evidence of coordinated activity or the emergence of an anchor institution that is central to the ecosystem. This has implications for vocational teachers. For example, public provision competes directly with well-established private providers and the Transnet SoE as there is little incentive for collaboration between existing incompany, private and public training providers. Consequently, programmes such as those at the uMfolozi Academy, and the vocational teachers working within them, remain in silos despite attempts to mediate. Even between the public colleges and universities, there is competition for students and consequently little interaction.

A final example on the horizontal dimension is that of the IBLN in the Alice case. As noted elsewhere (Chapters 5 and 8), the IBLN emerged in 2015 as a joint response to the knowledge needs of stakeholders within the region's smallholder farming system. As well as the public education anchoring institutions already introduced, the network is anchored by cooperative structures such as a dairy cooperative and a youth cooperative, as well as a dynamic collection of individuals including farmers, activists and state extension workers. The Alice case draws attention to the question of what functions are critical to the establishment and sustainability of a learning network, and whether certain types of institutions (and the vocational teachers within them) are needed to fulfil these functions.

Anchoring functions and the relative importance of specific institutions changed as the IBLN evolved. In the early network phase, the role of a well-resourced and established university (Rhodes) capable of planning, funding and convening initial vocational teaching and learning interventions in partnership with the local agricultural college and Local Economic

Development (LED) office was key. Subsequently, it was the network members (individuals and smaller organizations) who were involved in cocreating the curriculum through the questions they asked, the inputs and knowledge they shared and the activities they undertook. Significantly in the Alice case, the training-of-trainers' programme offered in the IBLN was designed to support social learning in a networked learning environment around a shared matter of concern (lack of water for food production). This was strengthened by the subsequent development of productive demonstration sites, in which the agricultural college lecturers provided conceptual and practical leadership that expanded into teaching practice-experiences for their students. This was a major driver of internal curriculum innovations and lecturer professional development (Lotz-Sisitka et al, 2021).

The IBLN illustrates how connections on the horizontal dimension shaped curriculum design and reform, and the role of vocational teachers within that. Core to this was a policy framework developed via a national review of agricultural education by the Academy of Science of South Africa (2017) that motivated the centring of the farmer in agricultural curriculum innovation, which provided institutional legitimacy (a vertical facilitating mechanism) for the VET teachers' roles and their subsequent curriculum innovations. There were also specific individuals outside of formal educational institutions who played an important (unprompted) role in motivating the lecturer group involved in the IBLN and providing positive affirmation and support, especially from the farmers' associations, extension service and the LED office. With adequate pedagogical scaffolding and contextual common sense, there could have been a wider variety of other actors and institutions that could theoretically have taken a lead in anchoring these expansive processes of vocational teaching and learning. What was also significant is that the engagement of Fort Cox Agriculture and Forestry Agricultural College (FCAFTI) with the IBLN led to a substantive philosophical and practical shift in the overall mandate, curriculum offerings and work of the institute. Before the IBLN, they had almost no offerings that attended to smallholder farming needs or sustainability challenges (see Chapter 2). Seven years after the IBLN was established, the college curriculum now directly and explicitly serves the needs of these farmers, which is effectively a curriculum transformation that has been internally driven by the lecturers. Moreover, the lecturers involved in the IBLN have been offering professional development to do the same in other agricultural training institutes (Lotz-Sisitka et al, 2021).

As the IBLN continues to evolve, the subsequent expression of a shared desire to stay connected led to a new set of functional requirements. As membership grew, and the interests of the group evolved beyond the initial focus on water-related issues, the need for specialist knowledge on one key issue (water for food) receded somewhat and the growing need for coordination structures came to the fore, as well as knowledge needs relating to a broader set of farming challenges (especially knowledge of agroecological methods, dealing with unknown farming impacts from pests, fungi and so on). The formal network infrastructure development involved channels of communication and institutional structures such as a steering committee comprising farmers, college faculty and agricultural extension officers. Members of FCAFTI faculty played a leading role in this committee, which became a cornerstone of the network's coordination and remained in place in 2022. The role and importance of the WhatsApp group as a knowledge mediating tool also expanded, with college lecturers and other experts often sharing expertise and deliberating on questions raised by farmers. Reflecting on the trajectory of the IBLN, it was felt that it was helpful, but not in any way essential, that an educational institution played a leading role in the committee that anchored much of the network. This raises a question about when and how links to vocational teachers within an established and well-resourced institution are necessary for convening and sustaining community-based learning networks.

Discussion: Vocational teachers as mediators?

Vocational teachers play a very complex role in any vocational system. In the social ecosystems we studied, this is extremely apparent. We sought to understand where vocational teaching occurred across the cases and the enablers and constraints on vocational teachers, particularly in terms of curriculum and pedagogical practice. We now turn to the question of the implications from our cases for vocational teachers' functioning in the mediation space within the skills ecosystem.

Vocational teachers need to have expertise as educationists, have mastery of their field of work, be able to understand vertical signals and interpret these for students and mediate that process and link this to day-to-day practices. To that end, vocational teachers are an invisible connection point right at the centre of the ecosystem. However, the constraints of the formal logics of curriculum, teaching institutions and educational systems can make it difficult for teachers to play that role.

Vocational teachers are directly impacted by a variety of signals, affordances and constraints that originate on the vertical axis. There were unintended consequences of vertically derived interventions across the cases. New policies or funding opportunities at times redirected resources away from core activities towards flagship projects and preferred institutions, thus weakening the institutional base that teachers were working in. This highlighted the role that vocational teachers needed to play as mediators of the different signals coming from policy documents. Having well-qualified and quality teachers is key in this mediation space.

There were also opportunities to enhance the role and positionality of vocational teachers that arose because of funder-driven interventions. Interventions (such as SOGA) that are not targeting systemic change can make a difference more quickly than reforms to national policies, and we saw how these interventions could support professional networks of vocational teachers. However, teachers also spoke of these interventions being disparate and uncoordinated. Furthermore, when these interventions are not institutionalized in some form, they can be difficult to sustain both in terms of finances and personnel. For example, once SOGA in the Hoima case and the maritime interventions in the eThekwini case moved on, it was unclear what would be left, and despite the success of the NGO's curriculum intervention, vocational teachers struggled to implement student-centred learning in their day-to-day practice.

Perhaps most critically, the ecosystem model assumes that economic activity exists that can be supported and developed, but what we observed in several cases were examples of top-down interventions for sectors and skills needs that did not currently exist. This reflects a belief that the presence of skilled people will generate demand for those skills, or more positively, an approach where economic interventions were planned, and skills development was being undertaken, to meet anticipated demands. Either way, this creates particular challenges for vocational teachers that need to be considered. For example, how they might play the mediating role between training and the labour market when that space does not really exist. From a transitioning perspective, we also need to ask how they might play a role in supporting VET transformation, particularly when the details of the end point are unknowable.

While we found good vocational teachers across the cases, their ability to make differences to the lives of the students was greatly enhanced where there were collective approaches to curriculum, pedagogy and the student experience that also motivated lecturers to contribute to such processes. This is mirrored in the call of the International Commission on the Futures of Education (2021: 4) for pedagogy to be 'organised around the principles of cooperation, collaboration and solidarity'. For vocational teachers to work most effectively, there needs to be a degree of autonomy that enables them to collaborate and be able to respond to their students' needs and to shifts in the world of work and employer needs, another set of issues highlighted by the International Commission on the Futures of Education. There is a persistent tension between institutional logics, standardizing processes because of national or international qualifications, resourcing mechanisms and the teachers' ability to adapt and adjust their teaching. We did find some evidence of vocational teachers being able to revise the curriculum and respond to local needs. Specific examples included:

- Curriculum 'bending', where teachers can respond to the needs of their learners but also bring new examples into the teaching (classroom and demonstration sites) as the field evolves. These are curriculum revisions that do not require a formal review every two to three years, but instead are more alive to shifts in the world of work. In the IBLN case, this was the 'first phase', which then led to wider institutional curriculum and educational philosophy and mandate reform reflecting the principle of emergence in the skills ecosystem model, as discussed in Chapter 4.
- Allowing much more local definition. For example, Farmer X's process of hands-on informal curriculum development and subsequent engagement with formal elements of the system, and the flexibility in curriculum design in the development of certification and new course and programme offerings in the IBLN and FCAFTI.

However, to be innovative and creative in their pedagogical practices, vocational teachers had to find the spaces within formal institutional expectations (such as curricula and assessment requirements). Some of the innovation in vocational teaching that we saw was dependent on particular individuals with vision and energy. Consequently, the role of leadership becomes key. This can be in relation to leading teaching, or leaders having a vision that recognizes the creative space that is needed for teachers to perform these roles. It is not just about the individual agency of vocational teachers, but also about the extent to which they are given the space to do this kind of work and build trust with key stakeholders and employers in the local ecosystem. We observed several examples of individuals in management positions encouraging curriculum innovation in ways that may not be tolerated in other institutions. While Spours writes of system leadership, what we see appears deeper and wider.

Moreover, although we did find innovative practices, for example vocational teachers who went out of their way to source equipment or mirror workplace settings, such small-scale good pedagogical practices were nevertheless quite constrained. There were also challenges in implementation where vocational teachers sought to simulate workplaces (for example, productive workshops in farming). Such constraints appeared less prevalent in nonformal settings. In workplace training, for example, such barriers do not exist because trainees are in a workplace and able to learn while working or in an internship or as an apprentice. This can make it easier for a vocational teacher to inhabit this space as a mediator between learning and working because they inhabit one space and do not have to cross boundaries. Across the cases, vocational teachers were most able to be creative in the spaces where they were not too tightly constrained by formal education requirements and were able to adapt and design the curriculum and learning processes. Examples here include Farmer X and the logic of farming cycles, and the Maritime SoE designing programmes that are closely aligned with actual work in the port because they are embedded in the port with access to both equipment and workers.

For teachers to maximize their own impact and effectively scaffold learning and work outcomes for their learners requires the building of strong relations on the horizontal axis of the social ecosystem. In our cases, we observed both siloed individualized practice – at times reinforced by competition in the system – and nascent collaborations in various forms, both within and between organizations. At times, these relations were built upon existing institutional relationships and facilitated by formal networks, anchor institutions or other mediators in the ecosystem. However, very often, the vocational teachers themselves had to actively build and maintain these connections. More importantly, vocational teachers (and the local ecosystem more generally) needed support to build such connections across formal, informal and nonformal modalities of VET. Our cases raised questions about who and what institutions and interventions are best placed to facilitate this, and the extent to which vocational teachers need to be linked to well-resourced and well-connected institutions (see also Chapter 8 for a discussion of VET and higher education institution links).

Finally, there was a tension between the autonomy required of teachers to collaborate horizontally and the fairly rigid traditional vocational system that gives teachers little scope for innovation because they are tied to national qualifications, curricula and assessment systems (as discussed in Chapter 2). Pressures to enrol specific numbers of students, cuts to funding or the arrival of newly funded programmes all generate tensions within the ecosystem that teachers must navigate. The sense of constraint was particularly marked in the public institutions. While some teachers were able to work creatively within these constraints, most teachers we interviewed and observed felt they had little freedom to mediate and do anything but teach to the national programme. Some evidence from the cases also indicates that VET lecturers do have agency for change, however, and that the skills ecosystem approach potentially has an informal role to play in providing collective support for the professional development of VET lecturers through connecting them better to other actors (see Pesanayi, 2019a; Lotz-Sistika et al, 2021).

Conclusion: An expanded notion of VET teachers

That there is so little discussion on the role of teachers in the literature on skills ecosystems is a clear gap. Teachers are central to all aspects of the ecosystem, as interpreters of curriculum, scaffolders of learning and connectors to work. A much tighter relationship is needed between the world of work and the world of teaching and learning. This would involve a constant process of introducing new ideas and new knowledge and new ways of teaching as both learning and work transform. This requires an expansion of the notion of teachers within the VET system: it is not just those formally part of the education system, but also those who do the training and support in formal, informal and nonformal workplaces. Recognizing that vocational learning happens in and across these places is key, as is ensuring that feedback loops exist between work and the formal system so that curriculum and what happens in the classroom is adjusted and changed as work evolves. This becomes even more vital from a transitioning perspective.

An ideal scenario would see a vocational teacher who is able to mediate between the world of education and the world of work, in terms of their own expertise and experience, so that they have a good understanding of the current workplace practice, equipment and technology and are also a well-equipped educator. In this scenario, the vocational teacher sits in the mediating space, able to cross boundaries between learning and work and help the student to make these connections while also bringing knowledge from the workplace into the educational space and using their educational skills to help scaffold student learning, as well as providing the social connections and social capital to enable the students to enter the labour market.

Recognizing the complexity of a vocational teacher's role poses a challenge to policymakers. One response is to focus on raising the status and professionalizing vocational teaching, but this can mean that it becomes more regulated and tied to issues of qualification requirements, as the Australian experience has shown. This sits in tension with the idea of broadening the notion of vocational teachers and their various positions within colleges, workplaces and communities. However, rather than seeing these as contradictory, we may be able to argue that in a social skills ecosystem geared towards just transitions, there needs to be a way of strengthening both. This might involve broadening our understanding to strengthen VET teachers wherever they are in the formal system, delivering formal qualifications with greater professionalization, while also strengthening the understanding of how teaching and learning works within a diverse range of work-based spaces and nonformal networks and supporting vocational teachers to become more skilled in these spaces.

Wider discussion about improving the quality of vocational teaching points to the fact that many interventions have been driven by relatively short-term programmes funded by international actors, NGOs, development agencies and corporations, seeking to catalyse something within the system. Vocational teachers have many experiences of interventions that are often disparate and uncoordinated. The importance of building horizontal relationships between vocational teachers across and within institutional boundaries is a key finding. Teachers tend to be quite siloed, with institutions often competing for access to funds or access to workplaces with few incentives to collaborate. This ultimately undermines the ability to improve the system.

Adopting an ecosystemic approach and developing horizontal relationships with better localized coordination around professional development activities that develop communities of practice among vocational teachers may be a way to build capacity among the teachers.

There is a need to strike a balance between having stable organizations that can act as anchor institutions, where teachers have a sense of security and professional identity, and enabling teachers to engage in creative work to be mediating actors in the middle of the system and innovators. From a policy perspective, a system is required that empowers vocational teachers to function in the mediating space and play this type of role. This means giving VET teachers some autonomy to work with curriculum, adjust and plan time differently.

For a reimagined VET in Africa, there is an urgent need to recognize the expanded notion of a vocational teacher and the centrality of this role in the skills ecosystems. Indeed, many of the vocational teachers we encountered carried out their work at the centre of largely dysfunctional skills ecosystems and did so in the face of an inexcusable lack of resources and limited support, both vertically and horizontally. Foregrounding the expanded notion of a vocational teacher, and understanding the varied positionality and functionality of vocational teachers in relation to the verticalities and horizontalities in a skills ecosystem, might be a useful first step in enhancing their role in mediation spaces.

7

Challenges in
Transitioning Processes

Presha Ramsarup and Jo-Anna Russon

Introduction

We have sought to expand the social ecosystems model in the last two chapters by broadening the focus to include vocational teachers and informal working and learning. In this chapter, we continue this broadening by looking at the experiences of young people as they seek to move through life, work and learning towards better imagined futures. We do this through examining the literature on transitioning from learning to working. It is important to note at the outset that this account of transitioning is different from the just transitioning one introduced earlier in this book. However, as Ramsarup and Lotz-Sisitka (2020; see also Ramsarup, 2017) show, it is important to locate the transitioning individual within a wider just transitions framework if we are to break out of the current productivist assumptions of the dominant literature and practice.

We have argued that the worlds of work are undergoing radical changes. In this context, it is unsurprising that researchers report that many occupations are experiencing a heightened sense of difficult transitions (Evetts, 2009; Sawchuk and Taylor, 2010; Fenwick, 2013). Given the complex interrelations between work, learning and life, the boundaries and expectations of transitions through the lifecourse are also changing, both at individual and societal levels (Field, 2012). Unsurprisingly, more difficult transitions are experienced more acutely by those already disadvantaged, and their path to decent work has become typically longer and harder (Sawchuk and Taylor, 2010), with a growing number of 'stepping stones' on the way (OECD, 2008).

Crucially, little is still known about transitions beyond accessing the first job. Equally, a gap exists in this literature on transitioning in the context of work that crosses formal and informal contexts and forms of work beyond institutional workplace contexts. These gaps are crucial to our story in this chapter. We argue for an expanded view of transitions that takes into account interinstitutional boundary crossing between formal and nonformal learning experiences as well as transitioning into different types of work, sectors and occupations, including in the informal sector.

We conceptualize transitions broadly to include those changes that occur as people take action to move between learning and work (and vice versa), between different disciplines of knowledge and between different levels of learning and levels of practice. We use a variety of vignettes that provide insight into dynamics of transitions across a range of educational, life and work settings including farming, tailoring, catering and marine engineering. Our vignettes explore work within a broad framing understood as formal employment and/or informal and subsistence livelihoods. Together, these reveal diverse perspectives on what transitions are, how and why they can be problematic, and how different groups experience them differently. We show that current vocational education and training (VET) models fail to take a broader view of work and tend to be focused on a single job. In the context of patterns of work in Africa (but also globally), we argue that a transitions approach within a skills ecosystem framing goes beyond current dominant approaches that focus on jobs or decontextualized entrepreneurship training. We explore the implications for reimagining transitions for VET graduates in skills ecosystems dominated by informal and nonformal work and limited opportunities for formal employment.

Reviewing the transitioning literature

Transitions to work are written about in a set of overlapping ways. Here we outline three major themes that emerge from these, which allow us a vantage point from both a macro and a micro level. First, they involve a process, an outcome, one or more individuals (as it can be individual or collective) and a context (Burns, 2010; Brzinsky-Fay, 2011; Fenwick, 2013). Second, they involve three distinct processes: navigating pathways, structures and systems; transitioning between two states of being; and a sense of the whole of life as a form of transition (Ecclestone, 2009). Third, Raffe (2008) points to the macro level, using the term transition system to refer to the institutional and structural factors that shape transitions at the national level. Taken together, these approaches clearly show that transition systems are about individuals within relational webs. These are broader than education and training and involve interactions related to the organization of labour markets, social welfare systems, family structures and cultural norms. Together, they show that mainstream notions of supply and demand to analyse entry and exit into jobs are insufficient for understanding transitions and especially transitions into jobs undergoing change.

Our focus will primarily be on how individuals experience and navigate transitions, while remembering the interplay of structure and agency as discussed in Chapter 4. This leads us to draw on two further schools of transitions work: lifecourse research and critical vocationalism.

Lifecourse research

The wider sociohistorical context, institutional arrangements and social inequality at the family level all play a role in shaping the contours of the lifecourse, setting up the potential pathways for individuals to aspire to and follow, specifying relevant requirements for achievement and defining key deadlines to do so (Heckhausen 2010; Buchmann and Steinhoff, 2017; Schoon and Heckhausen, 2019). From this perspective, transition experiences are largely shaped by opportunities and constraints presented by the sociohistorical context and economic conditions, and within this context are dependent on individual decision making and agency.

Every lifecourse is characterized by a course of events that gives shape to life stages, transitions and turning points. We find the focus on life events useful as it helps to connect the ordering of life events and relate them to the way trajectories unfold; key events can act as 'triggers', and this allows us to link events to transitions in later stages of the lifecourse (Elder, 1994). The focus on events in a lifecourse is not done in a disjointed way; rather events viewed over the lifecourse allow us to ascribe social meaning very differently. How these life events emerge, how they are recognized and how people adapt to life events are also crucial as the same event or transition followed by different adaptations can lead to different trajectories (Sampson and Laub, 1990; Elder, 1994; Elder et al, 2003).

This leads on to the notion of turning points. Hodkinson and Sparkes (1997) outline three main types of turning points: structural, self-initiated and forced. Structural turning points are the result of external structures of institutions. Self-initiated turning points occur when the person concerned is instrumental in precipitating a transformation in response to a range of factors in their personal life in the field. Sometimes turning points are forced as they can be precipitated by external events and/or the actions of others such as redundancy.

Critical vocationalism

Sawchuk and Taylor (2010) stress that transitions are differentiated and differentiating across social groups in response to fewer good jobs being available in primary labour markets (where formal, decent jobs are concentrated). Workers already in these labour markets largely retain the ability to positively cope with their transitions. However, those who can't access them are unlikely to have easy and positive transitions. This is not simply a matter of chance but hugely shaped by factors such as gender, race, ethnicity and disability.

Sawchuk and Taylor describe their approach as 'critical vocationalism'. They critique the vocationalist orthodoxy that workers need to be adapted to the needs of the economy (see our comments on human capital theory in Chapters 1–3). They argue that this individual and adaptive perspective has inherent difficulties in admitting structural contradictions rooted in both institutions of education and economy. Rather, they stress how the relationship between education systems and labour markets is 'shaped by the tensions, and contradictions inherent within processes of control, conflict, accommodation and occasionally resistance' (Sawchuk and Taylor, 2010: 9). Livingstone (2004) argues that a significant education–jobs gap remains under-recognized and misinterpreted within the orthodoxy. In contrast, critical vocationalism stresses the need for an understanding of context, social differences and power relations that 'define how learning capacities are productive and reproductive of uneven social and economic prosperity' (Sawchuk and Taylor, 2010: 1). Bynner (2001) notes that there is a lack of attention in the orthodoxy to the broader political climate, culture and the effects of other spheres of institutional and noninstitutional life as dimensions of the transition process.

Sawchuk and Taylor argue for a shift in gaze to highlight the variety of social variables that shape patterns of transitions. This is part of an expanded view of transitions that encompass interinstitutional transitions focused on formal and nonformal learning experiences within learning and work transitioning, as well as intra-institutional transitions that are focused on transitioning into different types of work, sectors and occupations (Ramsarup, 2017, 2020; Ramsarup and Lotz-Sisitka, 2020).

Vignettes: Transition experiences

In this section, we discuss eight transition vignettes (see Table 7.1 and Boxes 7.1–7.8) that tell the stories of a range of livelihood-based lifecourse transitions as they relate to vocational education (formal and informal), work (including survivalist occupations, formal employment and self-employment) and social and institutional life contexts. The vignettes were collated from more than 60 interviews and focus groups that sought to understand the relationship between a transition experience and social variables, macro structural and economic factors, personal and socioeconomic history, and learning experiences, all of which produce or impact transition processes and outcomes (Burns, 2010).

In what follows, we synthesize these stories of transition in relation to the following questions:

1. How did individuals transition to their current context?
2. What enabling and constraining factors influenced transition processes?
3. What were their current and future aspirations?
4. What were their perceptions of how transitions could be improved?

Stories of transition

We sought to understand participants' experiences of transitions across a range of life, educational and work settings, as summarized in Table 7.1. For many, the transition into their current occupational position was forced by a crisis, and their current position was characterized by limited prospects or opportunities for onward transition. The transition stories from Gulu of the small-scale farmers (see also Chapter 5) and informal market vendors were marked by social inequality at the family level and extremely challenging sociohistorical contexts and local political–ecology–economy conditions. For example, the prolonged civil war had disrupted their normal lives, with some losing parents and growing up in internal displacement camps, which also halted opportunities to stay in school or pursue higher education. In response, some turned to agriculture as a livelihood, often to support families. For others, situations of domestic violence and family breakdown forced them to find alternative sources of living. Most had little formal education and were early school leavers because of early pregnancy or marriage, or a lack of tuition fees (which were often spent on boys rather than girls). Moreover, subsequent learning opportunities tended to be restricted to various survivalist training programmes.

In Hoima, those employed in the catering sector had rarely chosen to enter the sector but were forced to choose catering as this is what the state, family or some other sponsor was prepared to fund. For example, one individual shared that their intention had been to work in the legal profession, but the government scholarship programme allocated them to hotel management. They were poor and felt that there was no alternative but to accept. Again, this parallels experiences from existing South African research (Powell and McGrath, 2019b). From a sectoral perspective, we also learnt that to gain entry to the sector many had to work as an intern for several months with no pay. Once this low-quality 'stepping stone' transition had been navigated and participants had received a formal contract, work conditions were often very challenging, including long hours and low pay. Some were also made redundant as the COVID-19 crisis unfolded and hotels had to close. Again, such slow transitions to poor-quality work have been found in South African research also (Powell and McGrath, 2018, 2019b).

Table 7.1: Transition vignettes

Name and location	Data demographics	Transition context	Role of VET
Artists *Uganda*	Interviews × 12, involved in creative arts *(5 female, 7 male)*	Individuals in formal (often white-collar) work but seeking to develop a career or earn extra income in the creative arts. The creative arts are underappreciated politically and culturally	Informal apprenticeship – learning from other artists
Crop farmer *South Africa*	Interview with a Black crop farmer	Black crop farmer in the Eastern Cape. Left employment in the construction sector in 1981 to buy the family farm when it was being sold by the White farmer in response to renewed anti-apartheid activism	Family apprenticeship
AEOs *South Africa*	Engagements with AEOs and Black farmers via the Amanzi for Food network	AEO–farmer learning transition: shared learning on water shortages and rainwater harvesting	Certificates/ diplomas relevant for entry into the AEO profession
Small-scale mixed crop and animal farmers *Uganda*	7 × interviews with small-scale farmers *(6 male, 1 female)*	Survivalist farmers. Impacted by socioeconomic challenges, and postwar NGO and government support for farming	Sporadic informal training. One participant received a diploma in agriculture
Fashion design *Uganda*	8 × trainees/ practitioners 3 × private VET directors – in the fashion industry *(all female)*	Tailoring training and apprenticeships in Gulu focused on quality 'fashion' and professional businesses as an alternative to low-quality training in basic mending and sewing	Private VET/ apprenticeships Low-quality public VET /short courses
Market vendors *Uganda*	Interviews with 7 × female subsistence-based market vendors	Survivalist market vendors in Gulu, with no alternatives and no funds for studies	No training, except informal learning in the market

(continued)

Table 7.1: Transition vignettes (continued)

Name and location	Data demographics	Transition context	Role of VET
TVET Maritime students *South Africa*	Interviews with 11 × maritime students (*10 male, 1 female*)	Training programmes linked to promotion of the Port of Durban maritime economy	VET students on a new maritime course
Catering sector employees *Uganda*	15 × interviews (*8 male, 7 female*) and a workshop with individuals in the catering sector	Hotels and restaurants in Hoima, low-paid, unstable work. Possible sector improvements linked to the oil and gas industry	A range of specialist VET training

From a lifecourse perspective, such stories illustrate how a series of events shape life transitions and turning points. However, we also heard stories of similar situations of crisis triggers and limited choice, but where other actors or events modified or redirected the lifecourse. For example, new opportunities to learn tailoring in Gulu (see Box 7.4) reoriented learners towards fashion design as a viable life choice. Equally, the introduction of a new (well-promoted and fully funded) maritime VET programme targeted at disadvantaged communities in the eThekwini case opened up a previously unimaginable route. These maritime students were Black and had either transferred from other courses or had chosen to join the course because they were unemployed despite having other VET qualifications. The availability of funding was cited as a major enabler for joining and remaining on the course in a context where many students experience problems of progression and attainment due to poverty (see also Powell and McGrath, 2018). In a similar vein, the community transition in the Alice case was initially spurred by conflict and dissonance linked to dysfunctionality and limited capacity within agricultural extension officer (AEO) services to support farmers in managing water and food shortages. The subsequent intervention created an opportunity for the cocreation of solutions between AEOs, farmers, VET and other learning network institutional partners (see also Chapters 5, 6 and 8; Lotz-Sisitka et al, 2016; Sithole, 2018). This type of community-based, boundary crossing, transitional learning experience counters the typical individualistic focus on transitions.

Finally, we also heard stories of transitions with more of a sense of self-initiated turning points, though still in response to challenging circumstances. For example, the Black crop farmer in the Eastern Cape (Box 7.1) left the construction industry to return to his lineal heritage, when he felt driven to buy the family farm as it was being sold by the White farmer.

Similarly, while the creative artists in Uganda chose to stay engaged in the creative arts, there was a recognition that to do so typically would be in addition to their 'real jobs'. The vignette in Box 7.2 shows the variety

Box 7.1: Crop farmer, Eastern Cape, South Africa

What made me leave the contracting industry was because I heard from my parents that the owner of the farm was selling the farm. That was at the peak of UDM movement* in the '80s. It was in 1981. I decided then that I would buy the farm. Growing up I never thought to be a farmer. My parents come from a long line of farm labourers. They never knew of any other life. We had a strong bloodline of farm labouring. Equally I witnessed first-hand the cruelty they and in fact all of us were subjected to. The White farmer who owned this property was not kind. When I heard that it was being sold, I vowed to myself that no other White farmer would come and subject my parents to cruelty in old age. I cashed in my pensions, sold my house in Port Elizabeth and took out a loan and bought this farm cash. My parents were experts in farming. It was in our blood, it was the only thing we knew how to do. I learned from my father, and he mentored me till he eventually passed on. I wanted my parents to die on the land that birthed them, not as labourers but owners.

Note: * This appears to refer to the United Democratic Front established in 1983 but actually to a more general rise in anti-apartheid activity immediately prior to its formation. UDM is the name of a political party, strongest in the Eastern Cape, but this was not formed till 1997.

of factors that restrict their vocational transitions within the creative arts. Here we see the confluence of Sawchuk and Taylor's institutional structural conditions rooted in education and the economy, mirrored in cultural attitudes towards what constitutes work, all of which restricted their progression as artists in terms of work and income. Nonetheless, they also sought to address specific community needs through the arts.

Enabling and constraining factors

Here we sought to understand the enabling and constraining factors influencing the transition stories. In the first instance, the previous section illustrates that individual stories of transition were constrained in ways that reflected Sawchuk and Taylor's critical vocationalism approach: gender injustices, uneven power relations and limiting political and cultural contexts. For example, we saw how sociocultural attitudes constrained individuals, particularly the artists who were not recognized socially or politically as belonging to a valid profession. This was also the case for those involved in catering. One chef commented: "In Uganda people despise catering, people think that maybe if you go for catering, you're a failure." This is particularly problematic for females, with some reporting that family members viewed the sector as being associated with prostitution.

Box 7.2: The creative arts, Uganda

Many initially worked as artists while unemployed, but over time recognized this was something they could continue long term, but on a part-time basis once they got a 'real job', ideally, a salaried white-collar position. Opportunities for formal training are limited, and the musicians were aware that they were unlikely to be financially sustainable (unless they become famous). They argued that, culturally, art is not considered as work or fully appreciated (except for fine art), and it is viewed as less important than the sciences and as something that is linked to the tourist industry. They complained that tax systems and copyright laws do not fully protect workers in the creative arts, which reinforces its position as a side business.

While their local communities were often dismissive of their work, they talked about developing their work in response to community needs and interests, for example, using used plastic to make art, writing poems and songs linked to community problems or promoting community awareness on particular social issues. It was also seen as a way that the artists could express themselves and deal with their own traumas in everyday life.

In both the eThekwini and Hoima cases, transition experiences illustrated the extent to which individual decision making and agency is severely constrained by sociohistorical and economic contexts, and it was not clear that targeted skills interventions sufficiently understood and were designed to account for this. For the VET students in maritime engineering in eThekwini, the fully funded nature of this policy-driven training intervention enabled students to transition into the course from either unemployment or other VET courses. Beyond this, however, students expressed concerns about the curriculum, and what they perceived as a lack of proper resources and problematic student–lecturer power dynamics. All these factors appeared to constrain their ability to learn. Some students felt overwhelmed by what they described as veiled threats of being thrown off the course. This needs to be understood within a wider level of mistrust between staff and students across South African education, and wider societal conflicts. Nonetheless, the students were confident that they would gain access to relevant occupations as a direct result of the programme. This possibly reflects a naive understanding of the role that international qualifications and sector-based experience play in transitioning into the primary labour market.

In Hoima, in line with the influx of donor and INGO investment in skills development in the region, an international donor had provided significant capital investment and supplementary technical management support and expertise to a specialist catering college. However, employees in the catering sector in Hoima cited various constraining factors in terms of learning-to-work transitions such as a lack of school fees and lack of practical experience due to overly theoretical VET training. While they recognized that oil and gas could increase demand for hotels and restaurants, they were also acutely aware of the broader structural issues constraining progress in the sector (see Box 7.7).

We did not see much to suggest that the investment in the catering college would mitigate this due to broader challenges in the local sector. Once in the sector, young people's day-to-day lifecourses were constrained by poor working conditions, negative perceptions of the sector, sexualized stereotypes for females and a lack of occupational standards. Despite the support given to the catering skills provider in Hoima, one graduate found that their qualifications were not recognized in Kampala, where the large hotels tend to only employ graduates from high-ranking training institutions. This waitress had to retake the certificate to work for an established hotel, which incurred further costs. This is despite the establishment of the Ugandan Vocational Qualifications Framework in 2008, which should have eliminated such problems but has not overcome this lack of trust by employers in certification from providers that they do not know.

In contrast, in Gulu and Alice, we saw how networks and locally initiated training can enable learning transitions for individuals and groups within a particular sector, but in ways that more specifically target the day-to-day constraints that individuals face (as we explored in Chapter 5). For example, farmers in both countries faced multiple constraints including unpredictable weather and limited resources to mitigate this, inadequate extension services, corruption and poorly designed financial support systems. One Gulu farmer reported: "Government grants dictate who will get it. I am seen as a single person business, so I need to form a group, but people just want to get the money from the grant, and it won't help your business." Such constraints were compounded by low levels of educational attainment and dysfunctional or nonexistent agricultural extension services. The crop farmer (Box 7.1) also reported that while financially he did not have to depend on the government to survive as a farmer, he was constrained by inadequate market protections, inability to access financial support and broader system failures. He noted that the government "[say] they want Black commercial farmers, but their actions say otherwise" (see also Maqwelane, 2021, who traces this to paradoxically bifurcated policy histories). However, within these stories we also saw enabling factors linked to community-based networks. In South Africa, the Amanzi for Food programme and its Imvothu Bubomi Learning Network enabled learning groups and interactions between farmers and AEOs to develop over time (see Box 7.3 and Chapters 5, 6 and 8; Sithole, 2018). In Gulu, it was often community-driven networking that provided

---

Box 7.3: AEOs and community learning transition, South Africa

The AEOs helped to mediate training materials and package information and knowledge that might otherwise have been difficult for farmers to engage with. One of the challenges identified in the field was bridging the technical divide of learning materials and farmers' knowledge, and it is here that the AEOs believed they played an important role. They saw that they were able to present this knowledge in the farmers' own language (isiXhosa) and advise on using practical examples so that farmers were able to translate this knowledge into practice on their farms.

---

a support system to the farmers, for example through the formation of associations to share knowledge and harness social media, and to encourage young people to develop their skills.

Similarly, the survivalist female market vendors in Gulu faced multiple constraining factors including high taxation from the local government, inadequate capital to expand their informal business, the poor reputation of market vendors, corrupt middlemen, theft, gender barriers and lack of family support. Poor road networks in rural areas also made the sourcing of goods from remote areas difficult. However, supportive informal and semiformal networks provided spaces of learning, knowledge exchange and cocreation, illustrating how informal and formal networks could play a role in helping workers (in what Sawchuk and Taylor refer to as secondary labour markets) adapt to the economy and manage complex learning to work transitions.

In Gulu, we have already noted that there are many national and international NGOs targeting livelihood development through short-term training courses. In the transition stories of the tailors, we observed that such courses offered the women inadequate training while simultaneously reinforcing a narrative that they are unstable victims who need help to live. This appears to be an example of how an intervention designed as a structural turning point can in fact continue reproducing uneven social and economic prosperity. However, we also saw a counterexample in the tailoring sector through training innovations designed and led by women who view fashion as a profession, as Box 7.4 illustrates.

Individual aspirations

We also sought to capture people's aspirations and a sense of whether individuals saw themselves as on a journey to some other work. This enabled us to take the analysis beyond the often–overemphasized consequences of early transitions.

Box 7.4: Tailoring/fashion design, Gulu

There are many informal tailors in small markets in and around Gulu, most of whom have had access to short-term training courses and now offer basic services (for example, mending and making school uniforms) in order to survive. Their sense of societal value appeared to be constrained by inadequate training that reinforces stereotypes (such as 'unskilled', 'victims') and does not promote fashion design as a viable and successful path in life. Such training programmes tend not to focus on quality or business skills, and women graduate without basic skills in tailoring. As one factory director explained:

'Most of the people I have taken on for apprenticeship have mostly been people who drop out of school, people who have failed to get a job in the field they tried to study in, and people who have gone through training, but have not really benefitted from the training they had earlier on, these are people who have gone through tailoring schools.'

New training programmes are emerging that explicitly focus on quality and empowerment, demanding that the women show this talent. All the directors spoke of the need of including counselling sessions and personal support for the women, all of whom have faced severe trauma in their lives. As one noted:

'We are trying to develop the programme to include a lot of things, marketing ... I feel like they should be teaching more in business skills, personal growth, communication skills, not just the tailoring aspect of it, but also all of these soft skills that are supposed to help a person grow, be confident and feel they have a really good career, to be empowered to build a really good career in tailoring, without feeling that this is the job that people do when they don't have anything else to do.'

The trainees are now developing an active interest in fashion.

One overarching observation was that conversations about the future encompassed a mix of aspirations for both personal and community success. For some, their personal wish was to succeed in their current occupational lifecourse, and to do so in a way that benefitted others (see Box 7.5). The crop farmer (Box 7.1) also wished to see his farm fully operating as a commercial entity that could supply the surrounding district and provide decent work. He was particularly concerned about upskilling local youth in ways that might help tackle high levels of alcohol abuse in local communities. These dual community and individual aspects confirm the

Box 7.5: Small-scale farmers, Gulu, Uganda

Whether it was passion for farming or negative life events that prompted the transition into small-scale farming, most participants wanted to continue farming for life. Some were glad to be following in their family footsteps and felt that agriculture was a good way to support their family. Dreams included expanding the farm, becoming progressive commercial farmers, further education such as a degree/diploma in agriculture or information and communications technology (ICT), and establishing a training facility for extension services in the community. Many spoke of a hope and desire to increase awareness of agriculture/farming as a form of employment, particularly among the youth. As one farmer said:

'If this could be a platform for advising the youth of my age then I would encourage them to take skills development in agriculture and putting it to practice as a very important strive in fighting household poverty, and those in agriculture should start thinking of value addition to what they produce.'

findings of recent capabilities work on aspirations (for instance, Powell and McGrath, 2019a; Mkwanazi and Cin, 2020) and reinforce the importance of relationality.

The young women involved in fashion design were not used to being listened to or asked about their career, reinforcing our earlier point about the importance of deliberately including individual voices in transitions work. However, on probing deeper, it became clear that they had aspirations for an improved future, for example to improve their skills as fashion designers and develop their business and management skills. Most of them indicated they would like to further their formal learning by entering a degree programme, which would enable them to become teachers. These examples illustrate that while the participants we engaged with faced extremely challenging structural and institutional forces that shaped their transitions and future opportunities, they were highly cognisant of the social variables that individuals within their communities confronted daily and aspired to respond to this in some way.

A second observation was the trend for virtually all participants involved in the catering sector aspiring to start their own business. One spoke of starting a bakery, another aspired to be a consultant in setting up commercial kitchens, and two others wanted to become managers in the sector. This demonstrates how linear notions of the supply and demand of skills are insufficient when considering transitions beyond the initial learning-to-work transition. For example, access to a broader array of skills related

Box 7.6: Maritime VET students, eThekwini

The students seem to be very happy with their current position, but it also appears that this sentiment will only persist if the programme manages to deliver on its promises. Students spoke of expectations related to transitioning from the bridging programme to maritime specific courses, the opportunity for work-based or experiential learning, continuing academic, financial and social support and ultimately the guarantee of employment opportunities.

In terms of career aspirations, the maritime student narratives all converge on the perception that they will end up in the engineering stream by virtue of the title of their qualification and the information they have received during career guidance or orientation programmes at the academy. On the other hand, a few students suggested that if the world of maritime work did not provide the promised benefits, they would use their general engineering skills to enter onshore industries or revert to their previous work pathways.

to business planning, entrepreneurship and business development may be relevant through the lifecourse.

Finally, we also saw a mixture of ideal aspirations tempered with pragmatic ideas for navigating the expected challenges, as we would expect from the recent aspirations literature. Among the informal market vendors, most expressed no interest in further learning, though one fruit and vegetable vendor in Gulu was interested in learning hairdressing and tailoring. She stated that being a market vendor involves periods of sitting around waiting for customers, and the extra time could be used for other income-generating activities. In Box 7.6, for example, the maritime students clearly aspired to be employed in the maritime sector, but they also shared ideas on how they might use their current training to adapt and find work elsewhere.

In contrast to the market vendors, some of the artists aspired to go back to education, though not necessarily in the arts given the government's prioritization of science-based learning. However, most wanted to see the creative arts gain more acceptance in society alongside government recognition that it is a valid form of education and work. This aspiration for professional recognition also featured among the individuals involved in catering. Wider recognition by family and society is an important strand of the capabilities approach to education (see, for instance, Walker, 2008; De Jaeghere, 2017; Powell and McGrath, 2019a) and can be seen here too. Several participants spoke of their desire to raise awareness about the variety of opportunities within the catering sector (for example, in the airline industry, tourism, railways, hospitals and schools) and to challenge people's perceptions. However, Box 7.7 shows the structural constraints to the sector that may hinder such aspirations. While individual agency may be severely constrained by structural and institutional factors, this does not necessarily diminish the ability of individuals or communities to observe these and construct aspirational narratives about how they might be navigated.

Improving transitions

Finally, we wanted to understand how individuals believed that their particular transition lifecourse could be improved, either prospectively or retrospectively. Were there certain mechanisms that did or could help, for example interventions by development agencies or informal training? As noted earlier, one theme was the perceived importance of government-led professional recognition of livelihoods and the associated legal and structural protections for the sector or occupation. For example, the individuals involved in the creative arts recognized its intrinsic value to society and had experienced the arts as a way to heal and express themselves, but their work was informal. Some saw it as a means to earn an income or additional income, and some as a potential livelihood (see Powell and McGrath, 2019b, for similar findings in South Africa). However, the sector was not monitored or properly regulated, which meant that formalizing their income stream or establishing basic structures for paying tax was not possible.

Tailoring is also viewed largely as unprofessional, and little more than a way to help vulnerable women cope with their life circumstances. However, building on the successful models of training for fashion design in Gulu (see Box 7.4), it was felt that access to more professional programmes in fashion design would assist transitions in the sector more broadly. Those in the catering industry also spoke of the need for more opportunities to professionalize the sector, alongside dealing with broader economic constraints that negatively impacted the sector in Hoima (see Box 7.7).

There were also calls for systemic and institutional structures that recognize the holistic nature of work (formal and informal) and their related transitions. This was particularly evident in farming. As argued by Maqwelane (2021), in South Africa, this included a call for more appropriate structural support to ensure that farmers can stay viable in the current market and compete competitively. This, in turn, requires a more effective agricultural extension system and public–private engagement that supports Black small- and medium-scale farmers in ways that embrace a more holistic response to the value chain. This would necessitate confronting persistent policy dualism between commercial and subsistence farmers and developing a better understanding of the roles and contributors of various stakeholders (Maqwelane, 2021; see also Lotz-Sisitka et al, 2016, 2021; Pesanyi, 2019a). In Uganda, participants spoke of the need to reduce top-down government directives on what to grow and when, because this

Box 7.7: Catering sector, Hoima

Participants called for more to be done to support the catering sector in Hoima to capitalize on the opportunities associated with the oil industry. In particular, there were calls for government investment in roads, power and ICT to help develop the sector and improve guest experience. Some participants also called for local people in the sector to be more entrepreneurial in meeting the needs and expectations of a growing international clientele, particularly those associated with the oil industry.

However, improving the sector as a whole was seen to be hampered by a lack of professional standards (for instance, in service, food and hygiene standards), a lack of supply chain storage and a fragmented or nonexistent supply chain, a lack of internal staff training and limited access to computers and ICT training.

Most participants had limited awareness of local content legislation linked to oil contracts, and while some hotels and restaurants have gained extra business as a result of the emerging oil sector in the region, there was limited evidence of local opportunities to capitalize on the oil industry within the catering sector. One factor in this was the need for a specialized vocational provider in Hoima with greater industry recognition.

approach does not take adequate consideration of farmers' needs. In addition, structural contradictions in education and the economy mean that those with agriculture degrees often fail to gain employment, which subsequently does not encourage farmers to enrol in formal education. Gender inequalities have also left women vulnerable and trapped in subsistence agriculture for home consumption rather than transitioning to commercial small-scale agriculture. There were also calls for better structures that protect market vendors in fruit and vegetables (see Box 7.8).

Finally, there were consistent calls for more support for localized colearning through communities of practice, knowledge hubs or by connecting higher education institutions and training opportunities with particular communities and sectors. Those involved in farming suggested that this might include more focused learning on how to apply and disseminate knowledge (general and specialist) in farmer-centred ways (see Chapters 5, 6 and 8 for more discussion on this). Participants involved in the catering sector in Hoima had also begun to recognize the need for collaboration and networking as a result of their engagement with the project and expressed their desire to form a local association to enhance their local bargaining power and support graduates in the sector.

Drawing on insights from the critical vocationalist perspective, it is possible to see how professional recognition of a role or sector and basic institutional structures and protections could play a role in improving

---

Box 7.8: Market vendors, Uganda

Vendors reported that there is a need to reduce extortion from corrupt local government officers who take advantage of the market vendors who are unaware of tax policies. They suggested that government can further improve on security to deter theft. Indeed, it was noted that the market with the highest levels of theft has a police station just behind it.

They argued that more opportunities should be given to market vendors through collaborations with training institutions. This includes training support to saving groups that offer rich sources of learning and sharing of experiences for the vendors. They felt that guiding and improving these networks could enhance opportunities to move beyond survivalist trading.

---

the transition experiences of individuals in the secondary labour market. Moreover, while the significant education–jobs gaps persists and simple cradle-to-grave training cannot overcome the problems in the labour market (Livingston, 2004; Sawchuk and Taylor, 2010), the stories underpinning this chapter show the capacity for locally derived learning experiences that support work-based transitioning in both formal and informal work. This is particularly the case where transitional learning can draw on inclusive local networks and bridge the formal and informal within a particular sector such as tailoring or farming.

Towards a differentiated approach to understanding transition processes

The vignettes, drawn from across the four cases, clearly indicate the increasing complexity of transitions that are evident across the lifecourse. Across the individual transition stories we engaged with, in voicing the enabling and constraining factors, there was an intuitive conflation of personal lifecourse with critical vocationalism. The stories thus reflect the importance of valuing the voices of intended beneficiaries on the transitioning process and deliberately including such voices from the outset when conceptualizing and planning transition-based programmes or interventions within VET.

The reality emergent from the vignettes shows that, despite extensive policy reforms and donor inputs, there appears to be a disconnect between vertical enablers, which have focused on technical issues like qualifications frameworks and recognition of prior learning policies, and the horizontal community networks and local labour markets that are actually needed to activate transitions. Maqwelane's (2021) research shows significant contradictions within vertical enablers as well. This has shaped a situation that has prevented a collaborative systems approach to individual transitions and poor local implementation and/or insignificant benefits to rural economies. All of these impact the creation of permanent and decent entry-level learning pathways, especially in rural areas and informal contexts. Some of the dimensions of these complexities are discussed further in what follows.

Education policy creates normative expectations about appropriate processes, outcomes and dispositions linked to transitions. However, these vignettes show clearly that young people are not homogenous, and they can experience an array of social and structural barriers to productive employment that may differ according to personal circumstances, social context or sector. This runs counter to the dominant school-to-work notion evident in the literature.

The stories illustrate the reality that very few youth succeed in accessing the formal economy in a seamless manner. They capture the nonlinearity of education–labour market transitions by highlighting individuals' difficult transition from the education system into employment and then subsequently transition into unemployment or back into the education system. The individuals in our transition stories broadly experienced fragile and exclusionary transitions characterized by sociohistorical contexts and economic conditions that restrict individual and community or sector-based agency, which are exacerbated by policy contradictions and failures. In the tailoring example, we saw how an intervention designed as a structural turning point can in fact continue reproducing uneven social and economic outcomes.

The transition from education to employment, and particularly the 'in-between' when young people find themselves in neither fully, is a particularly vulnerable time for youth, reinforcing the need for supportive horizontal networks as central to supporting transitioning experiences. These support systems, which are generally family, friends and colleagues, are fragile and sometimes inadequate as the youth attempt to negotiate transitions. This highlights the need to examine support for collaborative social partners and the need for supportive ecosystems. From the stories, we were able to observe instances where the complex mix of constraints was partly mitigated by enabling factors in the form of networks and bespoke training interventions and supportive informal and semiformal networks providing spaces of learning, knowledge exchange and cocreation. The transition vignettes indicate that most of the young South Africans and Ugandans we engaged with may have strong ties with members of their family or people in their community but do not necessarily have access to people outside of this immediate network who could help them to access opportunities. This recognizes a move from a focus on individuals only to a larger focus on collectives or networks that offer systems of support, as part of our wider relational story.

The role of identity, structure and agency are central issues in transitions. Oinas et al's (2018) book argues that this also involves attending more 'carefully' to young people's political activities. Transitions cannot be viewed as isolated from broader histories, politics of skills systems (and their ongoing exclusions) and structural conditions. This highlights the necessity of centring voices that reflect actual transitioning experiences and their related insights and expertise. The stories also reflected a pragmatic mix of aspirations for both personal and community success. Those we spoke to were highly cognisant of the social variables that individuals within their communities confronted on a daily basis, and they aspired to respond to these in some way. For example, aspiring to gain commercial viability, or the opportunity to teach others, reflected an ability to cite ideal aspirations tempered with pragmatic ideas for navigating the expected challenges.

Practice and policy tend to create a binary between formal and informal. However, the stories reflect formal–informal interactions and colearning, illustrating the need to explore transitions as a relational phenomenon, a type of (nonlinear) continuum. This observation works against policy and development imperatives that continually seek to support the transition from informal to formal, largely without success.

Too much of the transitions literature, particularly in the policy sphere, conceives of a first job as the terminal outcome and then looks backwards to see what is faulty before this. However, it is evident that outcomes of transitions need to be conceptualized more broadly. This means looking beyond a single job. In reality, individuals may be in a work-based transition that is not of their making to begin with, and/or that promotes ongoing transitions across the lifecourse, or that is hampered by contradictions in policy and practice systems. Equally, they may be straddling education and work, or flipping between them. We need to examine pathways not just as straight lines to jobs but multiple pathways to varied opportunities for sustainable livelihoods and for multiple pathways enabled by job families/ streams of work (connected jobs). This has implications for more innovative ways to build bridges to diverse pathways, with special consideration of the role of VET in this. A social ecosystem for skills may potentially offer a more grounded and reality-congruent approach to considering transitions than the linear transition to a job model does.

Qualifications have long been viewed as *the* link between education and the world of work. This appears most relevant in the maritime and oil and gas sectoral cases we have examined, which are highly formal and internationalized. However, most of the stories we have collected indicate that qualifications are often not the central life event or turning point of a trajectory, and various other spheres of institutional and noninstitutional life are important dimensions of the transition processes (see also Chapter 5).

To contend with the structural contradictions rooted in the economy and in educational policy and institutions, we suggest that, in the differentiated labour markets observed in our stories, we can never be certain about what specific skills are needed for a livelihood opportunity or job. We thus need a conceptualization of learning-to-work transition that centralizes how we prepare people to be adaptable. Buchanan (2020) argues that this capability is best built through mastering particular domains of expertise, which are broad streams. The challenge is to define these domains and educate people in ways that allow them to draw out the more transferable qualities that can be applied in other contexts. Hence, the building and nurturing of adaptability emerges as an important consideration, deepening adaptive capacity in youth so they can adapt to an uncertain future. We found the construct of adaptive capacity useful to think about learning and work transitions. Adaptive capacity has many different dimensions, but there seems to be consensus on the ability of a system, institutions, groups or actors to cope and adjust to changing circumstances (Phuong et al, 2018). Whether viewed at a collective or individual level, adaptive capacity involves learning. In other words, the 'capacity to learn' is the most important element and always has a positive effect on increasing adaptive capacity (Eakin et al, 2011). Individual perspectives of adaptive capacity focus on individuals' societal knowledge and technical skills (Bos et al, 2013) and their ability to harness and combine system attributes in adaptation processes. An important necessary condition for understanding the collective perspectives of adaptive capacity is the need for enabling social learning (for instance, knowledge coproduction, comanagement and sharing).

Conclusion

We have shown in this chapter why we follow authors such as Sawchuk and Taylor in rejecting the orthodox account of transitions to work. However, our approach goes further through our drawing on a relational social ecosystems approach. Our vignettes illustrate the need for a more critical and differentiated consideration of needs and local contexts. They stress how policies are too often nonfacilitating as are labour market realities. They highlight the role of networks on the horizontal dimension and the situating and conceptualizing of skills so that they facilitate and strengthen these networks. They also show that local network building is critical to supporting institution-building. The future stability of a social ecosystem depends not only on networks and relationships, but also on robust, agile and inclusive anchor organizations, like local skills providers, that are core to the networks that form the foundations of and strengthen local institutions. However, any attempt to develop local educational and training institutions needs to consider the community in which they are embedded.

This requires more support for localized colearning networks through communities of practice, knowledge hubs or connecting higher education institutions and training opportunities within particular communities and sectors. This draws attention to more locally derived learning experiences that support work-based transitioning in both formal and informal work, particularly where transitional learning can draw on inclusive local networks and bridge the formal and informal within a specific sector such as tailoring or farming. The cases illustrate that context and community change is central. Decontextualized notions of learning pathways and youth transitions are not advisable and cannot facilitate local transitions.

Ramsarup (2017) argues that learning pathways are best conceived as a complex phenomenon, constituted by dialectically interdependent planes (with a dynamic interplay between what is present and what is absent, and their interdependence). We agree. Dealing with the complexity depicted in these stories requires understanding transitions as a multiscalar phenomenon within a dynamic skills ecosystem.

8

The Role of the University as Mediator in a Skills Ecosystem Approach to VET

Heila Lotz-Sisitka, George Openjuru and Jacques Zeelen

Introduction

In this chapter, we focus particularly on the mediating role of the university, in close connection with vocational institutions and informal community actors, in developing an inclusive approach to vocational education and training (VET) through an expanded social ecosystem for skills model. Here we draw upon lessons learnt from the Alice and Gulu cases on community-based approaches to establishing an expanded skills ecosystem approach to VET in Africa. The main question guiding this chapter relates to the possible mediating role of the university to enhance a regional expanded ecosystem for supporting quality vocational education that is also relevant to its context, including emergent possibilities to build skills and livelihoods linked to just transitions.

Universities are not VET centres as conventionally understood, but they can contribute to VET in various ways. Most often, universities are identified as contributing to the qualifications and training of VET educators. In this chapter, we take a different angle and consider the role of engaged research and community engagement as two approaches that can contribute to the advancement of an expanded social ecosystem model with positive benefits for VET institutions. Drawing on insights gained in the earlier chapters of this book requires us to take into account several important realities as previously discussed, as well as key ingredients for the development of a regional skills ecosystem of vocational education, as demonstrated by the two cases considered in this chapter.

Existing realities

First, in terms of existing realities in many rural areas in Sub-Saharan Africa, we need to take account of the legacies of colonial and apartheid policies and marginalizations that have left many people struggling without adequate income in the formal economy. As we have already noted, people tend to rely heavily on the land and natural resources and engage in subsistence farming with little or no value chain development. As we detailed in Chapter 3, coupled to this, people experience environmental degradation, educational exclusion and marginalization. These affect everybody but most especially women and youths in the rural areas. The legacies of apartheid in South Africa and the violent conflict era in Uganda still have a tremendous impact on the lives of people across generations, including on their VET systems (Rampedi, 2003; Angucia, 2010; Angucia and Amone-P'Olak, 2010; Openjuru, 2010; Kraak et al, 2016; Lotz-Sisitka et al, 2016, 2021; Van der Linden et al, 2020).

Working on a renewed approach to VET in Sub-Saharan Africa also implies grounding the approach more adequately in skills development that can advance the huge informal economy, a recurrent argument of this book. South Africa and Uganda differ slightly here as the formal economy is substantially larger in the former, but South Africa has also excluded a focus on development of the informal economy in its formal approach to VET. Fortunately, there is recently an increasing recognition there that something must be done to include more young people in the economy through more proactive and diversified VET systems that also address some of the complex challenges faced by the sector. As we have argued earlier, the challenge will be to find useful connections between the informal, formal and solidarity economies with an awareness of the need for decent work and innovative forms of sustainable value chains that benefit the working, learning and living conditions of the rural population as well as the more formalized economic sectors. All of this must contribute to a move towards just transitions.

Key ingredients

In terms of ingredients for a renewed VET approach, the previous chapters offer an interesting harvest concerning theoretical concepts as well as lived experiences in the four different cases highlighted in this book. We reprise and develop these here because they are critical to our consideration of the university as a mediator within the skills ecosystem.

On the micro level, we refer to the central concept of agency, understanding people's actions not as behaviour but as intentional action of actors in their specific contexts. The concept of agency we have developed is not the traditional view of 'rational man' or voluntaristic agency advanced in the neoliberal economy, or a deterministic view of agency that was promoted by apartheid and colonial governments where people were reduced to labourers without volitional will and reflexive living, learning and working choicemaking. Instead, we advance a view of agency that recognizes the possibility for movement and change but that also recognizes structural constraints and historical realities.

We also advance a notion of relational agency (Edwards, 2005) to strengthen collective notions of VET and how VET systems can transform. The notion of relational agency is central to the concept of an expanded skills ecosystem model, and it involves both individual as well as corporate agents (such as universities) and their practices, a point that we will elaborate further later in the chapter.

Another important issue is the reframing of the concept of work and what it means for many young people and communities (see also Chapter 9). In Chapter 7, we discussed the transition from education to work, which showed that for most young people in Africa today, transition is not a straight pathway. It has been called a 'long and winding road' (Powell and McGrath, 2018) and an ongoing 'hustle' (Thieme, 2013; Jordt Jørgensen, 2018), as we saw in Chapter 5. This is not only found in Africa but is increasingly being experienced globally as economies become more precarious under neoliberal policies, and as new technologies produce diversified forms of work, and the popularity of the gig economy gains ground. However, in most African societies, transitions as forms of hustling relate to difficulties in accessing and retaining education and learning opportunities, as well as work and livelihood prospects (Cooper et al, 2021; see also Chapter 7).

Young people are also dealing with a complex mix of roles, responsibilities and identities, for instance a combination of being a student, an entrepreneur, an employee and a family head (Jjuuko, 2021), oftentimes simultaneously. Another important issue is that the widespread mindset of considering vocational education as preparing youth just for handwork or a particular type of artisanal skill with limited status in society needs to be overcome. As Sennett formulates it, the head, heart and hand are all central elements of craftsmanship, which 'cuts a far wider swath than skilled manual labour; it serves the computer programmer, the doctor and the artist' (Sennett, 2006: 9).

It is also important to elevate the status of artisanal artistry, agency and craftsmanship in the sphere of the teachers and other educators. Teaching is not just technical or cognitive knowledge and skills transfer but includes, through a dialogue with students, dealing with ethical and normative issues (Blaak, 2021; Jjuuko, 2021). Chapter 6 revealed some of the challenges VET teachers have to navigate, which include the competing demands and expectations of employers, students, the formal and informal curriculum, as well as the expectations of funders and government. Thus, shifting teaching practices in a VET system under pressure is a necessary, but not an easy task.

As we noted in Chapter 6, new types of professional development are needed where theory and practice are much more connected, and learning and working are much more integrated, supported by joint ventures between the world of work and the world of education. We need to bring different types of knowledge and ways of acting together, for instance between the teacher at a VET college, the student in her internship period and the experiences of the daily supervisor at the workplace, and we need to consider the realities and politics of young people's lives lived as these shape VET possibilities and experiences (Oinas et al, 2018; Swartz et al, 2021). Another key point mentioned earlier is that in an the expanded ecosystem approach in VET, skills demand analysis and the development of value chains in a specific region should feed curriculum innovation, for instance in the area of digitalization and new technologies, or in the area of specific types of agricultural development that are suited to the agroecological conditions (Jjuuko et al, 2019; Rosenberg et al, 2020; Lotz-Sisitka et al, 2021).

At the regional level, the earlier chapters have shown that a transformed VET sector cannot be built by separate actors in splendid isolation. The need for regional horizontal connectivity between VET institutions, universities, NGOs, business foundations, youth organizations and other societal actors is pivotal. Joint learning networks and communities as found in the Alice and Gulu case study sites and discussed in Chapter 5 are promising examples of that type of connectivity. It is in the formation of learning communities that relational agency (Edwards, 2005) proves to be a useful concept when attempting to understand how people can come together, however fleetingly, to interpret a problem and respond to it. As we discussed in Chapter 5, relational agency focuses more directly on the nature of the relationships that comprise a network of expertise (Edwards, 2005). This means an approach of viewing skills as residing in an individual without the other is simplistic. Learning how to work together in engaging with the world of work is a skill in its own right (Edwards, 2005). Chapter 5 offers a very interesting illustration of the relational value that learning networks can bring to rural vocational practitioners (see also Lotz-Sisitka et al, 2021).

For the understanding of the design of learning communities and the role of networks, the approach of Wenger and colleagues concerning communities of practice is another important conceptual tool (Wenger, 1998; Wenger et al, 2011). This stresses the importance of social learning of people who share a common passion, discover mutual interests and develop a joint practice. Wenger's more recent work aligns more with the learning network concept put forward in the Alice case and with the expanded social ecosystem model as it considers diverse communities of practice learning to advance a practice within and across a wider, networked landscape of practice (Wenger-Trayner and Wenger-Trayner, 2020). Here there is also consideration of the value that is created for diverse partners and communities of practice via this wider networked social learning approach. We will return to this issue later in our discussion on universities and their contributions to a social skills ecosystem.

For a transformed VET sector, as earlier discussed, boundary crossing is a key activity to reach innovative connectivity between the world of work and the world of education. The use of field theory is fruitful for a better understanding of this transformation in institutions and boundary crossing between sectors. This theory reflects a relational worldview (Lewin, 1939; Bourdieu, 1977; Friedman, 2011). Social reality is perceived spatially, viewing all actors and sectors as interdependent. Through social interactions, actors give meaning to relationships, and as interactions unfold and get patterns, fields emerge within the social space (see also Blaak, 2021). It is possible to create in partnerships new fields in or outside of your own field (Friedman et al, 2014). These new fields are called 'enclaves' and emerge through a process of differentiating a new field within an existing field, but with its own configuration of positions and different norms and rules of the game, an example being the agroecological learning network that formed in the Alice case as part of the Fort Cox Agriculture and Forestry Agricultural College's (FCAFTI) programme. This seems especially true for the spaces where learning communities are functioning. Where they can operate between different sectors and create democratic space less constrained by organizational hierarchical power structures, enclaves can be innovative learning and working spaces. For instance, the community cafés in Gulu, discussed in Chapter 5, have emerging features of an enclave. This approach could be very helpful to support boundary crossing and the establishment of learning communities in VET given the necessarily transboundary nature of the field. This is also shown in the Alice case and the work of Pesanayi (2019a), who described the boundary crossing processes in establishing VET networks of this type in great detail, both in the Alice case and in South Africa more widely and Zimbabwe. His argument was that such an approach offers relational, conceptual and practical support for multiple agents in the agricultural learning system, including lecturers and students. It also supports former graduates in contexts where the state's role fails to provide necessary support for innovation and change.

On the macro level, we discussed in earlier chapters the central role of facilitating verticalities, referring to policy and funding institutions that determine the realities in the current VET, for instance concerning curriculum reforms and financing. Unfortunately, facilitating verticalities most often means a top-down approach, typically informed and pushed by external organizations such as the World Bank and other international donor organizations and NGOs or government policy and structurally directed governance praxis (see Chapter 2). As noted in Chapter 6, curriculum reforms are mostly externally driven and fail to take seriously regional demands for VET or the experiences and expertise from local educators, businesspeople, youth organizations, universities or other societal actors. This means that they are often more vertical than facilitating.

In searching for more realistic alternatives, the development of a social ecosystem for skills approach in VET will only have a chance if the relevant social actors and stakeholders become much more involved in policy formulation and policy implementation. However, this will require that they hold capability to avoid being 'sucked in' to the existing style of reform and policy structuring. Instead of top-down or bottom-up processes, we need a more dialectically related approach to mobilizing facilitating verticalities and bringing them into engagement with horizontal connectivities that link learning, living and work experiences in more realistic ways. In the expanded social ecosystem model, universities have a potentially interesting mediating role with powers to mobilize facilitating verticalities in ways that more closely connect with, and therefore also support, horizontally collaborative VET partners and local economies and value chains being developed in regional contexts. This is accentuated if they can form strong partnerships with VET colleges, which are core learning institutions with the specific mandate of providing VET in localized contexts.

Main questions of this chapter

This brings us to the main questions for this chapter. How can a university contribute in a regional context to the development of a skills ecosystem in terms of strengthening horizontal connectivity between stakeholders and institutions, as well as supporting a transformative two-way vertical facilitation of relevant bodies for VET, for instance involving local and national government departments? To be more specific in relation to our interests in this book: what could be the role for a university in an expanded skills ecosystem model, in terms of conducting (practice-oriented) research; enhancing lifelong learning types of professionalization for educators in VET; cocreating learning communities for joint knowledge production; contributing to regional value chain development; supporting just transitions; and bridging gaps between formal, nonformal and informal institutions and networks? And how does this 'locate' itself in the mandates of the university in Africa (and elsewhere) today? As stated by Bourke, this is a tension-laden, and at times contradictory, question:

> The decisive tension is that universities around the world are being encouraged by governments to assume greater responsibility for economic development and to translate knowledge into products and

services for the market – whilst at the same time being tasked to work with communities in alleviating the social and economic excesses of the market. (Bourke, 2013: 499)

We will discuss the university's mediating roles and experiences in Alice and Gulu later in the chapter. But first there is a need to probe what kind of university concept could be appropriate to facilitate these types of new partnerships with community actors, given the tension outlined by Bourke (2013). The northern orthodoxy has shifted increasingly from seeing a university as an ivory tower to a notion of a corporate knowledge institution contributing to a knowledge economy. However, is this suitable to deal with the coconstruction of local sustainable development and associated economies? This question is especially relevant with reference to the contemporary demand for bridging political economies and political ecology as environmental degradation impacts on local economies, especially agriculture. The model of a community-engaged university, as being advanced in some spheres internationally and in South Africa and Uganda, may offer a more viable framing of universities in the contexts that we consider in this book. As Green, South African Council of Higher Education chief executive officer, has noted, 'this means that we must unbecome what we are currently to become what we need to be' (USAf, 2021).

Engaged research and the community-engaged university

Besides the roles of teaching and community outreach, universities in Sub-Saharan Africa see an important community-oriented role for research, which has been prominently described in many of their mission statements. For instance, the mission statement of the University of Limpopo in South Africa reads: 'A world class African university, which responds to education, research and community engagement needs through partnerships and knowledge generation – continuing a long tradition of empowerment.' The University of Dar Es Salaam in Tanzania puts it thus: 'The unrelenting pursuit of scholarly and strategic research, education, training and public service directed at attainment of equitable and sustainable socioeconomic development of Tanzania and the rest of Africa' (see Zeelen, 2012).

At a policy level, this is referred to as a 'scholarship of engagement' (HEQC/CHESP, 2006; Cooper, 2011) and in some circles as 'transdisciplinary scholarship' (Lang et al, 2012). In this spirit, we have been concerned not just to describe and analyse existing developments in the four cases, but also to contribute by means of practice-oriented research and community engagement to transformative change of the VET sector in the service of wider just transitions.

The teams in Alice and Gulu drew on cultural historical activity theory (CHAT) forms of expansive learning (Engeström, 2001; Engeström and Sannino, 2010; Engeström et al, 2014) and participatory action research (PAR) (McTaggart, 1991) shaped by Freirean-inspired dialogical approaches (Freire, 1970). Both approaches were particularly interesting to use because of their alignment with the concept of a mediating role for universities in advancing an expanded skills ecosystem through relational agency and collaboration on a landscape of practice with VET and other community and state actors. PAR favours developing the connection between knowledge production and social change by creating partnerships between researchers, practitioners and a variety of client stakeholders (Reason and Bradbury, 2008; Boog et al, 2008). This methodology brings together different kinds of knowledge (including indigenous) and experience from different types of stakeholders by means of opening conversational space for an intensive dialogue oriented towards creating practical solutions for existing social and educative problems (Angucia et al, 2010; Tukundane, 2014; Tukundane and Zeelen, 2015; Blaak, 2021; Jjuuko, 2021). CHAT gives attention to mediating processes and learning within and across interacting activity systems that share an object of activity such as improvement of local economies, livelihood and work opportunities through VET (Engeström, 2001).

Applied to the stimulating role for the university in the advancement of VET, these perspectives helped us move away from looking just at skills in an atomistic way, considering instead the regional use of skills in a specific location and the contexts within which skills are being demanded. This is a move away from the dominant VET approach that assumes that once skills are available then the economy will grow. However, on the contrary, under the expanded ecosystem concept, it is increasingly becoming apparent that it is the reverse that occurs, with the local economy driving skills demand (Payne, 2007). An ecosystem approach to VET, therefore, means vocational skills training driven by the current and potential skills demand in a geographical region or sector. This means that if universities are to play a mediating role in the advancement of a skills ecosystem approach, then they would need to be involved in research that is orientated towards advancing the local economy and its value chains, while also advancing the possibilities for a just transition, interpreted as inclusive sustainable development in particular regional contexts. This must be done in ways that take the local social-economic and social-ecological conditions and histories into account and that seek to move beyond current impasses in development as experienced in local or regional contexts, which may include forms of locked in 'path dependence' (such as reliance on industrial models of agriculture where they are often inaccessible to the majority).

Alice: Experiences with the role of two universities

In the case of Alice, two universities have been engaged with the advancement of the expanded social ecosystem model, namely the University of Fort Hare and Rhodes University. These two universities were both engaged in working with the Local Economic Development (LED) office of the Raymond Mhlaba Municipality. Both were working in support of advancing the local economy and supporting the inclusion of local communities in advancing the local economy and seeking out environmentally sustainable alternatives to unsustainable or ecological and socially degenerative praxis. Interestingly, the two universities, working mainly out of two different faculties (Agriculture at Fort Hare and Education at Rhodes), were able to support the development of a social ecosystem for skills in different ways. Their core local partner was FCAFTI. It was the three learning institutions, together with the LED office, that led the expansion and development of an expanded skills ecosystem that was able to cross boundaries between formal and informal VET programmes and processes.

The possibility for these cooperations to expand the VET skills ecosystem in the context of the local economy and environment was initiated by small-scale farmers, who were aiming to expand their production with the support of the LED office, but who found themselves struggling with water for their crops, as we have outlined in earlier chapters. They raised this concern with the LED office, and via relational agency connections between the LED office, Fort Cox and the universities, a meeting was held in which both universities joined the agricultural institute, the LED office and a number of farmers to consider this problem together. Out of this, it was decided to form a learning network, the Imvothu Bubomi Learning Network (see previous chapters), that would involve the farmers, the agricultural college and the universities in seeking out solutions to this problem.

From here, several expansive learning 'change laboratory' research workshops were hosted by Rhodes University following CHAT methodology, in which a formative intervention team (Engeström et al, 2014) of researchers coengaged with people's matter of concern (or object of activity) and helped to surface contradictions within and across their activity systems (Pesanayi, 2019a and b). This catalysed a dialectical learning process in which multiple stakeholders could work together to resolve challenges that were confronting them in their activity. In this case, the initial challenge that was identified for resolution was the challenge of water for food and advancing the local economic opportunities of the farmers. Rhodes University, as mediating contributor in the expanded skills ecosystem model, was able to mobilize resources from a national organization, the Water Research Commission, to support an extended social learning and curriculum innovation programme focusing initially on water harvesting and conservation in the agricultural training institute. Later, this was expanded to agroecological activity support as farmers continued to draw on the network and draw in resources to support their learning and practices via the learning network. The activity expanded further to support LED system development and socially acceptable digital learning practices (see Chapter 5).

To strengthen initial interactions and relational agency building in the learning network, Rhodes University offered a training-of-trainers' course that facilitated the development of an applied social learning approach to advancing farmers' water for food practices (Lotz-Sisitka et al, 2016, 2021). The University of Fort Hare's agricultural faculty agreed to support some of the water for food practices through their research and were also working with the LED office on researching and seeking out solutions for advancing the rural economy. This started an extensive process of ongoing engaged research where researchers from Rhodes and Fort Cox supported the expansion of the learning network's horizontal connectivities with various processes and tools such as learning materials, a website, radio programming, social media tools and ongoing training processes, with the most recent being establishment of an electronic resource centre in the area that is being run by a group of youth in a local agricultural cooperative (Lotz-Sisitka et al, 2021; and Chapter 5). Fort Cox played a leading role throughout in terms of local meetings, radio programming, curriculum and social learning activities leadership, while the universities worked together closely in support of their local leadership role in the skills ecosystem.

Via their role as mediating support partner, Rhodes University was again able to mobilize resources from the United Nations Environment Programme to support other tools development, such as a market transformation mobile phone application that indirectly supported market connections (Durr, 2020). Moreover, efforts were made to bring other national stakeholders such as the Spar retail chain into contact with the LED office to advance the concept of a regional hub for farmers' produce to extend the market and value chain in the area.

Not all the initiatives worked as well as planned. For instance, the Spar retail chain–LED office link up process did not lead to the anticipated regional hub, despite extensive research done by the university and the Fort Cox and farmers' association partners to support this (Durr, 2020). This pointed to the importance of the link between research and local policy and economic system support for the actual establishment of new value propositions in the skills ecosystem, not all of which can be done by the university. In this case, it was a decision by Spar head office (a verticality that was not ultimately facilitating) that led to the regional hub not being established, as the Spar group decided to establish regional hubs in other (presumably more profitable) areas.

Gulu: Experiences of a young university

It is important to note that the foundation of Gulu University was intended to address the challenges of the postwar situation after a conflict lasting from 1980 to 2006 (see Alava, 2018, for a description of the impact of this situation on young people). As part of its restoration strategy, in 2003, the Ugandan government established the university, which focused first on agriculture as a way of promoting quick recovery in the region. Thus, community engagement and transformation has been a high priority from the university's beginnings.

Community university engagement has been a guiding approach for the university, an intentional relationship development between the university and its larger community (Boyer, 1996). Gulu University's primary focus is to work with the community for their own improvement and the betterment of their daily social and economic lives. In terms of the focus of this book, this translates to a commitment to play a mediating role in developing a regional skills ecosystem.

The university works with external partners on several fronts. For example, it collaborates with the government's Operation Wealth Creation in efforts to improve household incomes. One noteworthy activity here was the mango juice extraction from the local fruit during peak season. This demonstrated the industrial value of local mangoes, found in all homesteads, to counter the existing situation in which many are left to rot in the absence of markets. In this activity, communities gather the mangoes, which are paid for by and transported to the university for processing into mango pulp. This is then sold back to the community to improve their household nutrition, as well as to the food industry and hotels.

Gulu University is working with refugees to improve their agricultural practice and with vocational educational institutions to improve their curriculum development and delivery. It is well known for the promotion of traditional Acholi medicinal practice, welcoming traditional medicinal practitioners to do research on the efficacy of their health remedies in its laboratories in collaboration with research pharmacists. In 2021, they were working together on looking for herbal remedies for dealing with COVID-19. In addition, students work on several projects on improvement of community nutrition to address the problem of malnutrition in the community by using nutritionally improved millet, sesame and soy composite. They also work together with local communities in the development of new products and improving the marketing of existing ones.

The VET Africa 4.0 project provided an opportunity to build on this socially engaged mission and culture of the university and the experiences in the specific field of VET, supporting the existing network around the university's UNESCO Chair in Lifelong Learning, Youth and Work. This is building specialists in participatory research methodologies, as well as theoretical and practical concepts in lifelong learning, vocational education and career guidance. In recent years, intensive partnerships have been established between more than a dozen universities, VET institutes, NGOs, businesses and community organizations to enhance the capabilities of and opportunities for the youth to develop meaningful learning and working career trajectories. Several doctoral studies have been completed contributing to innovations in lifelong learning and vocational education (see for instance, Angucia, 2010; Tukundane, 2014; Jjuuko, 2021). Moreover, ideas have been developed to bring vocational programmes more prominently into higher education. Overall, Gulu University strives to become a more skills-oriented university of greater relevance for the communities in Gulu and the Acholi region (Openjuru, 2020).

Examples of research activities in the VET Africa 4.0 project

To give more insight into the mediating role of the university towards a regional skills ecosystem, the following research experiences made in Gulu are relevant. In a first round of network mapping, researchers explored relationships and networks with key stakeholders, including vocational institutes, NGOs, private sector, local government and informal practitioners. It quickly became evident that the VET field in the Acholi region is disparate and chaotic. Deeper investigations, however, revealed rich networks of learning among youth in the informal spaces, as elaborated in Chapter 5. From the outset, a clear need and desire was identified for more explicit relationships and greater cooperation among stakeholders in the region. Thus, developing some enclaves of practice became a core objective of the research process, inspired by the PAR approach. Early cross-case sharing with the Alice team regarding the Amanzi for Food experience provided the Gulu researchers with a roadmap to follow. The similarities in the regional contexts of rural, agricultural-dependent areas facing particular environmental and socioeconomic challenges provided a natural synergy between the cases. Modelling, therefore, on a carefully developed community of practice in Alice led to engagement in planting the seeds for an emerging network of working, living and learning for young people.

Following two rounds of interviews and focus groups that helped to develop an understanding of the broad social ecosystem for skills in the region, a series of research engagement activities were started aimed at bringing interested people together in communities of practice to test and share potentially new practices in the vocational field. These were based on the emergent needs and challenges that were identified in the earlier rounds of research. In Chapter 5, the PAR component of the youth network and the ensuing lifelong learning cafés and radio programmes were discussed. These platforms gave the youth a forum to raise their concerns about the challenges they face and opened up a series of discussions among youth of diverse backgrounds as well as between youth and youth livelihood programme developers, including cultural leaders, NGOs and the private sector. This culminated in youth pointing out that they were misrepresented in a process whereby non-youth made decisions for them about their lives, involving them in non-agentic ways, with most resources going towards bureaucratic processes rather than reaching the youth themselves. They also challenged the fallacious stigma about skills and livelihood development with a multitude of examples of youth coming together despite limited formal education. This series of discussions brought out links between creative arts, environmental care, cooperation and social impact. It also initiated a pilot 'environmental innovation and prototyping in VET' programme where youth entrepreneurs outside of the formal system were invited to work with the private sector and Gulu University representatives to develop entrepreneurial solutions to environmental problems in the region.

Another emergent network that is worth considering here was initiated as a result of research in the formal sphere that revealed that many graduates from VET were not well prepared for real life work, and that there was a lack of resources for students to get much needed hands-on practice. This was especially apparent when it came to larger equipment such as modern cars and tractors. Therefore, it was decided to engage in a pilot virtual reality programme. Directors of several larger (public and private) VET institutes, Gulu University representatives, NGO staff, students and informal instructors decided together on a pilot programme to test the use of virtual reality in tractor driving and repair. Over a series of meetings, this small group of stakeholders developed a programme, filmed and tested it, and hosted several roundtable reflective discussions on the practical application.

At its Hoima satellite campus, Gulu University is promoting aquaculture, a new economic activity for the region yet premised on the indigenous knowledge system of fishing in rivers and lakes. The community training emphasizes practical skills development for predominantly fishing communities. It starts with an explanation of the concept of cage fish farming in the classroom to the community interest group members who will later start building the cages. Bamboo poles and nylon strings are used to construct very simple, square cages that are then mounted on floating Jerry cans. The groups then make nets, following their existing practices. These nets are then attached to the cages, which are then put in the lake and anchored by sandbags. Once ready, the cages are stocked with young fish. This is contributing both to livelihoods and nutrition in the Albertine Region.

Last but not least, the mediating role of the University became visible in the UNESCO chair conference 'Towards meaningful education and decent work for the youth in Eastern and Southern Africa', held in April

2021. The conference focused on discussing partnerships, democratization and sustainability of approaches and interventions in vocational education. All relevant stakeholders were present such as staff of universities and VET providers, development agencies, youth groups, NGOs, government departments, employers' organizations, farmers and businesspeople from the region and beyond. The overall goal of the conference was to learn from each other and to enhance collective knowledge production, innovations and practical actions to promote meaningful education and decent work for youth. It turned out to be a very lively conference that enhanced existing partnerships and stimulated new enclaves of communities of practice in the region.

Discussion and insights gained

Expanded ecosystem development via relational agency

From the preceding discussion, and in reference to the expanded skills ecosystem framing, we note that considerable impact was achieved in expanding the skills ecosystems via relational partnerships with VET institutions and networks (formal and informal) to engage with and help to address local sustainable development issues. The cases discussed in this chapter show that universities have significant resources to share, especially in terms of their human capacity and knowledge coconstruction roles (education and research). They also show that universities have capacity to mobilize facilitating verticalities (for instance, policy and potential innovation funding streams) and to bring these into contact with and into a process of coresourcing horizontal connectivities. Importantly, this is not a top-down imposition of interventions, but rather a relational expansion outwards from the local context to draw in influential partners, funding, knowledge resources and potential development partners that can help with expanding the local economy as well as the knowledge and learning system. By means of these horizontal connectivities, enclaves can be developed where innovative learning processes get a chance.

As we pointed out in Chapter 4, the social ecosystem model is a conceptual framework that points to a more complex configuration of actors involved in VET and the need to bring facilitating verticalities (such as policy and national funding streams) into relationship with the horizontal connectivities and relations necessary to support VET in real world settings. In this chapter, we have shown that learning institutions, universities and vocational institutions in partnership are important mediators in the expanded social ecosystem for skills. By definition, in an ecosystem there must be interconnectedness and interaction between the different existences in that location.

Our case studies also show that this has allowed the development of human capability for productive purposes, but also for social and social-ecological transformation purposes. The expanded skills ecosystem manifested as a regional social-ecological formation that was generated by, and held together in, a world of interconnectedness between people working, learning and living together (Grainger and Spours, 2018). In both cases, there was also a clear responsiveness to skills demands, which emerged from community livelihood construction and economic development needs, as well as inclusive sustainable development needs such as water harvesting and conservation for food production. This offers a perspective that skills demand is not just 'industry driven' but by multiple concerns that arise at the interface of living and working with implications for learning. This points to the need for a broader understanding of how skills demand influences skills development in skills ecosystem research. In more traditional versions of the skills ecosystem model, the main focus has been on skills alignment with local industry (Windsor and Alcorso, 2008), which, as we argue across this book, is inadequate for the vocational learning needs in Africa, where not all work is provided in and through industry. However, this is also of wider significance globally.

If an ontological perspective grounds our conception of work (see McGrath, 2012; Lotz-Sisitka and Ramsarup, 2020; and Chapter 9), the notion of 'demand' shifts from being market driven only to include social justice and livelihoods-driven notions of 'demand', which includes work for the household (care economy), and work for the common good (ecological and social wellbeing economy), in addition to work for the state and market (public management and formal economies) (see Chapter 1). This has significant implications for VET if reconceptualized with the UNESCO (International Commission on the Futures of Education, 2021) notion of 'education *as* a common good' *for* the common good in view. It ushers in a new social contract for VET institutions, as proposed by the International Commission.

We have also shown that the insights into the emergence of an expanded skills ecosystem in the two case study contexts are enhanced by the concept of relational agency, which forcefully presents the social nature of skills development and utilization, as well as the social-ecological dynamics of skills demand and utilization. We note too that Wedekind (2016) has argued for relational agency and collegiality as mechanism for this within public VET institutions themselves where hierarchies in social relations tend to dominate, as they have historically also done between universities and vocational providers due mainly to social stigma and the reproduction of elites by universities. Relational agency broadens from individual action or agency and brings in the element of social action in a regional social ecosystem for skills. It challenges established hierarchical relations and allows for the production of 'common knowledge' that integrates across disciplines and hierarchies. This concept of relational agency (Edwards, 2005; Burkitt, 2016) is well demonstrated in our earlier descriptions. As shown by the cases, relational agency is a capacity to work with others to expand the object that one is working on and trying to transform by recognizing and accessing the resources that others bring to bear as they interpret and respond to the transforming object. Relational agency focuses more directly on the nature of the relationships that comprise a network of expertise (Edwards, 2005). In our cases, we have shown the way in which universities can form part of the relational network in coconstruction of an expanded social ecosystem for skills approach for VET, supported by CHAT and PAR methodologies. This does not mean that universities need to become VET providers, but rather that they work relationally with VET providers and other actors in the local economic and social-ecological contexts to advance sustainable development and respond to associated skills demands. In other words, they can fulfil a role of 'scholarship of engagement'.

This approach brings a new dynamic and orientation to skills acquisition or VET in terms of not only how to work, but also learning how to work together in engaging with the world of work (Edwards, 2005). This process is supported by PAR, but also through dialogical and enquiry-based pedagogical methods of group work or social learning. During such learning processes, students' agency and its emergence in relation to context and questions of the day is a significant outcome (Lehtonen, 2015). We saw this in the Alice case where students became active agents in supporting farmers in the local agroecological system through their engagement in codesigned productive demonstration site activity. The same is evident via the expansive learning orientation of CHAT, which advances relational agency around shared objects of activity in multi-actor settings (Engeström, 2001) and supports transformative agency (Pesanayi, 2019a).

Innovation systems and social movement building, role of community actors and universities

The case study findings also show that the expanded social ecosystem for skills concept is closely aligned with innovation systems development, which entails that new products/processes/services or new technologies be brought into social use through the activities or interactions between the actors and network of organizations, institutions and policies needed to bring those ideas, products, processes and services or technologies on to the market or into sustainable development use (such as rainwater-harvesting technologies). It is therefore about a network of institutions in all sectors for the production, diffusion and use of new and economically and socially useful knowledge and informs the policy framework within which the innovation process can take place. It highlights the interconnectedness of the knowledge/technology-creating institutions (Post-Harvest Innovation Learning Alliance, nd). Our cases, which differ from much mainstream innovation literature, show the need to embed and support situated innovations through expansive learning in learning networks and enclaves conceptualized as a relational dynamic between actors in an expanded skills ecosystem. This brings dynamism and situational relevance to the innovation process logic and makes the innovation concept a learning-centred concept and not a top-down impositional concept. As Whitley (2001) argues, educational and training institutions, public and private sector or not-for-profit NGOs all need to be involved. As shown, this is more accurately a process of social movement building rather than a technology of innovation diffusion.

Community engagement in theory and practice

As indicated, the role of the university in providing mediating support in the establishment of expanded social ecosystems for skills also supports recent emphasis on community engagement as a core role and pillar of higher education. The relational agency deployed among the partners in the expanded social ecosystems described in our cases show universities practising community engagement. By being a key role player in the expanded ecosystem, the university is not an 'outsider' that is 'developing the community', as can be found in some examples of community engagement practice, but rather a key contributor to the local economy, community and skills system, without losing its role as knowledge producer and educator with contributions to make at national and international levels. In fact, these contributions can be brought home into the local skills ecosystem as was the case in Alice where the university was able to mobilize national and international resources (financial, social, partnerships, technology and so on) to advance the expanded ecosystem, while developing both academic research and community activity at the same time. Like work on the advancement of the expanded skills ecosystem concept, community engagement in universities often involves partnerships and coalitions that help mobilize resources and influence systems, change relationships among partners, and serve as catalysts for changing policies, programmes and practices.

We found this to be the case in our research. In the Alice case, the students involved in the programme and the programme as a whole won awards for community engagement as a form of 'scholarship of engagement', showing that the role of the university in advancing skills ecosystems and skills ecosystem research praxis offers strong contributions to the community engagement and scholarship of engagement role and practice in universities. Indeed, it integrates teaching, research and community engagement and does not separate these functions out in the university, as is often the case.

Conclusion and agenda for the coming years

Our intention in this chapter was to focus on the role of formal learning institutions in the formation of the expanded skills ecosystem approach to VET and skills for sustainable development. We focused particularly on the university, as the university has a key partnering role to play in skills ecosystem development work. We have shown how three universities, working together with VET learning institutions (formal and informal) in two case study sites (Alice and Gulu), were able to mobilize significant capacity, resources and new approaches (innovations) as well as contribute to social movement building through an approach that values and develops relational agency. This also centres university contributions to community via an engaged approach to teaching, research and local sustainable development praxis, reflecting a 'scholarship of engagement'. We have indicated the key role that universities can play, especially in helping to make verticalities more facilitating through bringing resources from national and international platforms into the local economy and skills development setting, but also to mobilize new knowledge resources and approaches to local development that can open up new VET learning opportunities. In our research, we have also shown that there is a need to reframe the notion of demand in an expanded social ecosystem for skills approach to be inclusive of productivity in the traditional industrial sense, but also of productivity and demand for social and social-ecological systems knowledge and praxis for livelihoods advancement, that is, the bringing together of work, learning and living. There is a need for further research and development of LED opportunities by university partners working with other LED partners, and for deeper and more substantive engagement with the facilitating verticalities, especially when their facilitating role fails local economies and learning processes. Universities are well placed to take up such research in interdisciplinary teams. As shown in this chapter, this aligns well with innovations system development, community engagement and engaged research, as well as knowledge sharing and coproduction roles of universities who take a scholarship of engagement seriously. This orientation also repositions universities as contributors to social movement building for sustainable development in the expanded skills ecosystem model, reducing their historical isolation from local communities.

Across the book, the concept of boundary crossing (see also Pesanayi, 2019a) has come to the fore for advancing VET in Africa if we are to meet the demand for meaningful VET that is available in both formal and more informal VET learning settings. Universities should not see themselves as divorced from the VET landscape, but rather as active contributors in partnership with VET institutions (formal and informal) to sustainable skills ecosystems. Interestingly, as this chapter was being finalized, UNESCO and the Southern African Development Community were hosting a 'Futures of Education' meeting to discuss exactly this: how VET institutions and universities can work more cohesively in support of local and regional development priorities while also fulfilling their respective mandates. A similar challenge for a restructuring of university–VET relations was voiced in the UNESCO report on Futures of Education (see Chapters 1 and 9). Engaging within the expanded social ecosystem approach as articulated across this book repositions universities not as VET institutions themselves, but as vital contributors to the emergence of a viable and relevant VET landscape in Africa, which includes emerging learning networks, learning communities and enclaves of innovation, directed at just transitions and inclusive sustainable development that embrace the links between and coconstruction of new ways of learning, working and living necessary for viable futures for Africa's young people and future generations.

9

Implications for VET Research, Policy and Practice

Simon McGrath

The state of vocational education and training

When you ask different actors with an interest in vocational education and training (VET) about its state, it is common, though not universal, to get complaints. Politicians and civil servants will typically bemoan the cost of public investments in VET and compare these unfavourably with the perceived social and economic benefits. Employers tend to complain about the inadequacy of curricula, the unresponsiveness of public providers and the workreadiness of graduates. VET leaders frequently bemoan inadequate state investment but also often express frustration at staff and their unions for their lack of flexibility. Staff, on the other hand, feel underpaid, under-resourced and increasingly overly constrained and undersupported by changes to curriculum, pedagogy and assessment. Learners are likely to complain about lack of facilities, including for extracurricular activities, and are often aware of a VET stigma. Moreover, they often know that there is a huge disparity in many countries between typical artisanal and professional incomes. In both their learning experiences and labour market outcomes, intersectional inequality plays out, and providers and the VET system are too often complicit in this. The stigma and income disparities are also widely perceived among parents and society at large. Thus, there is a powerful sense of VET not working.

Furthermore, as Chapter 2 demonstrated, the policy community have had successive waves of huge policy ambitions for the sector, resulting in a series of attempted transformations. As part of a wider international process that has its roots particularly in Australia and England, African VET systems have experienced recurring attempts at reform over the last quarter century that repeat the use of the same set of policy tools, apparently oblivious to having used them before (Allais et al, 2022). If VET is not working well, then neither is VET reform. This book contributes some starting points in extricating VET from conceptions that constrain it. While we ground our arguments empirically in African cases and contexts, many of the issues that we have outlined are more widely relevant, whether this is the wider political–economy–ecology or the international spread of the VET toolkit. Thus, in this chapter, we are talking into the international VET debate.

On top of the internal issues with the VET system come further, existential, challenges. As we charted in Chapter 2, the educational logic of African Ministries of Education has led to massification of public VET provision to the point where graduate outputs far exceed the economy's absorption capacity, even before we address any quality concerns from employers. While pockets of excellence remain, often very tightly linked to actual labour market possibilities, the bulk of formal VET is largely detached from older notions of training for a specific job and even from likely employment. At the same time, it is failing to take seriously the ways and circumstances in which people work, and meaningfully engage in what types of education would be most valuable. Again, this is not an issue for Africa alone.

Moreover, many labour market projections suggest that formal productive sector employment is likely to decline, with potentially serious implications for the artisanal and professional areas served by conventional VET. Brown et al (2020) suggest we are heading towards the 'takeover' of human labour by robots and digitalization. While some will be able to respond through building digitalization competences, they suggest basic income grants are going to be necessary in the near future. The further decline of intermediate and higher skills jobs as a result of digitalization and automation, and the growing argument in favour of basic income grants, together pose a further existential threat to conventional VET. While this will have contextual specificities, the challenge for VET globally is immense (Avis, 2020; Buchanan et al, 2020).

Our political–economy–ecology critique of conventional VET (Chapter 3) points to the further threat internationally that many of the programmes and occupational destinations of traditional VET programmes are in areas that are most compromised by a move away from fossil capitalism. In South Africa, for instance, the automotive and mining industries were central to industrialization, the rise of public VET and the emergence of the apprenticeship system. However, these are not the mass employment and production sectors of a future just transition. While there is an important role for greening existing occupations, it will be vital to retrain existing workers for new technologies and economic opportunities including renewable energy options (see, for example, Presidential Climate Change Commission, 2021).

Thus, VET as conventionally understood and established over the three generations articulated in Chapter 2 faces a challenging present and a complex, dynamically changing future, which this book seeks to inform. As outlined in Chapter 1, this dominant mode of VET is actually part of a wider regime that has existed for a relatively short period of time, compared to longer-term cultural patterns. Moreover, its dominance is less apparent the further one moves from metropolitan industrial centres, as our cases reveal. Vocational learning existed before it and will continue after this point in history.

While we are in a process of transitioning, however contradictory and hesitant this is, there will be a need to engage with currently conventional VET and seek to fit it for a better purpose while also potentially expanding its focus and reach and/or reimagining its purpose in ways that can respond more substantively to shifting conditions.

Adopting and expanding the social ecosystems for skills model

Reflections on adopting a skills ecosystems approach

As we noted in Chapter 1, the purpose of this book is not simply to critique but to explore the emergence of better approaches to VET. In it, we have drawn inspiration from the skills ecosystem approach. Though not uniquely, this approach has made an important contribution by making a spatial-sectoral shift and inserting a meso level analysis between previously dominant, but largely unconnected, micro and macro analyses. In so doing, it has reflected a wider trend towards understanding how actors operate within networks and the importance of evolving institutions that build collaboration and trust. It also reflects a wider place-based turn in educational research (see, for example, Gruenewald and Smith, 2014).

Finegold's formulation of skills ecosystems rather than equilibria provided a valuable elaboration of his earlier work, stressing how well-functioning regional and sectoral arrangements could emerge within wider contexts of dysfunctionality and distrust (Finegold and Soskice, 1988; Finegold, 1999). His four key characteristics (catalysts, nourishment, supportive environment and actor independence) remain important analytical and practical lenses for examining existing ecosystems and considering interventions therein. Indeed, an important factor in our initial case study selection was a sense that there might have been catalysts operating in all four settings. We also wanted to explore whether these catalysts could help strengthen the other dimensions.

However, as the project developed, it was Spours' work that seemed preferable to us as its emphasis on social ecosystems of skills reflected our concern to move away from privileging economic growth and towards the 'bringing together of a wide range of social partners around the relationship between working, living and learning' (Hodgson and Spours, 2018: 4). This move highlights the need to recognize that economies, labour markets and skills formation systems are embedded within wider social, spatial and ecological contexts in which a broader range of actors have legitimate voice (see, for instance, International Commission on the Futures of Education, 2021).

Readers will recall that this approach too has four key elements: collaborative horizontalities, facilitating verticalities, mediation through common mission and ecosystem leadership, and ecological time (Spours, 2021a). These became key to our analytical approach in this book.

We have shown examples of where collaborative horizontalities appear to exist. It is important to consider what brings them into existence and how wide and deep these relationships are. In the more formal sector cases of oil in Hoima and the maritime sector in eThekwini, a core group of employers have developed strong relations. Indeed, an international oil ecosystem exists with the oil companies themselves operating alongside a next tier of large international corporations that manage the actual construction process, and further tiers of subcontractors in various specialisms, including training. In eThekwini, we found a wider ecosystem of coordinating bodies, suppliers, training providers and so on that emerged over time around a major industrial activity that is strongly place-based. Yet, both also illustrate the challenges faced by other organizations, including public colleges, in entering these networks. This reflects existing South African research. For instance, social network diagrams of the automotive ecosystem in the Eastern Cape show the public VET colleges as existing on the periphery with weak ties to the core of the ecosystem (McGrath, 2015). In the less formalized settings of Alice and Gulu, our team comprised important actors in emerging or existing social ecosystems for skills, which took a different form from the more industry-driven ones and were more inclusive of communities and informal actors.

Examples of facilitating verticalities appear across the cases but alongside much that is nonfacilitiating. We observed a strong tendency for policies and environments to have contradictory effects, and for policies to run far ahead of implementation, due often to disjunctures between policy intention and practice. One of Spours' strong assumptions is that states are essentially developmental. Despite this being the state ideology in South Africa, developmental capacity is weak (and more so in Uganda). However, more needs to be made of power and self-interest than Spours allows for (Wedekind et al, 2021). Moreover, we need to remember the effects of path dependence resulting from the legacies of fossil capitalism, colonialism and apartheid, as discussed in Chapter 3. This takes us beyond the flatter accounts of the northern skills ecosystems literature.

Looking specifically at the extent that just transitions are being facilitated, we must note that policies are often contradictory. In both the large industrial cases, we see that much vertical activity is greenwashing. Nonetheless, there is also evidence of donors, NGOs and certain state agencies (such as the South African Water Research Council) who are more facilitative of moves towards just transitions in the less formal settings (see also Rosenberg et al, 2020; McGrath and Russon, 2021). However, Chapter 3 points to the very powerful dynamics that need to be challenged in such a transitioning.

Mediation and leadership were crucial notions informing our work. By taking a relational perspective, this work of bringing together the horizontal and vertical to achieve ecosystemic goals was brought to the forefront of our analysis. In earlier chapters, we showed examples of organizations seeking to play this role, including universities, as discussed in Chapter 8. However, this is often undermined by limited resources and remains too dependent on key individuals. From an institutional theory perspective, it is worth considering the extent to which new institutions (agreed rules and processes) have emerged in these ecosystems and the extent to which mediatory actors are still required to develop and enforce these.

Finally, the notion of ecological time is crucial. In the Hoima case, it creates the space to consider the skills of the past (such as lake fishing) and to imagine a future social skills ecosystem beyond oil and gas. Our research is necessarily time-bounded, yet these ecosystems have existence before and after they were subjected to the research gaze. In this light, as McGrath and Russon (2022) note, 'the notion of ecosystems contains within it an implicit awareness of dynamic rather than static reality. Ecosystems can flourish but they are always subject to change and a finite existence. Taking this into account when thinking about the transition to sustainable VET is crucial.' Thinking about ecological time reminds us that there are multiple temporalities operating simultaneously and interdependently (Braudel, 1986 [1949]). Time is crucial too for thinking about transitioning, whether of individuals, firms, economies or societies. The ecosystem metaphor helps remind us that change takes time and is unlikely to be linear or simple.

Expanding the approach

Skills ecosystems work started off by analysing the extreme case of Silicon Valley and then moved initially to other regions of advanced Anglophone economies. It is only since around 2020 that the approach has started to move to the BRICS countries (Brazil, Russia, India, China, South Africa) through work in India and South Africa (Lotz-Sisitka, 2020; Brown, 2022).

We take the South African work further and complement it with work in the economically poorer context of Uganda. Although these ecosystems have important contextual differences from their northern predecessors, the basic analytical tools hold, as we have argued here and throughout the book. Nonetheless, we have argued for a strong ontological grounding in constructing such social ecosystems for skills and including some of what has historically been excluded from VET thinking and praxis (such as responses to a wider notion of work).

While the social ecosystem model identifies the importance of thinking also about skills for life and environmental sustainability, these remain underdeveloped. We too have not taken these as far as we would have liked, and more remains to be done in developing a political–economy–ecology perspective further. However, we have sought to make a case in this book for the importance of such a task and have offered some pointers towards it.

We have attempted to make a more explicitly ontologically distinct account. This has three main dimensions. First, our more explicit engagement with political ecology issues and the challenge of just transitions, though not fully realized, points to a further development of an account of VET's purpose as being different from the productivist–human capital origins that still permeate much of VET thinking. To see VET's purpose as being about furthering collective human flourishing and integral human development is both an axiological and ontological move.

Second, although relationality is implicit in an ecosystems account, we seek to make this more explicit through our discussions and application of the notions of relational agency and relational capability. We believe that relationality is fundamental for an approach to VET for just transitions, a vital next move in the field. We argue that the social ecosystem for skills model can help to advance relationality in VET, a position that also seems to be emerging in international and regional African discourse (for example, the recent UNESCO/South African Development Community deliberation on VET–higher education relations).

Third, as we noted in Chapter 1 and reiterated in Chapter 4, we draw on critical realism to underlabour our approach. This is fundamental to how we see the vertical and the horizontal interacting, but it is most important in how we try to address the scalar question. Adding in a meso level focus is useful in itself but raises the question of how levels interact. By drawing on Bhaskar's laminated approach to multiscalarity, we are able to address this issue. And as shown in our cases, wider issues such as climate change impact on the VET system through new demands for curriculum innovations that support, for example, content and practices for water conservation and climate resilient agriculture in rapidly changing conditions (such as in Alice). This shows processes and relations across the multiscalar system presented in Chapter 4.

One important decision that we made in writing this book was that social ecosystems thinking was useful, but that it did not provide sufficient conceptual tools to drive all of our work. It may be conceived as providing the middle of three layers of our conceptual approach. At a more generalized level, we have located our expansion of the social ecosystems approach in critical realism, as noted earlier. Moreover, each of the empirical chapters also drew on other literatures that are present in substantive debates in those subfields. We show that the social ecosystems model is complementary to other approaches, on inclusion, transitions from education to work, human development and sustainability, for instance.

We have also sought to broaden the social ecosystem approach by adopting a set of lenses on our empirical cases that take the work further in ways that were not central to Spours' largely conceptual approach. Our first lens was that of informality, seeking to apply, and adapt, the model to the reality of the majority of African, and indeed global, economic life. In the informal economy contexts we considered in Chapter 5, there were many thousands of continually shifting individuals, microenterprises and families operating in complex webs of relationality. At the same time, potential anchor institutions and their partners are very few and their reach relatively small. Therefore, it was useful to think in terms of network catalysts, providing frameworks for fractal processes of deepening relationality, rather than anchor institutions. While much informal sector activity is survivalist, our story is one of possibilities for generating new ideas for the future. Given young people's need to find new paths through living, working and learning, relationships rather than formal learning providers came to the fore. It was the former that allowed people to develop better approaches to assembling, repurposing and reconfiguring knowledge into dynamic responses. Nonetheless, we also saw learning sites that are formalizing, and we saw influences from the informal sector on the formal VET institutions in more responsive curriculum innovations, with a broader role being taken on by VET teachers (see Chapter 6). Particularly interesting here was the case of Farmer X (who is also discussed in Chapter 6). Originally primarily a producer, he had increasingly become a trainer and was in the process of moving from providing informal learning opportunities to getting a study programme accredited. This is a rare example of such a formalization being initiated from below, a point we shall return to when we consider implications for policy and practice.

Second, in Chapter 6, we considered how the model could be extended to consider more explicitly the part played by vocational teachers, surely central actors in any social ecosystem for skills. Mindful of cases such as Farmer X, we took an expansive view of vocational teachers, seeking to get beyond the existing largely bifurcated literature of formal sector industrial trainers and public sector vocational lecturers. Instead, we insist vocational teaching and learning happen across learning spaces and working spaces of all formalities. We argue that teachers are central to all ecosystem aspects, as interpreters of curriculum, scaffolders of learning and connectors to work. Ideally, they are mediators, traversing boundaries between learning and work and guiding the vocational learner to the same, both in terms of vocational knowledge in the classroom and in navigating the labour market, both formal and informal. It is vital that curriculum and what happens in the classroom is adjusted and changed as work evolves, and teachers must be key actors in this. This becomes even more vital as we think about VET for just transitionings. In moving towards this, teachers need further support.

Unfortunately, key verticalities here have often been nonfacilitating, such as focusing on higher teacher qualifications without adequately considering why this should make a difference to learning or how existing teachers are to access or use these new qualifications meaningfully in their contexts. If we are going to meet the needs of VET teachers beyond formal public institutions, then tailored or boundary crossing approaches will be vital. This needs to bring vocational teachers together with farmers, local economic development officials and extension officers (see Chapter 8). An ecosystem approach thus helps us question the top-down bias of too many interventions in vocational teacher development. Our data points also to the importance that teachers placed on building horizontal relationships within and across institutions and community organizations, of building horizontal collaborations in the language of both the social ecosystems for skills approach and the International Commission on the Futures of Education (2021, discussed further later in the chapter).

Education policies are increasingly employing a rhetoric of innovation. However, innovation requires real facilitating verticalities that empower vocational teachers to function in the mediating space. This necessitates giving them sufficient autonomy to work with curriculum and delivery. They are too often faced with blame and stigma, yet there are many able and committed vocational teachers who need to be properly paid and resourced and given the support to build their individual and collective capacity to deliver good quality VET. What we are categorically not arguing is that teachers should do more without being recognized and rewarded for this.

Our third move, in Chapter 7, was to consider how the social ecosystem approach for skills could inform the education-to-work transitions debate. In positioning our work alongside those who problematize such transitions and point to nonlinear and blocked transitions, and the role of intersectional inequality therein, we returned to questions of how the vertical and horizontal, and mediation between them, contribute to facilitating transitions. Our stories illustrate the need for more critical and differentiated consideration of needs and local contexts. They stress the role of networks and their building as critical to supporting institutions and learning pathways.

While Chapter 5 highlights the importance of networks, here we argue that in more formal or hybrid labour market contexts, anchor organizations remain crucial. Even in the networks in our cases, leadership was being provided by diverse learning institutions including VET institutions. These need to be robust, agile and inclusive. Linking back to Chapters 5 and 6, this requires more support for localized colearning networks.

Finally, in Chapter 8, we make the rather unusual move of looking at the role of universities in supporting social ecosystems for skills and these localized colearning networks. The reason for this is that universities are also potential contributors to diverse skills ecosystems, and they have capabilities and mandates for engaged research and community engagement alongside more traditional teaching and research roles. Each of our four research partners is active in ecosystems development work, with two working particularly closely with a range of other actors at the local level in case study sites. Through our experience in these cases, we argue that universities can play a key role in helping to make verticalities more facilitating through the particular advantages that they have in convening other actors due to their social status, research abilities and their capacity to bring national and international resources to local settings. We also show that there is a need to reframe the notions of productivity and demand to include both how they are conceived conventionally and how they relate to social and ecological systems knowledge and praxis for livelihoods advancement. This orientation also repositions universities as contributors to social movement building for sustainable development in the expanded social ecosystem model. This reduces their historical isolation, deriving from an 'ivory tower' notion of the university. Instead, they are boundary crossers, active contributors in partnership with VET providers (of whatever level of formality) in supporting sustainable and inclusive social ecosystems for skills.

Some limitations to our approach

Nonetheless, this book does have limitations that we should highlight. We will not claim that our research design was perfect. Indeed, a desire to be democratic led to an iterative approach to design and required compromises within the team. Moreover, the operationalization of our approach was significantly affected by multiple lockdowns across our research and writing sites that were the result of the COVID-19 pandemic. We were far enough into data collection at the start of lockdown to adjust and continue, but there are data that we were not able to collect. This required some refocusing of target themes for the empirical chapters. Given our intention to motivate for and start the expansion of the social ecosystem model, this refocusing was not problematic.

While we have stressed that critical realism underlaboured our approach, we have also noted that we do not attempt a full critical realist analysis. Our revised intention, for instance, was not to try to build a specific account of what was working in VET, for whom and why in the realist evaluation tradition (as we noted in Chapter 1). Rather, we set out to develop a case for researching VET in a new way, one that was underpinned by critical realism. In this sense, the book is complementary to two other recent book length treatments of skills development in Africa (Powell and McGrath, 2019a; Rosenberg et al, 2020), both of which spend more time in outlining a critical realist approach.

We also had a strong ambition to focus on skills for just transitions. However, both the blockages on fieldwork and the very early stages of moves towards transitions in many settings meant that our ambition outstripped our ability. In the end, we still decided to reflect our ambition in this text because this is an area of existential importance. However, we decided to see just transitions more as a lens through which to critique the current state of VET, explore our findings and identify the road still to be travelled.

Our intention has been to contribute towards addressing the long history of colonial and extractive natures of VET as engaged scholars. However, we acknowledge in the afterword that we were only partially successful in developing a better practice. It can be questioned also whether an African account should be developed from a theoretical approach that began in the north. In our praxis, however, the social ecosystem approach developed out of a demand for supporting farmers to learn more about rainwater harvesting to bring water to their fields in a context where such knowledge was largely absent from the VET system (including extension graduates' knowledges). Only later did we begin to draw insights from skills ecosystem research (see Pesanayi, 2019a; Lotz-Sistka, 2020; Lotz-Sisitka and Pesanayi, 2020). We did this because the social ecosystem perspective resonated with, and helped to better explain, our work in the Imvothu Bubomi Learning Network (IBLN) and its grounded emergence over time. We were therefore not simply reinforcing a dependence on northern knowledge. Rather, we were drawing on this to enrich our own experience and generative research innovations, and as shown in this book, we were also advancing this theoretical perspective. We were curious to see the wider application of this concept, and so used it in this study. What was important in this process is that social ecosystem approaches to skills helped to re-establish disrupted African 'cultures of agriculture' as a decolonial praxis (Pesanayi, 2019a) in the Alice case; respond to youth challenges of exclusion in the Gulu case; articulate the complexity of youth transitioning experiences in the eThekwini case; and reveal the dominance of oil companies and conglomerates in structuring VET in exclusionary ways in the Hoima case. Our concern was not therefore to deliberate colonial versus decolonial theory but rather to enrich grounded decolonial praxis in and for VET with useful theory (see Tikly, 2020, who draws on Santos, 2014, to argue for establishment of wider ecologies of knowledge in and as decolonial praxis). Centring our extended model on relationality, informality and context, among other key elements, our approach offers ways of working up decolonial praxis. We also acknowledge that a more critical reading of our approach is entirely possible.

By using the ecosystem metaphor, we are implying some degree of a complexity-influenced approach. However, like many other social scientists, we are only nodding to complexity's radical implications rather than fully engaging with the concept. Our ontological critique of the Spours' model seeks to move us beyond its implicit linearity, a function in part of representing its message through a quasi-graph. However, there is more work to be done here. We also note that not all concepts from complexity theory are useful for advancing generative research.

The ecosystem metaphor can be overstressed. The skills systems we are working on are social, not natural, systems. They exhibit social phenomena such as power and mistrust and are partially shaped by conscious actions and by structural and cultural histories and emergent properties as well as agentive dynamics of those involved in the processes of building local social skills systems. Following Spours and colleagues, we use the metaphor consciously not simply to describe the current world but as a tool for imagining the future and for opening up the many historical, cultural, structural, agentive, relational, social and social-ecological dynamics that ultimately make up a social ecosystem model for skills. However, there is a danger in using the metaphor that we blur the boundaries between what is, what might be and what should be. Further research into the many intersecting dynamics that sit inside the metaphor needs to be continued beyond what could be achieved in this book.

Implications for VET policy and practice

In critiquing the internal logic of current VET approaches, and in seeking to reimagine VET, our work throws up a number of implications for current policy and practice debates.

System thinking

Part of our focus on an expanded approach to social ecosystems for skills is a stress on the importance of looking at the whole of skills formation systems and not at narrow elements thereof. Too often, VET policy is dominated by a focus on public providers, indeed those public providers under the jurisdiction of Ministries of Education. Even when formal enterprise-based training is included in policy considerations, we are still talking about a small fraction of overall provision. While there are important reasons for focusing strongly on state systems, our clear message is that we need to look at the totality of skills formation.

Considering the whole system permits us to understand better the complex question of who benefits from different parts of the system, who does not, and under what conditions. While there is rightly an argument that public provision has a particular mandate to reach the socially and economically excluded, it is apparent that many are not able to access it. Equally, while many face forms of marginalization and exploitation in the informal economy, it is a site of opportunity and innovation for others.

Rethinking VET's purpose

By emphasizing the word 'social', following Spours, we are also reiterating the point that the focus of our attention on skills systems should not just be on a narrow employability–entrepreneurship–productivity agenda, as has become dominant in public systems that appear to have forgotten the wider societal and educative dimensions of VET. At the Shanghai World TVET Conference in 2012 (UNESCO, 2012), the global VET community agreed that the economic rationale of VET had to be seen as only one strand, alongside social inclusion and sustainable development. With such an emphasis on a triple purpose comes a stressing of broader categories of social actors. Yet, the VET responsiveness agenda has remained narrow, thinking solely about the needs of formal employers and the economy, remaining locked in a fetishization of skill (Wheelahan et al, 2022). This has once again been challenged by the International Commission on the Futures of Education (2021; see also the background paper by Buchanan et al, 2020), but whether this will have any more traction with the VET mainstream remains to be seen. Perhaps, as shown in our cases, the ontological foundations of VET as experienced by communities may help to give these policy arguments 'life' and greater resonance, and thus also traction. More cases could therefore be developed to provide further empirical perspective on the arguments put forward in this book.

What a social ecosystems approach does is reiterate the importance of other actors in building skills networks and institutions. Thus, civil society organizations, for instance, need to be part of VET conversations. A good, though still very much emerging, example here is that of the Ker Kwaro Acholi (see Chapter 5), the Acholi cultural organization that is seeking to become an important actor in reimagining development in northern Uganda, and the role of skills formation therein. Other actors are important too. Parents and students are central actors, yet they are largely marginalized. Their attitudes towards VET are central to its possibilities for success. Churches are major players in provision in many countries, such as Uganda, as well as being important civil society organizations with strong contributions to make regarding social inclusion and environmental stewardship. These issues point to the need to revisit debates about governance and responsiveness. These have been major elements of the VET Africa 3.0 approach but have largely failed on their own narrow terms and need radical rethinking.

Addressing public provision

While we have stressed the importance of looking at the broad range of VET provision, our research does have a series of messages for public provision. The discussion about the need to revisit governance, of course, is hugely important for the public system. With it comes the need to address the issue of public provider autonomy. There is a literature critiquing the limited extent and problematic conceptualizing of such autonomy in South Africa (for instance, McGrath, 2010; Wedekind, 2010; Kraak, 2016). Our story is very much one of many public providers being unable to respond fully to local skills needs and opportunities as they do not have a mandate. This is likely to become even more acute as VET needs to respond to new and pressing challenges of sustainability as well as rapidly changing economic circumstances. Where public VET providers are most prominent in our story is in two particular ways that are worth reflecting upon. First, in both Hoima, through the Uganda Petroleum Institute, Kigumba (UPIK), and eThekwini, through uMfolozi Maritime Academy, responsiveness to local economic trends actually comes from central government direction and leads to the formation of a new structure (whether an entirely new institution or a new part of an existing one). It does not come from local institutions, as they lack the capacity and authority to do this. This is deeply problematic. Second, in Alice, it was an agriculture and forestry training institute – with a mandate to become more regionally responsive – rather than the regular public TVET college, that was a key actor in the social ecosystem for skills. This reflects the far greater level of autonomy this institution enjoys, and perhaps also its more focused interest in agriculture as the key local sector, compared to the TVET college that offers a wider range of qualifications that are not well integrated into the local economy and its development. There is no justification for institutions under other ministries being more responsive to local skills needs than those institutions under Ministries of Education.

Part of the reason why public providers have been found to be peripheral to other economic sector stories in South Africa is that public colleges are seen as unable to respond quickly to industry approaches despite this being the intention of VET Africa 3.0 reforms over a quarter century. This is seen too in the case of public TVET colleges in eThekwini metropolitan area and Alice. The ability of local providers to be responsive and anticipatory regarding skills needed to support economic transformation is partly also related to the ability of other local state structures. In eThekwini, such structures are relatively strong, and the problem seems to be more about the marginal position of skills thinking, and especially of public provision of skills, in such structures. In Alice, too, we see some engagement with the structures of the municipality, but one that is more limited in its capacity.

The three 'responsive' public structures, moreover, are specialist providers, whether at the whole institution or academy level. This leads us on to the debate about whether such providers may have advantages over general institutions. There certainly are merits in the argument that specialization is advantageous. A specialist institution is potentially more able to overcome issues of stigma. It is also able to put relatively more of its resources into linking with external partners and understanding labour market, societal and environmental trends. It also lowers the costs for other actors in engaging with the public system as it reduces the need to search among apparently similar providers. However, such specialist institutions can only work if they are genuinely centres of excellence, whether related to national or local needs, and are resourced and staffed accordingly.

This takes us back also to the autonomy issue. It is one thing for central government to mandate a provider to respond to sectoral needs; it is another to give this provider the freedom to do so as and when it judges this to be appropriate. However, our cases also point to the challenges of getting wider buy-in for such centres of excellence. Neither UPIK nor uMfolozi were asked for by industry partners, who had their own skills formation strategies in place. Thus, both face a significant challenge in convincing employers that they are worth engaging with.

Part of the credibility challenge for centres of excellence has to do with qualifications. Both UPIK and uMfolozi were in the process of developing their own qualifications that were seen as more attuned to industry needs than typical national vocational curricula and qualifications. Yet, there were already industry-recognized international qualifications available, and developing something that is at least as attractive as these will be challenging. These are two highly formalized and internationalized sectors where major employers and serious health and safety concerns shape a tendency towards highly standardized programmes.

Almost polar opposites that still reinforce the need for market acceptance of qualifications are provided by examples from Alice and Gulu. In the former, the IBLN saw a curriculum and qualifications developed by multiple actors that was clearly valued locally. Here, the relative autonomy of tertiary providers, in the form of Fort Cox and Rhodes, permitted something to be developed that creatively engaged with the national qualifications framework (NQF) in a way that did not straitjacket learning to fit the formal frame. In Gulu, the case of Farmer X points to a welcome flexibility on the part of the Ugandan Department for Industrial Training. Its willingness to investigate accrediting what started off as an informal programme is welcome. However, it is clear here that it took the charismatic and knowledgeable leadership of Farmer X to make this happen. Like the key staff of Fort Cox and Rhodes, he was able to cross the boundary between the formal and informal to mediate between them.

Both countries are firm believers in NQFs despite the lack of evidence for their efficacy (see Allais, 2014). However, what is apparent across the cases is that qualifications alone are not enough to secure successful and rapid individual transitions. Despite longstanding NQFs, respondents spoke of having employers not recognize their certificates. Many employers still do care which provider delivered the education despite NQF rhetoric. By ignoring the necessary grounding of qualifications recognition in social relations (Buchanan et al, 2020), the introduction of NQFs may make the situation worse.

Too much policy attention is given to school/college-to-work transitions in ways that imply some tinkering with the education side can quickly sort out the problem. This ignores the massive gap between supply of new labour market entrants and the demand from formal sector firms for employees both in quantitative and qualitative terms (see Allais and Wedekind, 2020). What is apparent is that transitions cannot be straightforward in such a context, except for the privileged or incredibly lucky. Interventions are needed but cannot be simple and cheap in the face of this challenge. What needs to be attempted are interventions that focus more on stable and decent livelihoods than the first moment of labour market insertion, a notion that makes little sense in many contexts in Africa and beyond. Particular attention must be given to those who are socioeconomically and/or educationally disadvantaged and how to support their transitions into specific occupations and sectors. The uMfolozi Academy is an attempt to do this, but it is unclear how well it will succeed.

Skills for the informal sector

The issue of transitions takes us forward to a consideration of the informal sector and its role in skills formation and social ecosystems. As we have stressed, most African youth will engage with informal work, whether it be in the informal sector as conventionally understood or through informal working for formal sector firms, as is increasingly becoming the norm in the north too. In Chapters 5 and 7, we try to reframe the issue of transition for a majority informal reality. Our data make clear that just because someone is in the informal economy does not necessarily mean that they are mired in survivalist activities with no hope of progression. While we do not want to romanticize informal sector activities, our research does point to examples of innovation and dynamism. This is important as it emboldens us to argue against the policy tendency to seek to formalize the informal. In many ways, this is the worst of empty policy rhetoric. Declaring formality without the means to transform economies and labour markets so that informal work is genuinely eradicated both offers false hope (which seems to be an issue in some of the data from Gulu) and denies existing lived realities.

In the skills arena, this has led to well-meaning but intensely naive interventions to give those working in the informal sector qualifications on the NQF. Again, this is deeply problematic as it both makes a false promise that formal qualifications will lead to formal jobs and allows for the blaming of those who don't choose to acquire these new formal qualifications. Our data, on the other hand, shows examples of dynamic learning processes within the informal sector. The policy and practice question, thus, becomes: how do we support informal learning in the informal sector to strengthen its quality in terms of knowledge content, inclusivity and livelihood outcomes? This may be possible. If so, it needs to start from listening to those already engaged in such activities, as our Gulu and Alice teams are doing, and working with them to build improved practices including those of sharing existing good practices horizontally in ways that can also draw on the resources and networks of formal learning institutions. This is what some of the best interventions in upgrading traditional apprenticeship did in the VET Africa 2.0 era. Such interventions were typically small-scale NGO projects. What worked far less effectively were later major national interventions, typically bankrolled by external donors, especially the World Bank, that flooded informal sectors with money and generated more corruption than training (King and McGrath, 2002).

A strong finding from our research, reflected particularly in Chapter 5, is that there is considerable vibrancy in informal sector learning that goes far beyond the usual focus on traditional apprenticeship. We see two main strands of this in our data.

First, in Gulu especially, we found several new training providers who were better geared to the sector's needs. The owners included graduates and those with experience of working with international development organizations, who could draw on various forms of capital. These characteristics very much reflect the Gulu context, with its history of humanitarian aid and its local university that together have generated more skilled people than the formal economy can currently absorb. Some of those we encountered had started as training providers, but others had increasingly shifted from production to training. As with other endogenous initiatives within the informal sector, there is potential to support these organizations to strengthen them, but also a great risk of interventions from state or donors that undermine them. At this point, overformalizing them by pushing them towards national curricula and qualifications is almost certainly a bad idea.

Second, we found that some in the informal sector were using social media to acquire and share knowledge both nationally and internationally. Again, this is a useful corrective to the tendency to see the sector as mired in poverty and ignorance. In the Alice case, learning network members use combinations of social media, formal training and informal learning processes, with the latter often being constructed via calling on members of the network to share productive demonstrations or knowledge around certain concerns. The contemporary informal sector is far from homogeneous, and any policy interventions need to start from this and consider the contexts in which they are intended to operate.

Knowledge, learning and teaching

This use of social media in learning and knowledge sharing is an important part of our story of social ecosystems. Indeed, some of the networks go far beyond the conventional understanding of a spatially bounded skills ecosystem. The growth in the use of social media has implications for policy and practice. In small-scale farming, catering, tailoring and food production, we have examples of trusted sources of new ideas and advice that go far beyond VET providers or the agricultural extension system. Such systems need to be reviewed for the consequences of this in terms of knowledge sharing, learning and vocational praxis development. Perhaps nowhere is this more urgent than in the case of agricultural extension. It is noteworthy in this respect that Fort Cox has fed its experiences of being part of the IBLN into its own radical curriculum reform process that seeks to respond to new needs of agriculture graduates. Here again, we need to note that Fort Cox has more autonomy to respond like this than a typical public VET provider.

The growth in access to and content of social media, and rapid digitalization, has potentially profound implications for the flow of vocational knowledge and for the status of vocational teachers as key knowledge actors, as the International Commission on the Futures of Education (2021) outlines for education as a whole. On the one hand, as we saw in Chapter 6, the possibilities of learning informally online can assist teachers in making their formal lessons stronger, as they can source information and knowledge otherwise absent from resource-poor institutions. However, as social media do become more ubiquitous, they reinforce existing challenges to notions of teachers as sole distributors of knowledge through speaking and writing their notes on a blackboard in the theory classroom. Our data appear to reinforce arguments about shifting the teacher to more of a guide to accessing and evaluating knowledge. As we note in Chapter 6, there are many possibilities for a different role for vocational teachers, but this requires a fundamental revisiting of their role and purpose; a radical reworking of their initial and continuing preparation; and an adequate resourcing of them. All of these will be challenging in under-resourced public VET systems and in societies where a digital divide is still acute, as in both Uganda and South Africa. How to reach private provision of all kinds is a further issue.

Moves, such as in England and Australia, to reduce the initial qualifications of public vocational teachers appear highly counterproductive. However, simply requiring higher qualifications (and potentially retrenching experienced teachers on the way) is also to be avoided. More important, arguably, is thinking about continuous professional development. As we noted in Chapter 6, too many interventions in this area have been through relatively short-term programmes that are often disparate and uncoordinated. Rather, we stress the importance of building horizontal relationships between vocational teachers across and within institutional boundaries. An ecosystemic approach points to the importance of developing these horizontal relationships through better localized coordination around professional development activities that develop communities of practice among vocational teachers and others who contribute to their professional learning. For instance, in the Alice case, it was the collaboration between farmers, extension officers, LED officers, university staff and students, and other college lecturers in an ongoing learning network structure, that led to professional development of the lecturers.

The role of social media in vocational learning takes us to the question of education technology in vocational learning. The pandemic has seen a further marketing push by edtech firms keen to get state investment in their schemes. It is clear that edtech can do some valuable things in VET, but there is need for caution about its efficacy and cost, let alone its collaboration with the state to project a sense of techno–utopianism that will solve all ills (Black, 2021). Rather, we suggest that a debate about harnessing the power of informal e-learning may be more fruitful when thinking of strengthening VET teaching and learning. The Alice case has also shown that there is need to give much attention to technical issues such as devices, software, data costs and other dimensions for e-learning assumptions to be realized in practice for staff and students alike, and to bring attention to the fundamental inequalities that still prevail in access to all of these and to safe and effective learning spaces outside formal classrooms (Allais and Marock, 2020).

Rethinking private provision

We have been concerned with public and private provision of VET at various points in this chapter, but it is important to come explicitly to the debate about the role of private provision in national training systems. Starting from the local ecosystems that are the heart of this book, it is evident that there is much private provision but that it is highly varied.

In both Ugandan cases, the strongest formal VET providers historically have been church-owned. Uganda has sought to integrate these institutions into the national system, and their provision is mainly of national qualifications. However, the coming of oil to Hoima has also seen the arrival of new actors, typically small and specialized, focusing on very specific areas of training such as health and safety. In between these two forms, there is a third, that of the more conventionally understood private provider specializing in business and information technology, which are relatively fragile in a poor location such as Hoima. However, in this setting, it is apparent that public providers also are weak. Apart from UPIK, it is difficult to see potential for them to play anchoring roles. Rather, the likely future trajectory here is for a very diverse provider fauna to be maintained. In Gulu, we have also noted the evolution of new private providers with origins in production, as detailed earlier. From a dynamic ecosystems perspective, it is difficult to predict where this provider mix will go, but again there is a richness of diversity from which policy needs to build.

In Alice, there is nothing like the same range of providers as in the more urbanized Gulu. However, the IBLN brings together individual and community actors, but the key institutional players are public tertiary institutions, with the local public TVET college being notable by its relative absence from this social ecosystem for skills, although it has interacted in the network a few times. This reflects both its limited autonomy and a history of policy bifurcation between industrial and agricultural training, with public TVET colleges focused on the latter even where there is far more agriculture than industry.

Finally, in eThekwini, we need to distinguish between what is happening around the Port of Durban and an initiative at the secondary port of Richards Bay. Around the long-established Port of Durban, we see a complex infrastructure of private skills providers of various sizes and a large parastatal training provider. This latter provider reflects the South African history of public sector apprenticeships as a key tool of economic and social policy stretching back a century to the 1922 Apprenticeship Act. Three large public TVET colleges are present in the city, but they are only weakly engaged with the maritime sector, though there are stronger historic links to other sectors such as automotives. Public tertiary providers are more aligned with the maritime ecosystem, providing high-level skills to the industry. There appears to be relatively limited opportunities for the public colleges to get involved in this well-functioning ecosystem. It is noteworthy, therefore, that the main public skills intervention as part of the maritime infrastructural investments was not in the Port of Durban but 100 miles north at Richards Bay. The uMfolozi Maritime Academy is a sizeable attempt to enter the maritime skills ecosystem of KwaZulu-Natal.

It is also deliberately intended to insert more of an equity and inclusion agenda into recruitment into the sector. However, it is too early to judge whether it will be able to move sufficiently into the core of the network to be able to meet its objectives.

All four ecosystems point to the complexity needed in thinking about private provision from a policy perspective (Akoojee, 2011). Clearly, context matters hugely. It is apparent that in none of these ecosystems do public VET providers play a dominating role, though UPIK and uMfolozi aspire to importance. This raises interesting questions about what the state should do when skills ecosystems are already reasonably strong without a large public provision presence. Does it make sense to try to insert public providers into such ecosystems, as in the UPIK and uMfolozi cases? If not, how does the state intervene to address equity concerns or, perhaps increasingly, environmental imperatives? Are there other sectors where the dynamics are different, making large-scale public interventions in provision more feasible? How do these get identified? In contexts where formal industry does not dominate, what is the role of public provision and what should its relationship with other forms of provision be? There are good historical examples of positive relationships between public providers and the informal sector, for instance around opening college workshops out-of-hours for use by local producers (King and McGrath, 2002). Can these be replicated?

Universities as social ecosystem actors

Our focus in this book is on VET, but in Chapter 8 we focus on universities as important actors in Alice and Gulu. This opens up some consideration of what these cases have to say for the debate about developmental universities. In parallel to VET 2.0, an African strand of a wider southern notion of the 'developmental university' emerged in the late 1960s (Yesufu, 1973). It sought to move higher education away from elite formation and the transmission of northern knowledge, advocating instead 'the grounding of universities' teaching and research agendas in the "real" problems of African development, around rural marginalisation, poverty and the emergence of urban informal settlements and work' (McGrath et al, 2021: 886). Our discussion in Chapter 8, however, perhaps can better be seen as part of a more recent global movement to see universities' development role as being about the promotion of social entrepreneurship. Their particular contexts, including the presence of key individuals, has allowed both Gulu and Rhodes universities to play a role as innovation catalysts in our case studies. Nonetheless, there are wider questions about how such activities are made more sustainable and are replicated.

Towards a new language for thinking about VET policy and practice

We have shown in this chapter how an expanded social ecosystems perspective on skills formation can inform existing debates about VET policy and practice. However, more radically, the approach points to a new way of thinking about what should be the key future debates. Here, we will very briefly introduce a new lexicon for VET thinking that can help us in the wider task of 'reimagining our futures together', as the title of the International Commission on the Futures of Education (2021) report puts it (see also Buchanan et al, 2020 for elements of a new VET lexicon). This phrase of 'reimagining our futures together' needs highlighting. Our intention in this book is to share some of our collective work of reimagining *and* to invite others to do this urgent task with us.

The language of ecosystems leads to the notion of nurturing and to the question of how we can nurture social ecosystems as a way of building VET institutions, both in the sense of providers and rules. This leads on to how we can promote facilitating verticalities and encourage collaborative horizontalities. From this flows a need to focus on strengthening mediators and mediating activity. Our approach recognizes that there are not just anchor institutions but also anchor individuals who are central to the well functioning of social ecosystems. This turns our attention to how we might cherish and nourish these individuals, who might also be thought of as catalytic, in Finegold's language. Our strong focus in this book on relational agency leads to the importance of thinking about how we unlock this agency. However, in stressing agency we must always remember the role that structure plays alongside this within a laminated whole, and that agency is a socially constituted collective act as much as an individual act (Lotz-Sisitka, 2018). In other words, agents act in activity systems around shared or partially shared motives, working with others to advance aspects of shared activity (such as mediation activity in the social ecosystem for skills). This is well explained by Sannino (2020), who shows how transformative agency emerges in collectives.

All of this moves beyond the conventional command and control approach of states without shifting to a celebration of market forces. Rather, it is at heart a relational approach that also contains a notion of subsidiarity in trying to emphasize that decisions should be made at the appropriate level rather than stressing either centralization or decentralization (Scoones, 2016).

We have stressed the importance of moving towards skills for just transitions, but we have also confessed that we are still at an early stage in that journey. In reflecting more on this, we build here particularly on Rosenberg et al (2020). We have followed their argument that we need to move towards a new conversation between political economy and political ecology, demonstrated most clearly in Chapter 3. We have argued that VET policy and practice has largely been complicit in environmental destruction; VET research, in turn, is complicit in this by refusing to engage with the consequences. A quick survey of the five leading VET journals, for instance, shows only eight sustainability-related articles in the past decade. It is only with Rosenberg et al that an attempt to conceptualize skills for just transitions has begun in earnest.

VET must be reconceptualized to think of what skills we need to learn for what work and for what lives, and these lives must be seen as being lived with other humans, with other species and with the planet. VET must impart skills for us to get from where we are today, facing an environmental and, hence, existential crisis, to a place of sustainability and flourishing. This requires VET systems that can be proactive in engaging with the challenge of just transition. We believe that social ecosystems for skills are at the heart of this, as neither marketized individualism nor state-led development will provide solutions. However, we also need to remember that 'skills will not save us' (see Allais, 2012; Buchanan et al, 2020) but must be part of wider efforts to deliver just transitions.

Following on from Shalem and Allais (2018), Lotz-Sisitka and Ramsarup (2020) propose thinking about green work at four levels, and we apply this to a reimagined VET here in Figure 9.1. First, there is a normative dimension, in which we need to think beyond the narrow, unquestioning belief in VET for employability and interrogate what VET should be for (see, for instance, McGrath, 2012). Our cases are particularly valuable in showing the failings of the orthodoxy, but they also point forward, albeit partially, to other possible visions. Here we argue that human flourishing within planetary boundaries (as in Raworth's [2017] doughnut) is what VET should be seeking to support.

Second, there is an epistemic dimension. It is clear that new forms of work bring with them new knowledge and new knowledge requirements. We cannot predict exactly what will happen to existing jobs or which new ones will emerge, but they will all be shaped by technological, environmental and societal change, and this will impact on their knowledge content. We have shown how the knowledge of many different occupations, including that of vocational teacher, is shifting rapidly and dramatically, and suggested that VET policy and practice needs to respond to new knowledge challenges but also new opportunities for different patterns of knowledge sharing.

Third, there is a social dimension. Our book highlights the importance of new configurations of social actors and new relationalities, seen here through a social ecosystems lens. To achieve just transitions, it will be crucial that socially inclusive and democratic deliberation and practice spaces are opened up and defended. Some of the ecosystems we examine, particularly in the Gulu and Alice contexts, point in this direction.

Figure 9.1: VET 4.0's ontological, epistemic, social and normative dynamics

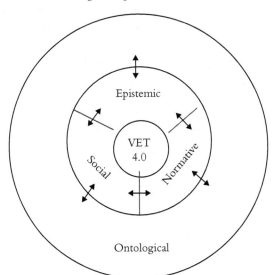

Fourth, Lotz–Sisitka and Ramsarup (2020) added a further dimension: the ontological. The existential nature of the environmental crisis calls us to think ontologically about how work contributes to the wellbeing of people, other species and the planet. This recalls some of the European VET tradition that has drawn on notions of *bildung*, of fulfilling one's purpose. In this view, VET is fundamentally about becoming fully human, about creating ways to live, work and learn in harmony with other humans, other species and the planet. Reimagining VET in this light is the single biggest challenge for the field today. Working our way into this is, however, not impossible, as also shown across the pages of this book. Importantly, our work resonates with a wider global call for a reimagined relational role for postschool VET. The International Commission on the Futures of Education (2021) says the following regarding VET:

> Post-secondary technical and vocational institutions, including community colleges and polytechnics, should also be seen not only as training institutions but as venues of applied research. They should give prominence to the importance of productive capabilities in our individual and collective lives, to the effective functioning of learning societies, to the numerous pathways for meaningful work, and to the potential for integration, partnerships, and cooperation between various sectors and communities. The local character of many vocational institutions closely connected to the community

provides an opportunity to foster thriving local cultures of learning. Local communities have distinctive connections to the knowledge commons, and technical and vocational institutes can contribute to developing insights about their application in distinctive, contextually relevant ways. (International Commission on the Futures of Education, 2021: 76)

Giving meaning to this recommendation is likely to require some of the approaches and considerations that we have given to reimagining a new social contract for VET Africa in this book. The exploratory nature of our work, as well as the caveats and recommendations for further research, therefore, could be taken forward within this wider framing of reimagining education for a more sustainable, just and inclusive future, and the reframed social contract that is needed for VET to become more relevant to the times that young people are growing up in, and the futures they face. While the need for this is pressing in the Ugandan and South African contexts we have discussed in this book, the same urgency applies globally.

Afterword: Towards a More Just and Sustainable Research Practice

VET Africa 4.0 Collective

In a blog post some of us wrote about the project, Monk et al (2021b) argue that '[t]he conjuncture of a renewed decolonisation debate, the pandemic and greater climate action urgency provide a moment for revisiting long standing aspirations towards just and sustainable research practices'.

In this short afterword, we reflect critically on how we tried to move towards more just practices both internally and externally. We will start by considering our internal practices.

The project was a partnership between four research chairs, and the team also included one vice-chancellor and two others with leadership roles within their schools. This helped reduce power imbalances at least at senior levels within the project. Although it was heavily driven in the application phase by a prospective principal investigator (PI) from the northern partner institution, the intention was always to give the funder an 'honest enough' account of what the project would do, while leaving considerable latitude for the team to decide on this subsequently. The seniority of some team members from each country meant that all major decisions had to be negotiated. Importantly, the key conceptual framing of ecosystems was implicit in the proposal but was made central later, based on work already started by the Rhodes team, as reflected upon in Chapter 9.

In the process of the project, there was a determination to maximize wider team involvement in decision making. A series of workshops punctuated the project, in Oxford, Gulu, Makhanda, Johannesburg, Kenton and online. Most team members participated in most of these events, and almost all travelled to at least one of the other two countries. However, presence is not the same as participation and, although attempts were made to run these events inclusively, existing power dynamics, of course, were not simply erased. At times, the meetings perhaps better resembled 'fish bowl' exercises in which an outer circle observed the discussions of an inner circle. As part of our practice, senior team members built a habit of checking in with others informally between sessions on what they had observed and what their reflections were. A good example of our practice came in January 2020 when, based in the Eastern Cape, we moved from fieldwork visits to teaching sessions on theory, to the development of four case-based visual representations of Spours' model showing collaborative horizontalities, facilitating verticalities and mediation. In the latter exercise, it was the more junior researchers who took the lead, particularly where their crucial knowledge about local dynamics came to the fore.

Inevitably, imbalances of power of multiple kinds did still exist. The bulk of the money flowed from United Kingdom Research and Innovation (UKRI) through the University of Nottingham, and the PI and the university were ultimately responsible for reporting and accounting. National allocations of funding were negotiated by the senior team members and reflected the very different costs of doing things in different settings. UKRI made COVID-adjustment funding available only to Nottingham, a clear injustice. However, a significant underspend in Nottingham's travel budget, also due to COVID-19, meant that the national budgets in both Uganda and South Africa got five figure (sterling) boosts, although without an extension of time in which to spend this. This did, however, provide additional and much welcomed funding for global south postgraduate scholars who also found themselves under pressure due to COVID-19 challenges.

Inequalities in resources were not just a north–south thing. Gulu is a much younger university than either of its South African counterparts, and Uganda has not been able to fund higher education initiatives in anything like the same way as the South African Research Chairs' Initiative. Both South African partner teams were organized around such chairs and had an ability to cofund aspects of the project and subsidize staff time. That working for a northern funder should require such cofunding, however, is problematic. There was also no direct capturing of the southern investment from a funding and time perspective, which often shows equal or high levels of both in-kind and actual expenditure investment from the global south in such partnership initiatives. This is an important 'corrective measure' that would facilitate a stronger sense of two-way investment and, thus, more equitable partnership constitution, rather than one-way funded investments from institutions such as the Global Challenges Research Fund, although the latter is appreciated.

There was an ambition in the project to support research capacity development, acknowledging that both South African partners were already well resourced in this regard. A writing workshop was delivered by the PI for the junior members of the team, and he was a resource person for a South African early career vocational education and training (VET) researchers' conference, hosted by the University of the Western Cape, at which the wider cohort of Wits' doctoral VET researchers were present. Other senior staff presented sessions for the wider team during the project's lifespan. Several of the more junior team members presented at conferences, both nationally and internationally, in so far as the distinction held in times of COVID. Several are working on journal articles jointly with senior team members, including some as lead authors. A number have received funding for further studies. Most notably, a Commonwealth Shared Scholarship allowed a team member who was a Rhodes doctoral student to spend a year in Nottingham, while one of the Gulu team went on to further studies at Wits.

You will have noticed that we describe the book as collectively authored and give 20 names in alphabetical order in the acknowledgements. You will also have seen that each chapter has a far smaller group of named authors. Both of these decisions were discussed and were not entirely unanimously supported. That the 20 of us were involved, though to different extents, is a fair reflection. Acknowledgement of this seemed preferable to the team as a whole to naming only some or announcing some hierarchy of involvement. Many of us would have also preferred not to have chapter author names. However, we decided that these were important for nonprofessorial colleagues who had been centrally involved in writing chapters, given the wider climate of performativity in universities internationally. These key chapter authors were relatively easy to identify, but we had more trouble over the notion of acknowledging editorial roles. While most of the team made some comments on draft chapters, a handful gave fuller editorial comments and even fewer did detailed editorial work across the book. The final decision was not to acknowledge these individuals directly and to see their work as collegial. It is also worth noting that this eventual editing was originally envisaged to be a more limited copyediting task as we had planned to get the core writing team together for a writing retreat. COVID-19 made this impossible, and so the editing process required more focus on tying the chapters more closely together. Delays and the ending of funding meant that only about half the team were active in this process, and only four of us did final reviews of the whole manuscript.

Turning to our external relations, as Monk et al wrote, 'Like VET itself, VET research in Africa has typically been extractive.' Much of VET research in Africa has been funded by international agencies or, in South Africa, by national government and local foundations. Indeed, several of us have done such research. However, we need to reflect that we often went into the field as the agents of the powerful, and that respondents perceived us thus. As Monk et al put it: 'Practitioners have largely believed that researchers exist to judge them, with most judgments being negative. This has generated a legacy of mistrust.' Moreover, such research has tended to take data away from the field and those whom it came from, to profit others in the wealthier parts of the south or, more usually, in the north.

The two more conventional VET case studies in this book did not fully escape from this extractive legacy. We came to the Hoima case because the PI had been the lead consultant for the Skills for Oil and Gas in Africa (SOGA) inception phase. His access to agency and oil company staff was important but clearly distorting of the research process. As there was an external evaluation of SOGA happening during our data-gathering phase, it was crucial to make it clear that we were not evaluating SOGA and were interested in it as part of a wider exploration of skills formation in the Albertine region. In eThekwini, we did not have any Wits staff on the ground, but one of our team was a well-known local industrial researcher. This again facilitated access to more senior and formalized contacts. However, in both cases we were far less grounded in the wider community or in the kinds of activities we were researching than was the case in Gulu and Alice. With limited embeddedness in the former two case study sites, lockdown constrained possibilities for trust building.

As will have become clear as you read the book, there was considerably greater embeddedness in the Alice and Gulu cases, which involved important elements of action research, both before and during the project. These point towards less extractive, more equitable ways of researching VET. In Chapter 8, we talk about this as part of as process of developing a scholarship of engagement.

In David Monk's contribution to the UKFIET blog, he notes from his perspective as a lecturer in Gulu:

> We decided from the outset that our research should practically contribute to youth livelihoods and community development by developing transdisciplinary and inclusive ecosystems of learning in VET, where research is but one component among many diverse learning needs.
>
> For example, in Gulu, it became apparent that institutions are short of equipment such as tractors. So, we gathered together a diverse group of people from agriculture who decided on, developed and tested a pilot programme for tractor driving and repair. The process required negotiation among parties with diverse backgrounds and differing needs. NGOs, government, university, private sector, traditional cultural leaders and students were all involved. In the process of working through the research we debated curriculum reform, pedagogy and assessment, extension work and history of cooperatives, funding and programme development and initiated a longer-term partnership for learning and advocacy in VET. The learning here was primarily oriented towards learning how to learn together, and empowering local communities to experiment with new ideas without fear of failure. The practical application of the research was far more visible and engaging

> for implementers than a policy document. We also gained credibility as did our findings of democratising overly hierarchical structures because we visibly engaged in democratising the research process ourselves. (Monk et al, 2021)

A similar scholarship of engagement characterized the work in Alice, which had a history of emergence since 2014 where a learning network formed involving multiple actors to address local challenges of water and food security among farmers who had been given back their land. The local agricultural institute, collaborating with universities in the vicinity, formed a social skills ecosystem that to this day continues its coengaged learning approach via both formal and informal means and means of boundary crossing between formal and informal learning institutions. This provided an emergent and grounded understanding of the potential for reflexively articulating this work over time within a social skills ecosystem approach as also reflected in earlier publications (Lotz-Sisitka and Pesanayi, 2020).

We found ourselves mirroring the social ecosystems approach in coming to operate within its mediation space between the vertical and the horizontal, with the research being led by anchor individuals in anchor institutions. The teams' combination of local and official knowledge allowed them to operate between formal and informal settings, and between national and local actors. Often, we needed to transgress the historically normative or 'proper' ways of acting to create

> spaces within and between institutions in order to follow the needs of the situation, rather than the protocols of the bureaucracy. Often, this meant working at the fringes of institutional mandates, to create wriggle room for ourselves and other actors in order to come together to form new connective tissues and ideas of what VET could and should be. (Monk et al, 2021)

It also required substantial empathy and social innovation, and a willingness to cross traditional institutional and normative boundaries. Here we learned from Pesanayi's (2019a) work showing the significance of these boundary crossing learning processes, often motivated by empathy and processes of reflexively coming to understand the limitations of past models for contemporary needs and demands.

Collaborative processes always mean letting go of control, and the pandemic made this even more necessary. We had to let the project evolve, like an ecosystem, and we had to follow its turns and tempos, while remaining mindful of official funder timelines and requirements. In attempting to genuinely value multiple knowledges, we needed to unlearn and reflect on what we simply took for granted regarding who and what mattered.

As university researchers, we must find ways of balancing the immediacy of the funded project and the need for stronger and longer-lasting bonds in the locations in which we research, while also forming new, oftentimes nontraditional, relations across our institutions and our related partner networks. This is particularly challenging for northern researchers and will be even more so in the light of our slow awakening to what the environmental crisis means for fieldwork and for international travel more generally.

References

Academy of Science of South Africa (2017) 'Revitalising agricultural education and training in South Africa: consensus study concise report', Pretoria: Department of Science and Technology.

Acemoglu, D. and Robinson, J. (2010) 'Why is Africa poor?', *Economic History of Developing Regions*, 25(1): 21–50.

Acemoglu, D., Johnson, S. and Robinson, J. (2001) 'The colonial origins of comparative development', *American Economic Review*, 91(5): 1369–401.

Acemoglu, D., Johnson, S. and Robinson, J. (2002) 'Reversal of fortune', *Quarterly Journal of Economics*, 117(4): 1231–94.

Adeyemi, M. and Adeyinka, A. (2003) 'The principles and content of African traditional education', *Educational Philosophy and Theory*, 35(4): 425–40.

African Union (2007) 'Strategy to revitalize technical and vocational education and training (TVET) in Africa', Addis Ababa: African Union.

Agarwal, A. and Narain, S. (1993) 'Towards green villages', in W. Sachs (ed) *Global Ecology*, London: Zed, 242–56.

Agbedahin, A. and Lotz-Sisitka, H. (2019) 'Mainstreaming education for sustainable development: elaborating the role of position-practice systems using seven laminations of scale', *Journal of Critical Realism*, 18(2): 103–22.

Akoojee, S. (2011) *Private Further Education in South Africa*, Saarbrücken: VDM.

Alava, H. (2018) '"Acholi youth are lost": young, Christian and (a)political in Uganda', in E. Oinas, H. Onoder and L. Suurpää (eds) *What Politics? Youth and Political Engagement in Africa*, Leiden: Brill, 158–78.

Alla-Mensah, J. (2021) 'A capability approach to the well-being of informal apprentices and journeypersons in the automotive trade in Ghana', unpublished PhD thesis, University of Nottingham.

Allais, S. (2007) 'Why the South African NQF failed: lessons for countries wanting to introduce national qualifications frameworks', *European Journal of Education*, 42(4): 523–47.

Allais, S. (2012) 'Will skills save us? Rethinking the relationships between vocational education, skills development policies, and social policy in South Africa', *International Journal of Educational Development*, 32(5): 632–42.

Allais, S. (2013) 'Understanding the persistence of low skills in South Africa', in J. Daniels, P. Naidoo, P. Pillay and R. Southall (eds) *New South African Review 3*, Johannesburg: Wits University Press, 201–20.

Allais, S. (2014) *Selling Out Education*, Rotterdam: Sense.

Allais, S. (2020a) 'Vocational education and inequalities in transitions from education to work in three African countries', in D. Francis, I. Valodia and E. Webster (eds) *Inequality*, Abingdon: Routledge, 141–80.

Allais, S. (2020b) 'Skills for industrialisation in sub-Saharan African countries', *Journal of Vocational Education and Training*, https://doi.org/10.1080/13636820.2020.1782455.

Allais, S. (2022) 'Enhancing skills linkage to the productive sectors in Africa', Geneva: ILO (forthcoming).

Allais, S. and Marock, C. (2020) 'Educating for work in the time of Covid-19: moving beyond simplistic ideas of supply and demand', *Southern African Review of Education*, 26(1): 62–79.

Allais, S. and Wedekind, V. (2020) 'Targets, TVET and transformation', in A. Wulff (ed) *Grading Goal 4*, Leiden: Brill, 322–38.

Allais, S., Shalem, Y., Marock, C., Ramsarup, P., Mlauzi, K., Khunou, B. et al (2022) 'New qualifications and competencies: trends in Sub-Saharan Africa TVET', technical report for UNESCO-UNEVOC, Centre for Researching Education and Labour, University of the Witwatersrand.

Altvater, E. (2016) 'The capitalocene, or, geoengineering against capitalism's planetary boundaries', in J. Moore (ed) *Anthropocene or Capitalocene?* Oakland: PM Press, 138–53.

Amanzi for Food (nd) 'Amanzi for food', https://amanziforfood.co.za, accessed on 26 July 2022.

Anderson, D. (2009) 'Productivism and ecologism', in J. Fien, R. Maclean and M.-G. Park (eds) *Work, Learning and Sustainable Development*, Dordrecht: Springer, 35–58.

Anderson, P. and Warhurst, C. (2012) 'Lost in translation? Skills policy and the shift to skill ecosystems', in D. Nash and A. Dolphin (eds) *Complex New World*, London: Institute for Public Policy Research, 109–20.

Angucia, M. (2010) *Broken Citizenship*, Amsterdam: Rozenberg.

Angucia, M. and Amone-P'Olak, K. (2010) 'The interface between early school leaving and the conflict in Northern Uganda', in J. Zeelen, J. van der Linden, D. Nampota and M. Ngabirano (eds) *The Burden of Educational Exclusion*, Rotterdam/Boston/Taipei: Sense, 127–41.

Angucia, M., Zeelen, J. and De Jong, G. (2010) 'Researching the reintegration of formerly abducted children in Northern Uganda through action research: experiences and reflections', *Journal of Community and Applied Social Psychology*, 20(3): 217–31.

Archer, M. (1995) *Realist Social Theory*, Cambridge: Cambridge University Press.

Archer, M. (1998) 'Realism and morphogenesis', in M. Archer, R. Bhaskar, A. Collier, T. Lawson and A. Norrie (eds) *Critical Realism: Essential Readings*, London: Routledge, 356–81.

Austin, G. (2008a) 'Resources, techniques, and strategies south of the Sahara', *Economic History Review*, 61(3): 587–624.

Austin, G. (2008b) 'The "reversal of fortune" thesis and the compression of history', *Journal of International Development*, 20(8): 996–1027.

Austin, G. (2015) 'The economics of colonialism in Africa', in C. Monga and J.-Y. Lin (eds) *The Oxford Handbook of Africa and Economics*, Oxford: Oxford University Press, 522–35.

Avis, J. (2020) *Vocational Education in the Fourth Industrial Revolution*, Cham: Palgrave Pivot.

Baas, L. (1998) 'Cleaner production and industrial ecosystems, a Dutch experience', *Journal of Cleaner Production*, 6(3–4): 189–97.

Barnett, R. (2006) 'Vocational knowledge and vocational pedagogy', in M. Young and J. Gamble (eds) *Knowledge, Curriculum and Qualifications for South African Further Education*, Cape Town: HSRC Press, 143–57.

Belay, M. and Mugambe, B. (2021) 'Bill Gates: stop telling Africans what kind of agriculture Africa needs; among other things, we might simply not agree', *Scientific American*, 6 July, https://www.scientificamerican.com/article/bill-gates-stop-telling-africans-what-kind-of-agriculture-africans-need/?previewid=0144FCCA-AADD-4DA3-A978B39874AD14D2, accessed on 26 July 2022.

Bhaskar, R. (1975) *A Realist Theory of Science*, Leeds: Leeds Books.

Bhaskar, R. (1979) *The Possibility of Naturalism*, Brighton: Wheatsheaf.

Bhaskar, R. (2013) 'Prolegomenon: the consequences of the revindication of philosophical ontology for philosophy and social theory', in M. Archer and A. Maccarini (eds) *Engaging with the World*, Abingdon: Routledge, 9–28.

Bjornlund, V., Bjornlund, H. and Van Rooyen, A. (2020) 'Why agricultural production in sub-Saharan Africa remains low compared to the rest of the world', *International Journal of Water Resources Development*, 36(S1): S20–S53.

Blaak, M. (2021) 'The normative practitioner', unpublished PhD thesis, University of Groningen.

Blaak, M., Openjuru, G. and Zeelen, J. (2013) 'Non-formal vocational education in Uganda', *International Journal of Educational Development*, 33: 88–97.

Black, S. (2021) 'Lifelong learning as cruel optimism: considering the discourses of lifelong learning and techno-solutionism in South African education', *International Review of Education*, https://doi.org/10.1007/s11159-021-09924-8.

Blom, R. (2016) 'Throwing good money after bad: barriers South African vocational teachers experience in becoming competent educators', in A. Kraak, A. Paterson and K. Boka (eds) *Change Management in TVET Colleges*, Cape Town: African Minds, 47–63.

Bond, P. (ed) (2002) *Unsustainable South Africa*, Pietermaritzburg: University of KwaZulu Natal Press.

Bond, P. and Hallowes, D. (2002) 'The environment of apartheid-capitalism: discourses and issues', in P. Bond (ed) *Unsustainable South Africa*, Pietermaritzburg: University of KwaZulu Natal Press, 23–44.

Boog, B., Preece, J., Slagter, M. and Zeelen, J. (eds) (2008) *Towards Quality Improvement of Action Research*, Rotterdam/Taipei: Sense.

Bookchin, M. (1990) *The Philosophy of Social Ecology*, Montreal: Black Rose.

Bos, J., Brown, R. and Farrelly, M. (2013) 'A design framework for creating social learning situations', *Global Environmental Change*, 23(2): 398–412.

Bourdieu, P. (1977) *Outline of a Theory of Practice*, Cambridge: Cambridge University Press.

Bourke, A. (2013) 'Universities, civil society and the global agenda of community-engaged research', *Globalisation, Societies and Education*, 11(4): 498–519.

Boyer, E. (1996) 'The scholarship of engagement', *Bulletin of the American Academy of Arts and Sciences*, 49(7): 18–33.

Branch, A. (2013) 'Gulu in war … and peace? The town as camp in northern Uganda', *Urban Studies*, 50(15): 3152–67.

Braudel, F. (1986) [1949] *The Mediterranean and the Mediterranean World in the Age of Philip II: Volume 1*, London: Fontana.

Brown, P., Lauder, H. and Cheung, S.-Y. (2020) *The Death of Human Capital?* Oxford: Oxford University Press.

Brown, T. (2022) 'Skill ecosystems in the global south: informality, inequality, and community setting', *Geoforum*, 132: 10–19.

Brzinsky-Fay, C. (2011) 'School-to-work transitions in international comparison', unpublished PhD thesis, University of Tampere.

Buchanan, J. (2020) 'Productivity Commission – Interim Report – National Agreement on Skills and Workforce Development Review', University of Sydney Business School.

Buchanan, J., Anderson, P. and Power, G. (2017) 'Skill ecosystems', in C. Warhurst, K., Mayhew, D., Finegold and J. Buchanan (eds) *Oxford Handbook of Skills and Training*, Oxford: Oxford University Press, 444–65.

Buchanan, J., Allais, S., Anderson, M., Calvo, R., Peter, S. and Pietsch, T. (2020) 'The futures of work: what education can and can't do', background paper for the UNESCO Futures of Education report, https://unesdoc.unesco.org/ark:/48223/pf0000374435, accessed on 2 December 2021.

Buchanan, J., Schofield, K., Briggs, C., Considine, G., Hager, P., Hawke, G. et al (2001) 'Beyond flexibility: skills and work in the future', NSW Board of Vocational Education and Training, http://www.bvet.nsw.gov.au/pdf/beyondflex.pdf, accessed on 1 November 2021.

Buchmann, M. and Steinhoff, A. (2017) 'Co-development of student agency components and its impact on educational attainment: theoretical and methodological considerations introduction', *Research in Human Development*, 14(2): 96–105.

Burawoy, M. (2013) 'Marxism after Polanyi', in M. Williams and V. Satgar (eds) *Marxisms in the 21st Century*, Johannesburg: Wits University Press, 34–52.

Burkitt, I. (2016) 'Relational agency: relational sociology, agency and interaction', *European Journal of Social Theory*, 19(3): 322–39.

Burns, E. (2010) 'Capturing the diversity of transition from a multidisciplinary perspective', *Australian Journal of Career Development*, 19(3): 43–51.

Busemeyer, M. (2014) *Skills and Inequality*, Cambridge: Cambridge University Press.

Buthelezi, Z. (2018) 'From policy to curriculum in South African vocational teacher education', *Journal of Vocational Education and Training*, 70(3): 364–83.

Bynner, J. (2001) 'British youth transitions in comparative perspective', *Journal of Youth Studies*, 4(1): 5–23.

Callaway, A. (1964) 'Nigeria's indigenous education', *Odu*, 1(1): 62–79.

Cerceau, J., Junqua, G., Gonzalez, C., Lopez-Ferber, M. and Mat, N. (2012) 'Industrial ecology and the building of territorial knowledge: DEPART, a French research action program implemented in harbor territories', *Procedia – Social and Behavioral Sciences*, 40: 622–30.

Cheru, F. (2016) 'Developing countries and the right to development: a retrospective and prospective African view', *Third World Quarterly*, 37(7): 1268–83.

Cheru, F. and Obi, C. (2011) 'Chinese and Indian engagement in Africa: competitive or mutually reinforcing strategies?', *Journal of International Affairs*, 64(2): 91–110.

Christensen, T. and Laegreid, P. (2007) 'The whole of government approach to public service reform', *Public Administration Review*, 67(6): 1059–66.

Cock, J. (2019) 'Resistance to coal inequalities and the possibilities of a just transition in South Africa', *Development Southern Africa*, 36(6): 860–73.

Coombs, P. and Ahmed, M. (1974) *Education for Rural Development*, New York: Praeger.

Cooper, A., Swartz, S. and Ramphalile, M. (2021) 'Youth of the Global South and why they are worth studying', in S. Swartz, A. Cooper, C. Batan and L. Kropff Causa (eds) *The Oxford Handbook of Global South Youth Studies*, Oxford: Oxford University Press, 32–54.

Cooper, D. (2011) 'The UCT idea of social responsiveness: engaged scholarship must be at its conceptual core for academic staff', Social Responsiveness Report 2010, University of Cape Town.

Cox, D. and Prestridge, S. (2020) 'Understanding fully online teaching in vocational education', *Research and Practice in Technology Enhanced Learning*, 15(16).

Cruikshank, J. (2003) *Realism and Sociology*, London: Routledge.

Deissenger, T. and Gonon, P. (2021) 'Towards an international comparative history of vocational education and training', *Journal of Vocational Education and Training*, 73(2): 191–6.

De Jaeghere, J. (2017) *Educating Entrepreneurial Citizens*, Abingdon: Routledge.

De Jaeghere, J. (2020) 'Reconceptualizing educational capabilities: a relational capability theory for redressing inequalities', *Journal of Human Development and Capabilities*, 21(1): 17–35.

Denov, M., Green, A., Lakor, A. and Arach, J. (2018) 'Mothering in the aftermath of forced marriage and wartime rape: the complexities of motherhood in post-war northern Uganda', *Journal of Motherhood Initiative*, 9(1): 158–76.

Department for International Development (2008) 'Climate change in Uganda: understanding the implications and appraising the response', https://reliefweb.int/report/uganda/climate-change-uganda-understanding-implications-and-appraising-response, accessed on 15 November 2021.

Department of Environment, Forestry and Fisheries (2019) 'National climate change adaptation strategy', Tshwane: DEFF.

Durr, S. (2020) 'Enabling social learning to stimulate value creation towards a circular economy: the case of Food for Us food redistribution mobile application development process', unpublished MEd dissertation, Rhodes University.

Eakin, H., Eriksen, S., Eikeland, P.-O. and Oyen, C. (2011) 'Public sector reform and governance for adaptation: implications of new public management for adaptive capacity in Mexico and Norway', *Environmental Management*, 47(3): 338–51.

Ecclestone, K. (2009) 'Lost and found in transitions', in J. Field, J. Gallacher and R. Ingram (eds) *Researching Transitions in Lifelong Learning*, London: Routledge, 9–27.

Edwards, A. (2005) 'Relational agency: learning to be a resourceful practitioner', *International Journal of Educational Research*, 43(3): 168–82.

Edwards, A. (2010) *Being an Expert Professional Practitioner*, Dordrecht: Springer.

Edwards, A. (2011) 'Building common knowledge at the boundaries between professional practices: relational agency and relational expertise in systems of distributed expertise', *International Journal of Educational Research*, 50(1): 33–9.

Elder, G. (1994) 'Time, human agency and social change: perspectives on the life course', *Social Psychology Quarterly*, 57(1): 4–15.

Elder, G., Johnson, M. and Crosnoe, R. (2003) 'The emergence and development of life course theory', in J. Mortimer and M. Shanahan (eds) *Handbook of the Life Course*, New York: Kluwer Academic/Plenum, 3–19.

Elhacham, E., Ben-Uri, L., Grozovski, J., Bar-On, Y. and Milo, R. (2020) 'Global human-made mass exceeds all living biomass', *Nature*, 588: 442–8.

Engeström, Y. (2001) 'Expansive learning at work: toward an activity theoretical reconceptualization', *Journal of Education and Work*, 14(1): 133–56.

Engeström, Y. and Sannino, A. (2010) 'Studies of expansive learning: foundations, findings and future challenges', *Educational Research Review*, 5(1): 1–24.

Engeström, Y., Sannino, A. and Virkkunen, J. (2014) 'On the methodological demands of formative interventions', *Mind, Culture, and Activity*, 21(2): 118–28.

Esteva, G. and Prakash, M. (1997) 'From global thinking to local thinking', in M. Rahnema and V. Bawtree (eds) *The Post-Development Reader*, London: Zed, 277–98.

Evetts, J. (2009) 'New professionalism and new public management: changes, continuities and consequences', *Comparative Sociology*, 8: 247–66.

Fafunwa, A. (1974) *History of Education in Nigeria*, London: George Allen and Unwin.

Fenwick, T. (2013) 'Understanding transitions in professional practice and learning: towards new questions for research', *Journal of Workplace Learning*, 25(6): 352–67.

Ferguson, J. (2006) *Global Shadows*, Durham, NC: Duke University Press.

Ferguson, N. (2003) *Empire*, London: Allen Lane.

Field, J. (2012) 'Transitions and lifelong learning: signposts, pathways, road closed?', *Lifelong Learning in Europe*, 1: 5–11.

Finegold, D. (1999) 'Creating self-sustaining, high-skill ecosystems', *Oxford Review of Economic Policy*, 15(1): 60–81.

Finegold, D. and Soskice, D. (1988) 'The failure of training in Britain: analysis and prescription', *Oxford Review of Economic Policy*, 4(3): 21–53.

Fitchett, J. (2021) 'Climate change has already hit southern Africa: here's how we know', The Conversation, 24 October, https://theconversation.com/climate-change-has-already-hit-southern-africa-heres-how-we-know-169 062, accessed on 24 October 2021.

Fluitman, F. (ed) (1989) 'Training for work in the informal sector', Geneva: ILO.

Forsyth, T. (2003) *Critical Political Ecology*, London: Routledge.

Foster, P. (1965) 'The vocational school fallacy in development planning', in A. Anderson and M. Bowman (eds) *Education and Economic Development*, Chicago: Aldine, 142–67.

Frayne, B. and Crush, J. (2017) 'Food supply and urban–rural links in Southern African cities', in B. Frayne, J. Crush and C. McCordic (eds) *Food and Nutrition Security in Southern African Cities*, London: Routledge, 34–47.

Freire, P. (1970) *Pedagogy of the Oppressed*, New York: Seabury.

Friedman, V. (2011) 'Revisiting social space: relational thinking about organizational change', *Research in Organizational Change and Development*, 19: 233–57.

Friedman, V., Sykes, I. and Strauch, M. (2014) 'Expanding the realm of the possible: "enclaves" and the transformation of field', paper presented at the Academy of Management Annual Meeting, Philadelphia, Pennsylvania.

Fynn-Bruey, R. (ed) (2021) *Patriarchy and Gender in Africa*, Lanham: Lexington Books.

Gamble, J. (2016) 'From labour market to labour process: finding a basis for curriculum in TVET', *International Journal of Training Research*, 14(3): 215–29.

Gamble, J. (2021) 'The legacy imprint of apprenticeship trajectories under conditions of segregation and Apartheid in South Africa', *Journal of Vocational Education and Training*, 73(2): 258–77.

German Agency for International Development (2015) 'Skills for Oil and Gas in Africa Programme: inception report', Eschborn: GIZ.

Gorz, A. (1989) *Critique of Economic Reason*, London: Verso.

Government of Uganda (2008) 'BTVET Act', Kampala: Government Printer.

Grainger, P. and Spours, K. (2018) 'A social ecosystem model: a new paradigm for skills development?', https://www.g20-insights.org/policy_briefs/a-social-ecosystem-model-a-new-paradigm-for-skills-development, accessed on 1/ November 2021.

Gruenewald, D. and Smith, G. (eds) (2014) *Place-Based Education in the Global Age*, London: Routledge.

Guha, R. and Martínez-Alier, J. (2013) *Varieties of Environmentalism*, London: Routledge.

Gupta, A. (2010) 'Grassroots green innovations for inclusive, sustainable development', in A. López-Claros (ed) *The Innovation for Development Report, 2009–2010*, London: Palgrave Macmillan, 137–46.

Habiyaremye, A., Kruss, G. and Booyens, I. (2020) 'Innovation for inclusive rural transformation: the role of the state', *Innovation and Development*, 10(2):155–68.

Hall, B. (2012) '"A giant human hashtag": learning and the #Occupy movement', in B. Hall, D. Clover, J. Crowther and E. Scandrett (eds) *Learning and Education for a Better World*, Rotterdam: Sense, 125–39.

Hall, R. and Lansbury, R. (2006) 'Skills in Australia: towards workforce development and sustainable skill ecosystems', *Journal of Industrial Relations*, 48(5): 575–92.

Hardt, M. and Negri, A. (2001) *Empire*, Cambridge, MA: Harvard University Press.

Hart, K. (1973) 'Informal income opportunities and urban employment in Ghana', *Journal of Modern African Studies*, 2(1): 61–89.

Heckhausen, J. (2010) 'Globalization, social inequality, and individual agency in human development: social change for better or worse?', in R. Silbereisen and X. Chen (eds) *Social Change and Human Development*, London: Sage, 148–63.

Higher Education Quality Committee/Community Higher Education Service Partnerships (2006) 'Community engagement in higher education', Pretoria: Council on Higher Education.

Hodgson, A. and Spours, K. (2016) 'The evolution of social ecosystem thinking: its relevance for education, economic development and localities', Centre for Post-14 Education and Work, Institute of Education, University College London.

Hodgson, A. and Spours, K. (2018) 'A social ecosystem model: conceptualising and connecting working, living and learning in London's New East', ELVET Research Briefing No 3, Centre for Post-14 Education and Work, Institute of Education, University College London.

Hodkinson, R. and Sparkes, A. (1997) 'Careership: a sociological theory of career decision-making', *British Journal of Sociology of Education*, 18(1): 29–44.

International Commission on Education for the Twenty-First Century (1996) 'Learning: the treasure within', Paris: UNESCO.

International Commission on the Futures of Education (2021) 'Reimagining our futures together', Paris: UNESCO.

International Labour Office (1976) 'Employment, growth and basic needs', Geneva: ILO.

International Labour Office (2018) 'Women and men in the informal economy', Geneva: ILO.

Isenberg, D. (2010) 'How to start an entrepreneurial revolution', *Harvard Business Review* (June): 1–11.

Jjuuko, R. (2021) 'Youth transition, agricultural education and employment in Uganda', unpublished PhD thesis, University of Groningen.

Jjuuko, R., Tukundane, C. and Zeelen, J. (2019) 'Exploring agricultural vocational pedagogy in Uganda: students' experiences', *International Journal of Training Research*, 17(3): 238–51.

Jjuuko, R., Tukundane, C. and Zeelen, J. (2021) 'Reclaiming the educative power of vocational placements: experiences from agriculture education practice in Uganda', *International Journal of Training and Development*, 25(2): 144–59.

Johanson, R. and Adams, A. (2004) 'Skills development in sub-Saharan Africa', Washington: World Bank.

Jones, T. (1926) *Four Essentials of Education*, New York: Scribner's Sons.

Jordt Jørgensen, N. (2018) 'Hustling for rights: political engagements with sand in Northern Kenya', in E. Oinas, H. Onodera and L. Suurpää (eds) *What Politics? Youth and Political Engagement in Africa*, Leiden: Brill, 141–57.

Joseph, J. (2002) *Hegemony*, London: Routledge.

Jütting, J. and De Laiglesia, J. (eds) (2009) 'Is informal normal?', Paris: OECD.

Kallaway, P. (2001) 'The need for attention to the issue of rural education', *International Journal of Educational Development*, 21(1): 21–32.

Kallaway, P. (2020) *The Changing Face of Colonial Education in Africa*, Abingdon: Routledge.

Kaneene, J., Haggblade, S. and Tschirley, D. (2015) 'Sub-Saharan Africa's food system in transition', *Journal of Agribusiness in Developing and Emerging Economies*, 5(2): 94–101.

Kilelu, C., Klerkx, L., Leeuwis, C. and Hall, A. (2011) 'Beyond knowledge brokerage: an exploratory study of innovation intermediaries', Economic and Social Research Institute on Innovation and Technology Working Paper Series 22, Maastricht.

King, K. (1971) *Pan-Africanism and Education*, Oxford: Clarendon.

King, K. (1977) *The African Artisan*, London: Heinemann.

King, K. (2020) 'Skills development and the informal sector', in J. Charmes (ed) *Research Handbook on the Informal Economy*, Cheltenham: Edward Elgar, 347–62.

King, K. and McGrath, S. (2002) *Globalisation, Enterprise and Knowledge*, Oxford: Symposium.

Klerkx, L., Hall, A. and Leeuwis, C. (2009) 'Strengthening agricultural innovation capacity: are innovation brokers the answer?', *International Journal of Agricultural Resources, Governance and Ecology*, 8: 409–38.

Kraak, A. (1993) 'Free or co-ordinated markets?', unpublished PhD thesis, University of the Western Cape.

Kraak, A. (ed) (2009) *Sectors and Skills*, Cape Town: HSRC Press.

Kraak, A. (2016) 'Three decades of restructuring in further education colleges', in A. Kraak, A. Paterson and K. Boka (eds) *Change Management in TVET Colleges*, Cape Town: African Minds, 1–22.

Kraak, A., Paterson, A. and Boka, K. (eds) (2016) *Change Management in TVET Colleges*, Cape Town: African Minds.

Lang, D., Wiek, A., Bergmann, M., Stauffacher, M., Martens, P., Moll, P. et al (2012) 'Transdisciplinary research in sustainability science: practice, principles, and challenges', *Sustainability Science*, 7(1): 25–43.

Langthaler, M., McGrath, S. and Ramsarup, P. (2021) 'Skills for green and just transitions: reflecting on the role of vocational education and training for sustainable development', Briefing Paper 30, ÖFSE, Vienna.

Lauglo, J. and Lillis, K. (eds) (1988) *Vocationalising Education*, Oxford: Pergamon.

Lauglo, J. and Maclean, R. (eds) (2005) *Vocationalisation of Secondary Education Revisited*, Dordrecht: Springer.

Lave, J. (1977) 'Cognitive consequences of traditional apprenticeship training in West Africa', *Anthropology and Education Quarterly*, 18(3): 177–80.

Lawson, N. (2019) '45° change: transforming society from below and above', Compass, https://www.compassonline.org.uk/wp-content/uploads/2019/02/Compass_45-degree-change.pdf, accessed on 11 September 2021.

Leff, E. (2015) 'Political ecology: a Latin American perspective', *Desenvolvimento E Meio Ambiente*, 35: 29–64

Lehtonen, A. (2015) 'Evaluating students' agency and development of ownership in a collaborative playmaking project', *European Journal of Social and Behavioural Sciences*, 14(3): 1885–901.

Lewin, K. (1939) 'Field theory and experiment in social psychology: concepts and methods', *American Journal of Sociology*, 44(6): 868–96.

Livingstone, D. (2004) *The Education-Jobs Gap*, Toronto: Broadview.

Losch, B. (2016) 'Structural transformation to boost youth labour demand in sub-Saharan Africa: the role of agriculture, rural areas and territorial development', Employment and Market Policies Working Paper 204, International Labour Organization, Geneva.

Lotz-Sisitka, H. (2009) 'Why ontology matters to reviewing environmental education research', *Environment Education Research*, 15(2): 165–75.

Lotz-Sisitka, H. (2011) 'The "event" of modern sustainable development and universities in Africa', in Global University Network for Innovation (ed) *Higher Education in the World 4*, Basingstoke: Palgrave Macmillan, 41–57.

Lotz-Sisitka, H. (2018) 'Think piece: pioneers as relational subjects? Probing relationality as phenomenon shaping collective learning and change agency formation', *Southern African Journal of Environmental Education*, 34: 61–73.

Lotz-Sisitka, H. (2020) 'Probing the potential of social ecosystemic skills approaches for Expanded Public Works Programme green skills research', in E. Rosenberg, P. Ramsarup and H. Lotz-Sisitka (eds) *Green Skills Research in South Africa*, Abingdon: Routledge, 113–27.

Lotz-Sisitka, H. and Pesanayi, T. (2020) 'Formative interventionist research generating iterative mediation processes in a vocational education and training learning network', in E. Rosenberg, P. Ramsarup and H. Lotz-Sisitka (eds) *Green Skills Research in South Africa*, Abingdon: Routledge, 157–74.

Lotz-Sisitka, H. and Ramsarup, P. (2020) 'Green skills research: implications for systems, policy, work and learning', in E. Rosenberg, P. Ramsarup and H. Lotz-Sisitka (eds) *Green Skills Research in South Africa*, Abingdon: Routledge, 208–23.

Lotz-Sisitka, H., Pesanayi, T., Weaver, K., Lupele, C., Sisitka, L., O'Donoghue, R. et al (2016) 'Water use and food security: knowledge dissemination and use in agricultural colleges and local learning networks for home food gardening and smallholder agriculture; volume 1', WRC Research Report No 2277/1/16, Water Research Commission, Pretoria.

Lotz-Sisitka, H., Pesanayi, V. (late), Sisitka, L., Metelerkamp, L., Chakona, G., van Staden, W. et al (2021) '"Amanzi for Food": a social learning approach to agricultural water knowledge mediation, uptake and use in smallholder farming learning networks', Research and Development Report No TT 868/21, Water Research Commission, Pretoria

Lucas, W., Spencer, E. and Claxton, G. (2012) 'How to teach vocational education: a theory of vocational pedagogy', Centre for Real World Learning, University of Winchester.

Lund, H. and Karlsen, A. (2020) 'The importance of vocational education institutions in manufacturing regions: adding content to a broad definition of regional innovation systems', *Industry and Innovation*, 27(6): 660–79.

Mabasa, A. (2018) 'South Africa's energy policies will fail due to lack of co-ordination', Daily Maverick, 14 May, https://www.dailymaverick.co.za/opinionista/2018-05-14-south-africas-energy-policies-will-fail-due-to-lack-of-co-ordination, accessed on 5 December 2021.

Malm, A. (2016) *Fossil Capital*, London: Verso.

Maqwelane, L. (2021) 'Towards reconfiguring the agricultural expert system (AES) for black small to medium farmer development for commercialisation: a progressively focused policy literature review and social learning dialogue in the Eastern Cape Raymond Mhlaba Local Municipality', unpublished MEd thesis, Rhodes University.

Marshall, A. (1890) *Principles of Economics*, London: Macmillan.

Martínez-Alier, J. (1997) 'Environmental justice (local and global)', *Capitalism, Nature, Socialism*, 8(1): 91–107.

Martínez-Alier, J. (2003) *The Environmentalism of the Poor*, Cheltenham: Edward Elgar.

Mastercard Foundation (2020) 'Secondary education in Africa', Toronto: Mastercard Foundation.

McGrath, S. (1996) 'Learning to work?', unpublished PhD thesis, University of Edinburgh.

McGrath, S. (2010) 'Beyond aid effectiveness: the development of the South African further education and training college sector, 1994–2009', *International Journal of Educational Development*, 30(5): 525–34.

McGrath, S. (2012). 'Vocational education and training for development: a policy in need of a theory?', *International Journal of Educational Development* , 32(5): 623–31.

McGrath, S. (2015) 'Understanding interactive capabilities for skills development in sectoral systems of innovation: a case study of the Tier 1 automotive component sector in the Eastern Cape', LMIP Report No 7, Human Sciences Research Council, http://hdl.voced.edu.au/10707/409 829, accessed on 28 October 2021.

McGrath, S. (2018) *Education and Development*, Abingdon: Routledge.

McGrath, S. (2020a) 'Skilling for sustainable futures: to SDG8 and beyond', TESF background paper, University of Bristol, https://doi.org/10.5281/zenodo.4022328, accessed on 15 November 2021.

McGrath, S. (2020b) 'What can be learnt from the international right to education movement?', https://right2learn.co.uk/content-hub/simon-mcgrath-the-right-to-learn-what-can-be-learnt-from-the-international-right-to-education-movement, accessed on 22 September 2021.

McGrath, S. and Badroodien, A. (2006) 'Beyond aid effectiveness: the development of the South African further education and training college sector, 1994–2009', *International Journal of Educational Development*, 30(5): 525–34.

McGrath, S. and Lugg, R. (2012) 'Knowing and doing vocational education and training reform', *International Journal of Educational Development*, 32(5): 696–708.

McGrath, S. and Powell, L. (2016) 'Skills for sustainable development', *International Journal of Educational Development*, 50: 12–19.

McGrath, S. and Russon, J.-A. (2022) 'Towards sustainable vocational education and training: thinking beyond the formal', *Southern African Journal of Environmental Education*, forthcoming.

McGrath, S., Thondhlana, J. and Garwe, E. (2021) 'Internationalisation of higher education and national development: the case of Zimbabwe', *Compare*, 51(6): 881–900.

McGrath, S., Badroodien, A., Kraak, A. and Unwin, L. (eds) (2004) *Shifting Understandings of Skills in South Africa*, Cape Town: HSRC Press.

McGrath, S., Powell, L., Alla-Mensah, J., Hilal, R. and Suart, R. (2020b) 'New VET theories for new times: the critical capabilities approach to vocational education and training and its potential for theorising a transformed and transformational VET', *Journal of Vocational Education and Training*, https://doi.org/10.1080/13636820.2020.1786440, accessed on 9 July 2022.

McGrath, S., Akoojee, S., Gewer, A., Mabizela, M., Mbele, N. and Roberts, J. (2006) 'An examination of the vocational education and training reform debate in Southern Africa', *Compare*, 36(1): 85–103.

McGrath, S., Ramsarup, P., Zeelen, J., Wedekind, V., Allais, S., Lotz-Sisitka, H. et al (2020a) 'Vocational education and training for African development', *Journal of Vocational Education and Training*, 72(4): 465–87.

McIntyre, B., Herren, H., Wakhugu, J. and Watson, R. (eds) (2009) 'International Assessment of Agricultural Knowledge, Science and Technology for Development (IAASTD): synthesis report', Washington: Island Press.

McLaughlin, S. (1979) 'The wayside mechanic', Centre for International Education, University of Massachusetts.

McTaggart, R. (1991) 'Principles for participatory action research', *Adult Education Quarterly*, 41(3): 168–87.

Meinert, L. and Whyte, S. (2017) 'These things continue: violence as contamination in everyday life after war in northern Uganda', *Ethos*, 45: 271–86.

Metelerkamp, L. (2018) 'Learning for change', unpublished PhD thesis, Stellenbosch University.

Metelerkamp, L. and van der Breda, J. (2019) 'LGSETA informal economy skills study data report', Cape Town: Siyakhana.

Metelerkamp, L., Biggs, R. and Drimie, S. (2020) 'Learning for transitions: a niche perspective', *Ecology and Society*, 25(1): 14.

Metelerkamp, L., Sisitka, L., Pesanayi, T. (late), Matambo, C. and Lotz-Sisitka, H. (2021) 'Guidelines for establishing and supporting an effective learning network', Environmental Learning Research Centre, Rhodes University.

Mikkonen, S., Pylväs, L., Rintala, H., Noelainen, P. and Postareff, L. (2017) 'Guiding workplace learning in vocational education and training: a literature review', *Empirical Research in Vocational Education and Training*, 9(9).

Ministry of Education and Sports (2011) 'BTVET "Skilling Uganda" strategic plan 2011–2020', Kampala: MoES.

Ministry of Education and Sports (2019a) 'Technical Vocational Education and Training (TVET) policy', Kampala: MoES.

Ministry of Education and Sports (2019b) 'Uganda Skills Development Project', http://www.education.go.ug/uganda-skills-development-proj ect-usdp, accessed on 16 August 2021.

Ministry of Energy and Mineral Development (2015) 'Workforce skills development strategy and plan for oil and gas sub-sector in Uganda', Kampala: MEMD.

Ministry of Gender, Labour and Social Development (2020) 'A situational analysis of persons with disability in Uganda', https://www.developmentp athways.co.uk/wp-content/uploads/2020/09/Webready-DP1294-ESP-Disability-Uganda-Sept-2020.pdf, accessed on 8 December 2021.

Mkwananzi, F. and Cin, M. (2020) 'From streets to developing aspirations: how does collective agency for education change marginalised migrant youths' lives?', *Journal of Human Development and Capabilities*, 21(4): 320–38.

Monk, D. (2013) 'John Dewey and adult learning in museums', *Adult Learning*, 24(2): 63–71.

Monk, D., Davidson, M. and Harris, J. (2021) 'Gender and education in Uganda', *Oxford Research Encyclopedia of Education*, https://oxfordre.com/ education/view/10.1093/acrefore/9780190264093.001.0001/acrefore-9780190264093-e-1289, accessed on 16 July 2021.

Monk, D., Metelerkamp, L., McGrath, S. and Molebatsi, P. (2021) 'VET Africa 4.0: integrating community research praxis', UKFIET, 26 August, https://www.ukfiet.org/2021/vet-africa-4-0-integrating-community-research-praxis, accessed on 14 November 2021.

Moodie, G. (2002) 'Identifying vocational education and training', *Journal of Vocational Education and Training*, 54(2): 249–66.

Moodie, G., Wheelahan, L. and Lavigne, E. (2019) *Technical and Vocational Education and Training as a Framework for Social Justice*, Brussels: Education International.

Moore, J. (ed) (2016) *Anthropocene or Capitalocene?* Oakland: PM Press.

Moore, J. (2017) 'The Capitalocene part II: accumulation by appropriation and the centrality of unpaid work/energy', *Journal of Peasant Studies*, 45(2): 237–79.

Muwaniki, C. and Wedekind, V. (2019) 'Professional development of vocational teachers in Zimbabwe: the past, present, and future', in S. McGrath, M. Mulder, J. Papier and R. Suart (eds) *Handbook of Vocational Education and Training*, Cham: Springer, 1649–65.

National Christian Council of Kenya (1967) 'After school what?', Nairobi: NCCK.

National Planning Commission (2012) 'National Development Plan', Cape Town/Pretoria: Government Printer.

Nguimkeu, P. and Okou, C. (2020) 'A tale of Africa today: balancing the lives and livelihoods of informal workers during the COVID-19 pandemic', Africa Knowledge in Time Policy Brief Issue 1.3, Washington, World Bank.

Norrie, A. (2010) *Dialectic and Difference*, London: Routledge.

Nyerere, J. (1979) 'Adult education and development', in H. Hinzen and V. Hundsdorfer (eds) *The Tanzanian Experience*, Hamburg: UNESCO Institute for Education, 49–55.

Ocitti, J. (1973) *African Indigenous Education as Practised by the Acholi of Uganda*, Nairobi: East African Literature Bureau.

Oinas, E., Onodera, H. and Suurpää, L. (eds) (2018) *What Politics? Youth and Political Engagement in Africa*, Leiden: Brill.

Oketch, M. (2014) 'Education policy, vocational training, and the youth in Sub-Saharan Africa', WIDER Working Paper 2014/069, World Institute for Development Economics Research, United Nations University, Helsinki.

Okumo, I. and Bbaale, E. (2018) 'Technical and vocational education and training in Uganda: a critical analysis', *Development Policy Review*, 37(6): 735–49.

Omolewa, M. (2007) 'Traditional African modes of education', *International Review of Education*, 53: 593–612.

Openjuru, G. (2010) 'Government education policies and the problem of early school leaving: the case of Uganda', in J. Zeelen, J. van der Linden, D. Nampota and M. Ngabirano (eds) *The Burden of Educational Exclusion*, Rotterdam/Boston/Taipei: Sense, 17–34.

Openjuru, G. (2020) 'Foreword', in J. van der Linden, A. Rodrigues-Vasse, M. Kopp, B. Abraham and F. Dier (eds) *Youth, Education and Work in (Post-) conflict Areas*, Groningen: University of Groningen, vii–x.

Operation Phakisa (nd) 'Operation Phakisa', https://www.operationphakisa.gov.za/pages/home.aspx, accessed on 26 July 2022.

Organisation for Economic Co-operation and Development (2008) 'Employment outlook 2008', Paris: OECD.

Palmer, R. (2020) 'Lifelong learning in the informal economy', Geneva: ILO.

Papier, J. (2017) 'Improving college-to-work transitions through enhanced training for employment', *Research in Post-Compulsory Education*, 22(1): 38–48.

Parenti, C. (2016) 'Environment-making in the capitalocene: political ecology of the state', in J. Moore (ed) *Anthropocene or Capitalocene?*, Oakland: PM Press, 166–84.

Patel, S. (2017) 'Colonial modernity and methodological nationalism: the structuring of sociological traditions in India', *Sociological Bulletin*, 66(2): 125–44.

Pawson, R. and Tilley, N. (1997) *Realistic Evaluation*, London: Sage.

Payne, J. (2007) 'Skill ecosystems: a new approach to vocational education and training policy', SKOPE Issues Paper 14, University of Oxford.

Payne, J. (2008) 'Skills in context: what can the UK learn from Australia's skill ecosystem projects?', *Policy and Politics*, 36(3): 307–23.

Pesanayi, T. (2019a) 'Boundary-crossing expansive learning across agricultural learning systems and networks in Southern Africa', unpublished PhD thesis, Rhodes University, Grahamstown.

Pesanayi, T. (2019b) 'Boundary-crossing learning in ESD: when agricultural educators co-engage farmers in learning around water activity', in J. Armon, S. Scoffham and C. Armon (eds) *Prioritizing Sustainability Education*, London: Routledge.

Phelps Stokes Fund (1922) *Education in Africa*, New York: Phelps Stokes Fund.

Phelps Stokes Fund (1925) *Education in East Africa*, New York: Phelps Stokes Fund.

Phuong, L., Wals, A., Sen, L., Hoa, N., Van Lu, P. and Biesbroek, R. (2018) 'Using a social learning configuration to increase Vietnamese smallholder farmers' adaptive capacity to respond to climate change', *Local Environment*, 23(8): 879–97.

Post-Harvest Innovation Learning Alliance (nd) 'Innovation systems: what are they?', http://projects.nri.org/phila/innovationsystems, accessed on 7 August 2021.

Powell, L. and McGrath, S. (2018) 'The long and winding road to the labour market: South African public TVET college students' experiences of system failure', in C. Nägele and B. Stalder (eds) 'Trends in vocational education and training research', Vocational Education and Training Network (VETNET), https://doi.org/10.5281/zenodo.1319704.

Powell, L. and McGrath, S. (2019a) *Skills for Human Development*, Abingdon: Routledge.

Powell, L. and McGrath, S. (2019b) 'Capability or employability: orientating VET toward "real work"', in S. McGrath, M. Mulder, J. Papier and R. Suart (eds) *Handbook of Vocational Education and Training*, Cham: Springer, 369–92.

Power, M. (2004) 'Social provisioning as a starting point for feminist economics', *Feminist Economics*, 10(3): 3–19.

Presidential Climate Change Commission (2021) 'First report: recommendations on South Africa's draft updated Nationally Determined Contribution (NDC)', https://a9322a19-efe3-4459-9a6c-ab806fededa3.filesusr.com/ugd/1eb85a_896d0493b6284743b2ff3986b36be622.pdf, accessed on 14 November 2021.

Presidential Infrastructure Coordinating Commission (2012) 'National Infrastructure Plan', Cape Town/Pretoria: Government Printer.

Price, L. (2012) 'Interdisciplinarity and critical realist research', paper presented at the PhD Week, Education Department, Rhodes University, Grahamstown, March.

Psacharopoulos, G. (1981) 'Returns to education', *Comparative Education*, 17(3): 321–41.

Psacharopoulos, G. (1985) 'Returns to education', *Journal of Human Resources*, 20(4): 583–604.

Raffe, D. (2008) 'The concept of transition system', *Journal of Education and Work*, 21(4): 277–96.

Rampedi, M. (2003) 'Implementing adult education policy in the Limpopo province of South Africa', unpublished PhD thesis, Groningen: University of Groningen.

Ramsarup, P. (2017) 'A critical realist dialectical understanding of learning pathways associated with two scarce skill environmental occupations within a transitioning systems frame', unpublished PhD thesis, Rhodes University.

Ramsarup, P. (2020) 'Learning pathways into environmental specialisations', in E. Rosenberg, P. Ramsarup and H. Lotz-Sisitka (eds) *Green Skills Research in South Africa*, Abingdon: Routledge, 81–96.

Ramsarup, P. and Lotz-Sisitka, H. (2020) 'Transitioning into work: a learning and work transitioning process perspective', in E. Rosenberg, P. Ramsarup and H. Lotz-Sisitka (eds) *Green Skills Research in South Africa*, Abingdon: Routledge, 97–112.

Raworth, K. (2017) *Doughnut Economics*, London: Random House.

Reason, P. and Bradbury, H. (eds) (2008) *The Sage Handbook of Action Research*, London: Sage.

Rodney, W. (1972) *How Europe Underdeveloped Africa*, London: Bogle-L'Ouverture.

Rogers, A. (2019) 'The homelessness of adult education', *Studies in the Education of Adults*, 51(1): 15–35.

Rosenberg, E., Ramsarup, P. and Lotz-Sisitka, H. (eds) (2020) *Green Skills Research in South Africa*, Abingdon: Routledge.

Sachs, W. (ed) (1993) *Global Ecology*, London: Zed.

Sampson, R. and Laub, J. (1990) 'Crime and deviance over the life course: the salience of adult social bonds', *American Sociological Review*, 55: 609–27.

Sannino, A. (2020) 'Transformative agency as warping: how collectives accomplish change amidst uncertainty', *Pedagogy, Culture and Society*, 30(1): 9–33.

Santos, B. (2014) *Epistemologies of the South*, London: Routledge.

Santos, F. and Eisenhardt, K. (2005) 'Organizational boundaries and theories of organization', *Organization Science*, 16(5): 491–508.

Satgar, V. (ed) (2018) *The Climate Crisis*, Johannesburg: Wits University Press.

Savage, I. (2019) '10 facts about farming in Africa', Borgen Project, https://borgenproject.org/tag/subsistence-farming, accessed on 5 December 2021.

Sawchuk, P. and Taylor, A. (2010) 'Understanding challenging transitions in learning and work', in P. Sawchuk and A. Taylor (eds) *Challenging Transitions in Learning and Work*, Rotterdam: Sense, 1–25.

Scheidel, A., Temper, L., Demaria, F. and Martínez-Alier, J. (2018) 'Ecological distribution conflicts as forces for sustainability: an overview and conceptual framework', *Sustainability Science*, 13(3): 585–98.

Schmidt, T. (2021) 'Teacher as person: the need for an alternative conceptualisation of the "good" teacher in Australia's vocational education and training sector', *Journal of Vocational Education and Training*, 73(1): 148–65.

Schoon, I. and Heckhausen, J. (2019). 'Conceptualizing individual agency in the transition from school to work: a social-ecological developmental perspective', *Adolescent Research Review*, 4: 135–48.

Scoones, I. (2016) 'The politics of sustainability and development', *Annual Review of Environment and Resources*, 41: 263–319.

Senge, P., Hamilton, H. and Kania, J. (2015) 'The dawn of system leadership', *Stanford Social Innovation Review* (Winter): 1–18.

Sennett, R. (2006) *The Craftsman*, New Haven: Yale University Press.

Shalem, Y. and Allais, S. (2018) 'Linking knowledge, education and preparation for work: exploring occupations', Centre for Researching Education and Labour, University of Witwatersrand.

Sheffield, J. and Diejomaoh, V. (1972) 'Non-formal education in African development', New York: African-American Institute.

Shiva, V. (1994) 'Conflicts of global ecology: environmental activism in a period of global reach', *Alternatives*, 19: 195–207.

Sithole, P. (2018) 'Investigating the role of extension officers in supporting social learning of rainwater harvesting practices amongst rural smallholder farmers in Nkonkobe Local Municipality, Eastern Cape', unpublished MEd thesis, Rhodes University.

Smith, E. and Yasukawa, K. 2017 'What makes a good VET teacher? Views of Australian VET teachers and students', *International Journal of Training Research*, 15(1): 23–40.

Spielman, D., Ekboir, J. and Davis, D. (2009) 'The art and science of innovation systems inquiry: applications to Sub-Saharan African agriculture', *Technology in Society*, 31(4): 399–405.

Spours, K. (2019) 'A social ecosystem model: conceptual developments and implications for VET', working discussion paper, Centre for Post-14 Education and Work, Institute of Education, University College London, https://discovery.ucl.ac.uk/id/eprint/10082170, accessed on 12 October 2021.

Spours, K. (2021a) 'Building social ecosystem theory', https://www.kenspours.com/elite-and-inclusive-ecosystems, accessed on 5 October 2021.

Spours, K. (2021b) 'The dynamics of the Social Ecosystem Model (SEM) in cities – connecting working, living and learning', http://www.kenspours.com/set-and-cities, accessed on 5 October 2021.

Standing, G. (2016) *The Corruption of Capitalism*, London: Biteback.

StatsSA (2021) 'Quarterly labour force survey quarter 2: 2021', http://www.statssa.gov.za/publications/P0211/P02112ndQuarter2021.pdf, accessed on 15 November 2021.

Steffen, W., Crutzen, P. and McNeill, J. (2007) 'The Anthropocene: are humans now overwhelming the great forces of nature?', *AMBIO: A Journal of the Human Environment*, 36(8): 614–21.

Steffen, W. Grinevald, J., Crutzen, P. and McNeill, J. (2011) 'The Anthropocene: conceptual and historical perspectives', *Philosophical Transactions of the Royal Society A: Mathematical, Physical and Engineering Sciences*, 369: 842–67.

Stevenson, H. (2020) 'Education union renewal', in M. Soskill (ed) *Flip the System US*, New York: Eye on Education, 154–60.

Olsen, D. and Tikkanen, T. (2018) 'The developing field of workplace learning and the contribution of PIAAC', *International Journal of Lifelong Education*, 37(5): 546–59.

Swartz, S., Cooper, A., Batan, C. and Kropf Causa, L. (2021) *The Oxford Handbook of Global South Youth Studies*, Oxford: Oxford University Press.

Swilling, M. (2020) *The Age of Sustainability*, London: Routledge.

Swilling, M. (2021) 'It's the green train now – and you're on the wrong platform, Gwede Mantashe', Daily Maverick, 23 May 2021, https://www.dailymaverick.co.za/article/2021-05-23-its-the-green-train-now-and-youre-on-the-wrong-platform-gwede-mantashe, accessed on 5 December 2021.

Swilling, M. and Annecke, E. (2012) *Just Transitions*, Cape Town: Juta.

Taylor, E. (2010) 'Cultural institutions and adult education', *New Directions for Adult and Continuing Education*, 127: 5–14.

Tetrault, D. (2017) 'Three forms of political ecology', *Ethics and the Environment*, 22(2): 1–23.

Thieme, A. (2013) 'The "hustle" amongst youth entrepreneurs in Mathare's informal waste economy', *Journal of Eastern African Studies*, 7(3): 389–412.

Tikly, L. (2013) 'Reconceptualizing TVET and development: a human capability and social justice approach', in UNEVOC (eds) *Revisiting Global Trends in TVET*, Bonn: UNEVOC, 1–39.

Tikly, L. (2020) *Education for Sustainable Development in the Post-Colonial World*, Abingdon: Routledge.

Tomaney, J. (2017) 'Book review: *Fossil Capital: The Rise of Steam Power and the Roots of Global Warming* by Andreas Malm', LSE, https://blogs.lse.ac.uk/lsereviewofbooks/2017/07/07/book-review-fossil-capital-the-rise-of-steam-power-and-the-roots-of-global-warming-by-andreas-malm, accessed on 17 November 2021.

Tukundane, C. (2014) *Education and Skills for Development*, Groningen: University of Groningen.

Tukundane, C. and Zeelen, J. (2015) 'Using participatory action research to improve vocational skills training for marginalised youth in Uganda: experiences from an early school-leavers' project', *International Journal of Training Research*, 13(3): 246–61.

Tukundane, C., Minnaert, A., Zeelen, J. and Kanyandago, P. (2015) 'Building vocational skills for marginalised youth in Uganda', *International Journal of Educational Development*, 40: 134–44.

United Nations Development Programme (2021) 'The next frontier: human development and the Anthropocene; Human Development Report 2020', New York: UNDP.

United Nations Educational, Scientific and Cultural Organisation (2012) 'Shanghai consensus: recommendations of the Third International Congress on Technical and Vocational Education and Training', https://unevoc.unesco.org/home/UNESCO+Publications/lang=en/akt=detail/qs=5457, accessed on 8 November 2021.

United Nations Environmental Programme (2020) *The Little Book of Green Nudges*, Nairobi: United Nations Environment Programme and GRID Arendal, https://www.unep.org/resources/publication/little-book-green-nudges?_ga=2.166977466.587143638.1638695914-890871891.1637604 503, accessed on 5 December 2021.

Universities of South Africa (2021) 'Engagement is transformation: the university and community engagement', https://www.usaf.ac.za/eng agement-is-transformation-the-university-and-community-engagement, accessed on 29 November 2021.

Vaganova, O., Bakharev, N., Kulagina, J., Lapshova, A. and Kirillova, I. (2020) 'Multimedia technologies in vocational education', *Amazonia Investiga*, 9(26): 391–8.

Van der Linden, J., Rodrigues-Vasse, A., Kopp, M., Abraham, B. and Dier, F. (eds) (2020) *Youth, Education and Work in (Post-)conflict Areas*, Groningen: University of Groningen.

Van Rensburg, P. (1974) 'Report from Swaneng Hill', Uppsala: Dag Hammarskjold Foundation.

Van Staden, W. (2020) 'Climate responsive innovation within the agricultural curriculum and learning system', *Southern African Journal of Environmental Education*, 36: 73–87.

Walker, M. (2008) 'A human capabilities framework for evaluating student learning', *Teaching in Higher Education*, 13(4): 477–87.

Wedekind, V. (2010) 'Chaos or coherence? Further education and training college governance in post-Apartheid South Africa', *Research in Comparative and International Education*, 5(3): 302–15.

Wedekind, V. (2016) 'A climate for change? Vertical and horizontal collegial relations in TVET colleges', in A. Kraak, A. Paterson and K. Boka (eds) *Change Management in TVET Colleges*, Cape Town: African Minds, 64–82.

Wedekind, V. (2019) 'Curriculum responsiveness and student employability: an institutional analysis', in G. Kruss, A. Wildschut and I. Petersen (eds) *Skills for the Future*, Cape Town: HSRC Press.

Wedekind, V. and Mutereko, S. (2016) 'Employability and curriculum responsiveness in post-school education and training, LMIP Report No 22, http://lmip.org.za/document/employability-and-curriculum-respons iveness-post-school-education-and-training, accessed on 29 October 2021.

Wedekind, V., Watson, A. and Buthelezi, Z. (2016) 'Lecturers in distress: fractured professional identity amongst TVET college staff in South Africa', *SAQA Bulletin*, 15(1): 117–42.

Wedekind, V., Russon, J.-A., Ramsarup, P., Monk, D., Metelerkamp, L. and McGrath, S. (2021) 'Conceptualising regional skills ecosystems: reflections on four African cases', *International Journal of Training and Development*, 25(4): 347–62.

Wenger, E. (1998) *Communities of Practice*, Cambridge: Cambridge University Press.

Wenger, E., Trayner, B. and De Laat, M. (2011) 'Promoting and assessing value creation in communities and networks: a conceptual framework', Ruud de Moor Centrum, Open Universiteit Nederland.

Wenger-Trayner, E. and Wenger-Trayner, B. (2020) *Learning to Make a Difference*. Cambridge: Cambridge University Press.

Wheelahan, L. (2007) 'How competency-based training locks the working class out of powerful knowledge: a modified Bernsteinian analysis', *British Journal of Sociology of Education*, 28(5): 637–51.

Wheelahan, L. (2015) 'Not just skills: what a focus on knowledge means for vocational education', *Journal of Curriculum Studies*, 47(6): 750–62.

Wheelahan, L., Moodie, G. and Doughney, J. (2022) 'Challenging the skills fetish', *British Journal of Sociology of Education*, 43(3): 475–94, https://doi.org/10.1080/01425692.2022.2045186.

Whitley, R. (2001) 'National innovation systems', in N. Smelser and P. Baltes (eds) *International Encyclopedia of the Social and Behavioral Sciences*, Oxford: Pergamon, 10303–9.

Windsor, K. and Alcorso, C. (2008) 'Skills in context: a guide to the skill ecosystem approach to workforce development', NSW Government, https://www.training.nsw.gov.au/forms_documents/industry_programs/workforce_development/skill_ecosystem/skills_in_context.pdf, accessed on 29 October 2021.

Winkler, N., Ruf-Leuschner, M., Ertl, V., Pfeiffer, A., Schalinski, I., Ovuga, E. et al (2015) 'From war to classroom: PTSD and depression in formerly abducted youth in Uganda', *Frontiers in Psychiatry*, 6(2): 1–10.

Wise, T. (2020) 'Failing Africa's farmers: an impact assessment of the Alliance for a Green Revolution in Africa', Working Paper No 20–01, Global Development and Environment Institute, Tufts University.

Wright, E. (2010) *Envisioning Real Utopias*, London: Verso.

World Bank (2021) 'Climate risk country profiles', Climate Change Knowledge Portal, https://climateknowledgeportal.worldbank.org, accessed on 12 November 2021.

Yesufu, T. (1973) *Creating the African University*, Ibadan: Published for the Association of African Universities by Oxford University Press.

Yu, C., De Jong, M. and Dijkema, G. (2014) 'Process analysis of eco-industrial park development – the case of Tianjin, China', *Journal of Cleaner Production*, 64: 464–77.

Zeelen, J. (2012) 'Universities in Africa: working on excellence for whom? Reflections on teaching, research and outreach at African universities', *International Journal of Higher Education*, 1(2): 157–65.

Zeelen, J., van der Linden, J., Nampota, D. and Ngabirano, M. (eds) (2010) *The Burden of Educational Exclusion*, Rotterdam: Sense.

Ziderman, A. (2016) 'Funding mechanisms for financing vocational training', IZA Policy Paper 110, Institute for the Study of Labor, Bonn.

Index

References to figures appear in *italic* type;
those in bold type refer to tables and boxes.

M

Mabase, A. 41

Makerere University 26

Malawi 28

Malm, A. 2, 17, 37, 41–2

Maqwelane, L. 132, 134

Maritime Academy, uMfolozi TVET
College 10, 66, 102, 170, 171, 176–7

maritime sector 106–7, 109–10, 161

maritime transport 41

maritime VET students 124, 126, **131**

market vendors 122, 128, 131, 133, **134**

Marshall, A. 56

Martínez-Alier, J. 44

Marx, K. 47, 52

Marxism 43

McGrath, S. 1, 4, 11, 25, 27, 28, 30, 31, 34,
56, 57, 77, 78, 84, 161, 177

McIntyre, B. 53

McTaggart, R. 146

mediation 5–6, 60–1, 69–70, 73–4, 101,
162

by universities 20, 139, 144–6, 156–7, 166

Alice (case study) 147–8, 155

Gulu (case study) 149–52

by vocational teachers 112–15, 116

Metelerkamp, L. 6, 78, 91

migration 28–9

Millennium Development Goals 30

minerals 46

Ministry of Energy and Mineral Development
(MEMD), Uganda 12

Mkwananzi, F. 90

Monk, D. 77, 81, 182, 184, 185–6

Moodie, G. 7, 33

Moore, J. 17, 42, 47, 52

multiscalarity 71, 163

N

Namibia 25, 32

National Christian Council, Kenya 29

national qualification frameworks
(NQFs) 171–2, 173

natural fundamentalism 52

neocolonialism 44–50

neoliberal growth model 58

neoliberal transnational governmentality 46

neoliberalism 9, 30, 35, 45

networks *see* learning networks

Nguimkeu, P. 76

Norrie, A. 73

Nyerere, J. 29

O

Oceans Economy 102

Ocitti, J. 23

oil and gas sector 10–12, 41, 46, 48, **49**,
103, 161

Oinas, E. 52, 136, 142

Oketch, M. 34

Openjuru, G. 140, 150

Operation Phakisa **49**, 102

Operation Wealth Creation 149

P

Palmer, R. 35

Parenti, C. 47–8

participatory action research (PAR) 146, 150

Patel, S. 1

Pawson, R. 17

Payne, J. 58, 146

Pesanayi, T. 46, 101, 143, 147, 154, 167,
186

Phelps Stokes Foundation 25–6

Phuong, L. 137

political ecology 45, 163

political economies 46–7

political-economy-ecology 41–4, 48, **49**,
50, 159

politics of work and life 52

'poor White problem' 27

Powell, L. 7, 122, 141, 167

power relations 44

precolonial skills development 23–5

Presidential Climate Change Commission
(PCCC), South Africa 51

Price, L. 71

primary education 28, 30

private-for-profit education and training 32

private provision 175–7

productivity 156, 166

Psacharopolous, G. 98

public provision 170–2, 176

public sector employment 27

Q

qualifications 136, 171–2, 173

R

Raffe, D. 119

Rampedi, M. 140

Ramsarup, P. 118, 121, 138

Raworth, K. 43

real, domain of the 71

real utopias 43, 53

Reason, P. 146

recolonisation by invitation 46

refugees 149

relational agency 20, 90, 141, 142, 153–4,
155, 178

relationality 163

reliability 83

renewable energy 41

research practices 182–7

Rhodes University

'Amanzi [Water] for Food' programme 14

Imvothu Bubomi Learning Network
(IBLN) 67, 86, 87, 89, 110

university as mediator 147, 148

university as social ecosystem actor 177